Designing Components with the C++ STL

Designing Components with the C++ STL

A new approach to programming

Ulrich Breymann

Addison-Wesley

Harlow, England • Reading, Massachusetts • Menlo Park, California • New York
Don Mills, Ontario • Amsterdam • Bonn • Sydney • Singapore • Tokyo • Madrid
San Juan • Milan • Mexico City • Seoul • Taipei

First published by Addison Wesley Longman Verlag (Deutschland) GmbH 1996 as
Die C++ Standard Template Library: Einführung, Anwendung, Konstruktion neuer Komponenten

Addison Wesley Longman Limited
Edinburgh Gate
Harlow
Essex CM20 2JE
England

and Associated Companies throughout the World.

Translated and typeset by 46
Cover designed by Designers & Partners, Oxford, UK
Printed and bound in the United States of America

First printed 1998. Reprinted 1998.

ISBN 0–201–17816–8

British Library Cataloguing-in-Publication Data
A catalogue record for this book is available from the British Library

To Lena, Niko and Anne

Foreword

Ironically, it was in Waterloo that the STL was adopted as part of the ISO/ANSI Standard C++ Library, and from that day on it went onto a triumphal march. Alexander Stepanov and Meng Lee had proposed the result of years of research at Hewlett-Packard, a standard template library, to the standards committee. The committee gracefully adopted the STL as part of the C++ standard at a committee meeting in Waterloo in the summer of 1994, after countless controversial discussions and much work spent by committee members on making the STL fit for a standard. Most importantly, the adoption was tied to the condition that the source code had to be made publicly available. Since then the STL has become more and more popular in the C++ community and conquered the hearts of quite a number of programmers. Personally, I know of software developers who cannot imagine getting their work done anymore without a general-purpose library like the STL. Obviously, not all Waterloos are the same. This Waterloo was in Ontario – seemingly a good omen.

Much of the merit, however, is not seriously due to picking the right location for presenting a library. The STL is an invaluable foundation library that makes programmers more productive in two ways. It contains a lot of different components that can be plugged together, so it provides a flexible and extensible framework. Plus, it has an elegant, consistent, and easy to comprehend architecture.

When Ulrich asked me in fall 1995 whether I would feel like writing this book with him, my first thought was: Does the world really need another STL book? Three books had already been out at that point in time; I had volunteered for writing a regular column about the STL for a magazine of high renown like *C++ Report*; numerous conference organizers invited me to speak about the STL; even my employer had me prepare and conduct courses on the STL. In sum, there were countless resources available to meet the growing interest in the C++ community. I simply questioned the need for yet another STL tutorial. About a year later, I held the German edition of his book in my hands, skimmed through the pages, and started reading – with increasing enjoyment. And I must admit, he convinced me. This book goes beyond the tutorials I had seen up to then and has an approach and appeal of its own: it explains techniques for building your own data structures and algorithms on top of the STL and this way appreciates the STL for what it is – a framework. I had been looking for this aspect in tutorials, often in vain.

As can be expected, the book starts off with an introduction to the STL. Already the initial explanations provide you with insights into the internals of the STL that you miss in other introductory material. For instance, Ulrich explains what the implementation of an iterator typically looks like. This kind of information is profound enough to lay the foundations for leaving the realm of simple STL usage, and enables you to understand and eventually extend the STL framework by adding your own containers and algorithms. The most distinguishing part of this book is Part III: Beyond the STL. You will see demonstrations of elegant and sophisticated usage of the STL – well-known data structures like matrices and graphs built on top of the STL, as well as examples of additions to the STL, like hash-based containers.

I would also want to acknowledge that this English edition of the book is the most accurate and up-to-date source of information on the STL currently available. It reflects the ISO C++ Standard Draft as of January 1997. In fact, since its advent in 1994, the STL underwent quite a number of minor and major changes, all of which were introduced in the process of improving and standardizing the STL. Unfortunately, many, if not most compilers are currently not yet capable of understanding the full range standard C++, and consequently today's standard library implementations provide workarounds for not yet supported language features. Keep up with the language standard and learn how the standard STL of tomorrow will differ from available implementations of today.

In sum, I enjoyed the book and appreciate it as a sound and serious reference to the STL. I hope you will also.

Angelika Langer
September 1997

Preface

The Standard Template Library (STL)

One reason for the success of C++ is that today a large number of libraries is available on the market which greatly facilitate the development of programs, because they offer reliable and well-proven components. A particularly carefully constructed library is the *Standard Template Library*, which has been developed at Hewlett-Packard by Alexander Stepanov, Meng Lee, and their colleagues. It has been accepted by the ANSI/ISO committee as part of the coming C++ standard (ISO/IEC, 1997).

The emphasis of the STL is on data structures for containers, and the algorithms that work with them. The technical reference document of the STL (Stepanov and Lee, 1995) has practically, with some modifications, become a part of the C++ standard proposal (ISO/IEC, 1997). Both are the basis for the first two parts of this book. The document can be freely used, as long as the copyright conditions are quoted. These conditions plus references to sources can be found in the Appendix from page 286.

The C++ Standard Library and the STL

The STL does not include the entire C++ Standard Library nor all its templates; it represents, however, the most important and most interesting part. The C++ Standard Library includes several areas:

- Generic data structures and algorithms
  - containers
  - algorithms
  - iterators
  - functional objects

- Internationalization

- Diagnosis (exceptions)

- Numeric issues
  - complex numbers
  - numeric arrays and related operations

- Input and output library (streams)

- Miscellaneous
  - memory management (allocators) and access
  - date and time
  - strings

The area shaded in gray constitutes the subject of this book – in other words, the book does not deal with the historic STL, but with that part of the C++ Standard Library that has originated from the STL. Besides an introduction, the emphasis is on sample applications and the construction of new components on the basis of the STL.

Owing to several requirements by the ISO/ANSI standard committee, this part of the C++ Standard Library no longer matches the original STL exactly. Thus, a more precise – albeit too long – title for this book would be *Generic algorithms and data structures of the C++ Standard Library – introduction, applications, and construction of new components*. The changes affect only some details, but not the concept; therefore the name *Standard Template Library* and the abbreviation STL have been retained. Furthermore, the standard has not yet been passed, and the standard proposal is still subject to changes. These changes to and differences from the original STL will be indicated where they occur.

Aims of this book

The book has two aims. As a technical reference, the reference document mentioned earlier is hardly suited to explain the concepts of the STL. Therefore, the first aim is to present how the STL can be used in a sensible way. Internal details of the STL are described only to the extent needed to understand how it works.

However, this book is more than a simple introduction. With the aid of comprehensive examples, the STL is presented as a tool box for the construction of more powerful and sometimes even faster components. These components are more complex data structures and algorithms which can be efficiently implemented by means of the modules contained in the STL. The algorithms are evaluated with respect to their run time behavior relative to the amount of data to be processed (time complexity). However, not only the modules themselves and their combination are of interest, but also the programming techniques employed in the STL and in this book.

Readership

This book is intended for all those involved in the development of software in C++, be they system designer, project manager, student of computer science, or programmer. To make the software portable, maintainable, and reusable, it is highly recommended that valid standards are adhered to and thoroughly exploited – otherwise, they would not be needed. The use of prefabricated components such as those of the STL increases both the reliability of the software and the productivity of the developers. The precondition for understanding this book is knowledge of the C++ programming language and its template mechanisms which can be gained by reading good text books on the subject, such as *C++ Primer* (Lippman, 1995).

Structure of the book

The book is divided into three parts. Part I is an introduction to the STL and describes its concepts and elements, with the emphasis on iterators and containers. The concept of iterators and containers is essential for the working of the algorithms.

Part II discusses the standard algorithms, where almost every algorithm is illustrated with an example. Because of the large number of algorithms described, it should be viewed as a catalog.

Part III describes applications and extensions. Extensive examples help to show how the components supplied by the STL can be used to design more complex data structures and algorithms and powerful abstract data types.

Examples

Not only is the functioning of STL elements described, but for almost every element and all the applications of Part III an executable example is presented that can be run on the reader's computer. This gives the reader a chance to experiment and achieve a deeper understanding.

The examples are available via FTP or the Internet, see:

```
ftp.informatik.hs-bremen.de/pub/brey/stl or
http://www.informatik.hs-bremen.de/~brey
```

Remarks

The public domain implementation of the STL by Hewlett-Packard is very similar to the C++ standard proposal, since modifications and extensions have been carried out since the integration of the STL. The differences are pointed out throughout the book. It can be expected that after publication of the C++ Draft International Standard, probably towards the end of 1997, all compiler producers will supply an STL implementation conforming to the standard, so that differences in various implementations will play only a very marginal role.

In the text, programming issues such as variables, keywords, and program examples can be recognized by `this type style`. Explanations that interrupt the text of a program are marked as indented comments `/* ... */`. Names of files are printed in *italics* and screen displays in *slanted characters*. A little lightbulb indicates an important hint or tip for programming.

Suggestions and criticism

are more than welcome. If you want to point out errors or make suggestions or critical remarks, you can contact the author either through the publisher or directly via e-mail (`brey@informatik.hs-bremen.de`).

Acknowledgements

I have received many suggestions from my colleagues Ulrich Eisenecker (Fachhochschule Heidelberg), Bernd Owsnicki-Klewe (Fachhochschule Hamburg), and Andreas Spillner (Hochschule Bremen), and I am very grateful to them for their critical and thorough review of the manuscript and for their helpful hints and tips. All weaknesses and errors rest solely with the author.

Contents

Part I
Introduction

The concept of the C++ Standard Template Library

Summary: There are several libraries for containers and algorithms in C++. These libraries are not standardized and are not interchangeable. In the course of standardization of the C++ programming language, a template-based library for containers and optimized algorithms has been incorporated into the standard. This chapter explains the concept of this library and describes it with the aid of some examples.

The big advantage of templates is plain to see. Evaluation of templates is carried out at compile time, there are no run time losses – for example, through polymorph function access in case genericity is realized with inheritance. The advantage of standardization is of even greater value. Programs using a standardized library are more portable since all compiler producers will be oriented towards the standard. Furthermore, they are easier to maintain since the corresponding know-how is much more widespread than knowledge of any special library.

The emphasis is on *algorithms* which cooperate with *containers* and *iterators* (Latin *iterare* = repeat). Through the template mechanism of C++, containers are suited for objects of the most varied classes. An iterator is an object which can be moved on a container like a pointer, to refer either to one or another object. Algorithms work with containers by accessing the corresponding iterators. The concepts will be presented in more detail later.

References: Owing to its very nature, this book is based on well-known algorithms of which several – those used in the examples – are described in detail. This book cannot, however, provide a detailed presentation of all the algorithms used in the STL. For example, readers who want to know more about red-black trees or quicksort should refer to other books about algorithms. The authors of the STL refer to Cormen *et al.* (1994) which is a very thorough book and well worth reading. An introduction to the STL is provided by Musser and Saini (1996), published while I was working on this book. Josuttis (1996) gives an introduction to the *entire* C++ standard library, including an introduction to the STL, but without the applications and the extensions presented in this book.

1.1 Genericity of components

An interesting approach is not to emphasize inheritance and polymorphism, but to provide containers and algorithms for all possible (including user-defined) data types, provided that they satisfy a few preconditions. C++ templates constitute the basis for this. Thus, the emphasis is not so much on object orientation but on generic programming. This has the very important advantage that the number of different container and algorithm types needed is drastically reduced – with concomitant type security.

Let us illustrate this with a brief example. Let us assume that we want to find an element of the `int` data type in a container of the `vector` type. For this, we need a `find()` algorithm which searches the container. If we have n different containers (list, set, ...), we need a separate algorithm for each container, which results in n `find()` algorithms. We may want to find not only an `int` object, but an object of an arbitrary data type out of m possible data types. This would raise the number of `find()` algorithms to $n \cdot m$. This observation will apply to k different algorithms, so that we have to write a total of $k \cdot n \cdot m$ algorithms.

The use of templates allows you to reduce the number m to 1. STL algorithms, however, do not work directly with containers but with interface objects, that is, iterators which access containers. Iterators are pointer-like objects which will be explained in detail later. This reduces the necessary total to $n + k$ instead of $n \cdot k$, a considerable saving.

An additional advantage is type security, since templates are already resolved at compile time.

1.2 Abstract and implicit data types

Abstract data types encapsulate data and functions that work with this data. The data is not visible to the user of an abstract data type, and access to data is exclusively carried out by functions, also called methods. Thus, the abstract data type is specified by the methods, not by the data. In C++, abstract data types are represented by classes which present a tiny flaw: the data that represents the state of an object of this abstract data type is visible (though not accessible) in the `private` part of the class declaration for each program that takes cognizance of this class via `#include`. From the standpoint of object orientation, 'hiding' the private data in an implementation file would be more elegant.

Implicit data types can on the one hand be abstract data types themselves, on the other hand they are used to implement abstract data types. In the latter case they are not visible from the outside, thus the name 'implicit.' For example: an abstract data type `Stack` allows depositing and removing of elements only from the 'top.' A stack can, for instance, use a singly-linked list as implicit data type, though a vector would be possible as well. Users of the stack would not be able to tell the difference.

Implicit data types are not important in the sense of an object-oriented analysis which puts the emphasis on the interfaces (methods) of an abstract data type. They are, however, very important for design and implementation because they often determine the run time behavior. Frequently, a non-functional requirement, such as compliance with a given response time, can be fulfilled only through a clever choice of implicit data types and algorithms. A simple example is the access to a number of sorted addresses: access via a singly-linked list would be very slow compared to access via a binary tree.

The STL uses the distinction between abstract and implicit data types by allowing an additional choice between different implicit data types for the implementation of some abstract data types.

1.3 The fundamental concept

The most important elements of the STL are outlined before their interplay is discussed.

1.3.1 Containers

The STL provides different kinds of containers which are all formulated as template classes. Containers are objects which are used to manage other objects, where it is left to the user to decide whether the objects are deposited by value or by reference. 'By value' means that each element in the container is an object of a copyable type (value semantics). 'By reference' means that the elements in the container are pointers to objects of possibly heterogeneous type. In C++, the different types must be derived from a base class and the pointers must be of the 'pointer to base class' type.

A means of making different algorithms work with different containers is to choose the same *names* (which are evaluated at compile time) for similar operations. The method `size()`, for example, returns the number of elements in a container, no matter whether it is of `vector`, `list`, or `map` type. Other examples are the methods `begin()` and `end()` which are used to determine the position of the first element and the position *after* the last element. These positions are always defined in a C++ array. An empty container is characterized by identical values of `begin()` and `end()`.

1.3.2 Iterators

Iterators work like pointers. Depending on the application, they can be common pointers or objects with pointer-like properties. Iterators are used to access container elements. They can move from one element to the other, with the kind of movement being hidden to the outside (control abstraction). In a vector, for example, the `++` operation means a simple switch to the next memory position, whereas the same operation in a binary search tree is associated with a traversal of the tree. The different iterators will be described in detail later.

1.3.3 Algorithms

The template algorithms work with iterators that access containers. Since not only user-defined data types, but also the data types already existing in C++, such as `int`, char, and so on are supported, the algorithms have been designed in such a way that they can also work with normal pointers (see the example in the following section).

1.3.4 Interplay

Containers make iterators available, algorithms use them:

Containers ⟺ Iterators ⟺ Algorithms

This leads to a separation which allows an exceptionally clear design. In the following example, variations of one program will be used to show that algorithms function just as well with C arrays as with template classes of the STL.

In this example, an int value to be entered in a dialog is to be found in an array, by using a find() function which is also present as an STL algorithm. In parallel, find() is formulated in different ways in order to visualize the processes. The required formulation is approached step by step by presenting a variation *without* usage of the STL. The container is a simple C array. To show that a pointer works as an iterator, the type name iterator is introduced with typedef.

```
//  k1/a3.4/main.cpp
//  (file names refer to the examples which are available via FTP)
//  variation 1, without using the STL
#include<iostream>   //  the new calling conventions for header
                     //  files can be found in Section 1.7.3


//  new type name Iterator for 'pointer to int'
typedef int* Iterator;

//  prototype of the algorithm
Iterator find(Iterator begin, Iterator end, const int& Value);

int main()
{
    const int Count = 100;
    int aContainer[Count];          //  define container

    Iterator begin = aContainer;    //  pointer to the beginning

    //  position after the last element
    Iterator end = aContainer + Count;

    //  fill container with even numbers
    for(int i = 0; i < Count; i++)
        aContainer[i] = 2*i;

    int Number = 0;
    while(1)
    {
        cout << " enter required number (-1 = end):";
```

```
        cin >> Number;
        if(Number == -1)                        //  program abort
            break;

        Iterator position = find(begin, end, Number);

        if (position != end)
            cout << "found at position "
                << (position - begin) << endl;
        else cout << Number << " not found!" << endl;
    }
}

//  implementation
Iterator find(Iterator begin, Iterator end,
            const int& Value)
{
    while(begin != end          //  pointer comparison
        && *begin != Value)     //  dereferencing and object comparison
        ++begin;                //  next position
    return begin;
}
```

It can be seen that the `find()` algorithm itself does not need to know anything about containers. It only uses pointers (iterators) which need to have very few capabilities:

- The `++` operator is used to proceed to the next position.
- The `*` operator is used for dereferencing. Applied to a pointer (iterator), it returns a reference to the underlying object.
- The pointers must allow comparison by means of the `!=` operator.

The objects in the container are compared by means of the `!=` operator. In the next step, we cancel the implementation of the `find()` function and replace the prototype with a template:

```
//  variation 2: algorithm as template (see k1/a3.4/maint1.cpp )
template<class Iteratortype, class T>
Iteratortype find(Iteratortype begin, Iteratortype end,
                const T& Value)
{
    while(begin != end          //  iterator comparison
        && *begin != Value)     //  dereferencing and object comparison
        ++begin;                //  next position
    return begin;
}
```

The rest of the program remains *unchanged*. The placeholder `Iteratortype` for the iterator's data type may have an arbitrary name. In the third step, we use a container of the STL. The iterators begin and end are replaced with the methods of the vector<T> class which return a corresponding iterator.

```cpp
// variation 3 : a container as STL template (see k1/a3.4/maint2.cpp )
#include<iostream>

// please include STL-directory!
#include<vector>   // STL

// new type name 'Iterator' for 'pointer to int'
typedef int* Iterator;

// algorithm as template
template<class Iteratortype, class T>
Iteratortype find(Iteratortype begin, Iteratortype end,
                  const T& Value)
{
    while(begin != end               // iterator comparison
          && *begin != Value)        // object comparison
        ++begin;                     // next position
    return begin;
}

using namespace std;

int main()
{
    const int Count = 100;
    vector<int> aContainer(Count);   // define container
    for(int i = 0; i < Count; i++)   // fill container with
        aContainer[i] = 2*i;         // even numbers

    int Number = 0;
    while(1)
    {
        cout << " enter required number (-1 = end):";
        cin >> Number;
        if(Number == -1)             // program abort
            break;

        // use of container methods:
        Iterator Position =
            // use our global find(), not the one in namespace std
            ::find(aContainer.begin(),
                aContainer.end(), Number);
```

```
        if (Position != aContainer.end())
           cout << "found at position "
                 << (Position - aContainer.begin()) << endl;
        else cout << Number << " not found!" << endl;
     }
  }
```

This shows how the STL container cooperates with our algorithm and how arithmetic with iterators is possible (formation of a difference). In the last step we use the `find()` algorithm contained in the STL and replace the whole template with an additional `#include` instruction:

```
//   variation 4: STL algorithm (k1/a3.4/maintstl.cpp )
#include<algorithm>
//   ... the rest as variation 3, but without find() template
```

In addition to this, it is not necessary to define an iterator type with `typedef` because every container of the STL supplies a corresponding type. Instead of `Iterator`, you may write `vector<int>::iterator` in the above program. An interesting fact is that the algorithm can cooperate with *any* class of iterators that provides the operations `!=` for comparison, `*` for dereferencing, and `++` for proceeding to the next element. This is one reason for the power of the concept and for the fact that each algorithm has to be present in only *one* form, which minimizes management problems and avoids inconsistencies. Thus, algorithms and containers of the C++ Standard Template Library come quite close to the ideal concept that one can simply plug together various software components which will then function with each other.

The use of the large number of algorithms and containers of the STL makes programs not only shorter, but also more reliable, because programming errors are prevented. This helps to increase productivity in software development.

1.4 Internal functioning

How does the STL function internally? To show this in detail, the example from the previous section will be used, not with a container of the STL, but with a user-defined class which behaves exactly as the classes of the STL. To ensure that an iterator of this class cannot simply be identified with a pointer, the example must be made slightly more complex: instead of the vector, we take a singly-linked list. The class will be called `slist` (for simple list).

Thus, we have no random access to the elements via the index operator. Therefore, the container is filled by means of the method `push_front()`. Furthermore, to keep the class as simple as possible, no run time optimization is considered. This class for a simple list is not complete; it provides only what is needed in the example.

The predefined `find()` algorithm is used to show that the user-defined class really behaves exactly like a class of the STL.

```
//   file k1/a4/slist : list template for singly-linked lists
//   T is a placeholder for the data type of a list element
```

```
//  incomplete (only functions needed for the example are implemented)
#ifndef simplelist
#define simplelist
#include<cassert>

template<class T>
class slist
{
  public:
    slist() : firstElement(0), Count(0) {}
```

/*

Copy constructor, destructor, and assignment operator are omitted. The implementation of `push_front()` creates a new list element and inserts it at the beginning of the list:

*/

```
    void push_front(const T& Datum) //  insert at beginning
    {
      ListElement *temp =  new ListElement(Datum, firstElement);
      firstElement = temp;
      ++Count;
    }

  private:
    struct ListElement
    {
        T Data;
        ListElement *Next;
        ListElement(const T& Datum, ListElement* p)
        : Data(Datum), Next(p) {}
    };

    ListElement *firstElement;
    size_t Count;
```

/*

The list consists of list elements whose type is defined inside the `list` class as a nested public class (`struct`). In a structure, direct access to internal data is possible, but this is not a problem here because the data is located in the private section of the `slist` class. Each list element carries the pertinent data, for example a number, together with a pointer to the next list element. `firstElement` is the pointer to the first list element. The class `slist` provides an iterator type `iterator` which is located in the `public` section since it is to be publicly accessible. It is also used in the following `main()` program. An iterator object stores the current container position in the `current` attribute. The methods satisfy the requirements for iterators formulated on page 7.

*/

```
public:
  class iterator
  {
    public:
      iterator(ListElement* Init = 0)
      : current(Init){}

      T& operator*()                // dereferencing
      {
          return current->Data;
      }

      const T& operator*() const    // dereferencing
      {
          return current->Data;
      }

      iterator& operator++()        // prefix
      {
        if(current) // not yet arrived at the end?
          current = current->Next;
        return *this;
      }

      iterator operator++(int)      // postfix
      {
        iterator temp = *this;
        ++*this;
        return temp;
      }

      bool operator==(const iterator& x) const
      {
        return current == x.current;
      }

  private:
    ListElement* current; // pointer to current element
}; // iterator
```

/*

As can be seen above, in the postfix variation of the ++ operator, the copy constructor is needed for initialization and return of temp. For this reason, the prefix variation should be preferred where possible. Some methods of the slist class use the iterator class:

*/

```
iterator begin() const { return iterator(firstElement);}
iterator end()   const { return iterator();}

/*
```
Some types of the iterator get public names. Then it is possible to use them outside the class without knowing the implementation.
```
*/
typedef T value_type;
typedef ptrdiff_t difference_type;
typedef T* pointer;
typedef T& reference;
// etc. See text.
};
#endif // slist
```

Sometimes it is advantageous to write

```
// internal type definition may be unknown
slist<myDataType>::difference_type Dist;
```

in a program instead of

```
// predefined type
long Dist;
```

This is especially useful if there are possible later changes in the internal type structure of class `slist`. Using the public type names avoids changing an application program which uses the list. More advantages will be described in Section 2.1.

At this point we only need the subtraction operator to be able to calculate differences between list iterators. The subtraction operator might be global because it does not have to know any internals of an iterator to fulfil its tasks:

```
template<class iterator>
int operator-(iterator a, iterator b) { ... }
```

On the other hand, conflicts with other `operator-()` templates may occur since the name `iterator` is only a placeholder for a data type and name spaces are not considered here. For this reason, the operator is restricted to `slist` iterators by inserting it into the `slist::iterator` class as an element function.

```
// insert into slist::iterator above
int operator-(iterator fromWhere)
{
    int Count = 0;
    while(fromWhere.current != current // not yet reached
          && fromWhere != iterator())  // not yet at the end
    {
        ++Count;
        ++fromWhere;
    }
```

```
        /*
        The difference between the iterator and the fromWhere iterator is determined
        by incrementing fromWhere until the iterator is reached. Thus, the condition
        is that fromWhere lies before the iterator. In other words: fromWhere must
        be able to reach the iterator by means of the ++ operator.
        */
    assert(current == fromWhere.current);

        /*
        In case of inequality, it is not possible to reach *this from fromWhere by
        means of ++.
        */
    return Count;
}
```

The loop condition involving `iterator()` (together with the assertion) ensures that the loop does not run endlessly and that the program aborts when the iterator cannot be reached from the iterator `fromWhere` by means of the ++ operation.

The following `main()` program strongly resembles the one on page 8 and uses the user-defined class in the same way as a class of the STL. Try using this example to get a clear idea of the functioning details, and you won't have any great problem understanding the STL.

```cpp
//  k1/a4/mainstl2.cpp
#include<algorithm>      //  contains find()
#include<iostream>
#include"slist"   //  user-defined list class (see above)
using namespace std;

int main()
{
    const int Count = 100;
    slist<int> aContainer;                // define the container

        /*
        Change of order because the container is filled from the front! This example differs
        from those in Section 1.3.4, because elements are inserted, that is, the container is
        expanded as needed.
        */

    for(int i = Count; i >= 0; i--)   // fill the container with
        aContainer.push_front(2*i);   // even numbers

    int Number = 0;
    while(true)
    {
        cout << " enter required number (-1 = end):";
        cin >> Number;
```

```
    if(Number == -1)                          //  program abort
        break;

    //  use of container methods:
    slist<int>::iterator Position =
        find(aContainer.begin(),
            aContainer.end(), Number);

    if (Position != aContainer.end())
        cout << "found at position "
            << (Position - aContainer.begin()) << endl;
    else cout << Number << " not found!" << endl;
    }

}
```

Exercise

1.1 Complete the `slist` class using the following:

- A method `iterator erase(iterator p)` that removes the element pointed to by the iterator `p` from the list. The returned iterator is to point to the element following `p` provided it exists. Otherwise, `end()` is to be returned.
- A method `void clear()` that deletes the whole list.
- A method `bool empty()` that shows whether the list is empty.
- A method `size_t size()` that returns the number of elements.
- A copy constructor, a destructor, and an assignment operator. The latter might use `clear()` to their advantage.

1.5 Complexity

The STL has been developed with the aim of achieving high efficiency. Run time costs are specified for each algorithm depending on the size and kind of the container to be processed. The only assumption made is that user-defined iterators can move from one element of a container to the next element in constant time.

This section gives a brief introduction to the concept of complexity as a measure for computing and memory requirements.

An algorithm should obviously be correct – this is, however, not the only requirement. Computer resources are limited. Thus, another requirement is that algorithms must be executed on a real machine in a finite number of cycles. The main resources are computer memory and available computing time.

Complexity is the term that describes the behavior of an algorithm with regard to memory and time consumption. The efficiency of an algorithm in the form of a running program depends on:

- the hardware,
- the type and speed of required operations,
- the programming language, and
- the algorithm itself.

The concept of complexity exclusively concerns the algorithm. Machine properties and programming language details are ignored, since they modify the time needed for an algorithm by a constant factor if we assume a von Neumann architecture. There are two ways of analyzing the efficiency of an algorithm:

1. Measurements

    (a) Carry out measurements of the run time behavior for different sets of input data.

    (b) The best, worst, and average cases are of interest. The cases depend on the properties of the input data, the system environment and the algorithm, so that corresponding knowledge must be available.

2. Analysis of the algorithm

    (a) The algorithm is analyzed. Machine and compiler are ignored.

    (b) The frequency of executed instructions is an index of the speed. This frequency can be directly derived from the algorithm.

    (c) Again, the best, worst, and average cases are of interest.

Only the second way will be described. Wherever the term 'complexity' appears, it is intended to mean *time complexity*. Examples can be found in Table 1.1. Since they are independent of any special programming language, they are written in pseudo-code notation. The symbol $\propto$ stands for 'proportional to.'

The loop variables i and j are of no importance in this context. The frequencies with which the instructions $x = x + y$ and $n = n/2$ in Table 1.1 are executed differ by *orders of magnitude* which are not dependent on any machine or programming language. Only these orders of magnitude are of interest here.

1.5.1 O notation

The 'O notation' describes an order of magnitude. In the examples of Table 1.1, the orders of magnitude $O(1)$, $O(n)$, $O(n^2)$, and $O(\log n)$ occur. Apart from a constant factor, the 'O notation' describes the maximum execution time for large values of n, thus indicating an *upper bound*. What 'large' means depends on the individual case, as will be shown in one of the following examples.

> *Definition:* Let $f(n)$ be the execution time of an algorithm. This algorithm is of (time) complexity $O(g(n))$ if and only if two positive constants c and n_0 exist so that $| f(n) | \leq c \, | g(n) |$ applies to all $n \geq n_0$.

Algorithm	Frequency	(Time) complexity
$x = x + y$	1	constant
for $i = 1$ to n *do* $x = x + y$ *od*	$\propto n$	linear

for $i = 1$ to n
 do
     for $j = 1$ to n
     do $x = x + y$
     od
 od
	$\propto n^2$	quadratic

$n =$ natural number
 $k = 0$
 while $n > 0$
 do
     $n = n/2$
     $k = k + 1$
 od
	$\propto \log n$	logarithmic

Table 1.1 Algorithms and frequency.

Example

Let us assume an algorithm for vectors whose execution time $f(n)$ depends on the length n of the vector. Let us further assume that

$$f(n) = n^2 + 5n + 100$$

applies. The execution time could now be estimated with a simpler function $g(n) = 1.1n^2$. If we now compare $f(n)$ with $g(n)$, we see that $g(n) > f(n)$ for all $n \geq 66$. Obviously, we could have chosen different values for c and n_0, for example $c = 1.01$ and $n_0 = 519$. Therefore, complexity of $f(n)$ is $O(n^2)$. The complexity says *nothing* about *actual* computing time.

Example

Let A be an algorithm of execution time $f_A(n) = 10^4 n$ and B be an algorithm of execution time $f_B(n) = n^2$. It can easily be seen that algorithm A is faster for all values $n > 10^4$, whereas B is faster for all $n < 10^4$. Algorithm A is therefore to be recommended for large values of n, where in this case, the word 'large' means $n > 10^4$.

Therefore, algorithms of low complexity should normally be preferred. Exceptions are possible, depending on the value of the constants c and n_0. In order to select an appropriate algorithm for a given problem, the size n of the input data set must be known.

Some rules

Example:

1. $O(const * f) = O(f)$ $\qquad$ $O(2n) = O(n)$

2. $O(f * g) = O(f) * O(g)$ $\qquad$ $O((17n) * n) = O(17n) * O(n)$
$$= O(n) * O(n) = O(n^2)$$

$O(f/g) = O(f)/O(g)$ $\qquad$ $O((3n^3)/n) = O(3n^2) = O(n^2)$

3. $O(f + g)$ = dominating function
of $O(f)$ and $O(g)$ $\qquad$ $O(n^5 + n^2) = O(n^5)$

Examples

Linear search

Let us assume an unordered sequence of names together with addresses and phone numbers. The task is to find the phone number for a given name.

- The number to be found can lie at the beginning, the end, or somewhere in the middle.

- On average, we must compare $n/2$ names when the total number of names is n.

- The time complexity is $O(n/2) = O(n)$.

Binary search

Now, we look for a name in a normal, thus sorted, phone book.

- We look in the middle of the book and find a name. If this is the name we are looking for, we have finished. If not, we continue our search in the left or right half of the book, depending on whether the name we are looking for is alphabetically located before or after the name we just saw.

- We repeat the previous step with the chosen half of the book until we have found the name we are looking for, or we find out that it does not occur in the book at all. With each of these steps, the number of possible names is halved: $n/2, n/4, n/8, ..., 4, 2, 1$.

- There exists a number k so that $n \geq 2^{k-1}$ and $n \leq 2^k$. We do not need more than k comparisons.

- The algorithm is of complexity $O(k) = O(\log_2 n) = O(\log n)$.

Travelling salesman problem (TSP)

A travelling salesman wants to visit n towns. He wants to save time and money and looks for the shortest route that connects all towns. One method to find the optimum solution is an analysis of all possible routes. What is the complexity of this method?

As his first town, he can choose one out of n towns. From this point, he can choose between $n - 1$ towns to drive to next. When he has reached the next town, he can choose between $n - 2$ towns, and so on. When he has visited $n - 1$ towns, only one choice remains: town number n. The total number of routes to connect n towns is $n \cdot (n - 1) \cdot (n - 2) \cdot \ldots \cdot 2 \cdot 1 = n!$

If 20 towns are to be visited, there are 20! = 2,432,902,008,176,640,000 different routes to compare. The complexity of the algorithm is $O(n!)$.

This well-known problem is an example of a class of similar problems which are called NP complete. NP is an abbreviation for 'non-deterministic polynomial.' This means that a non-deterministic algorithm (which 'magically' knows which is to be the next step) can solve the problem in polynomial time ($O(n^k)$). (A more extensive and more serious treatment of the subject can be found in Hopcroft and Ullman (1979).) In the end, it does not matter at all *in which order* the next town to be visited is chosen, but if you *do* know the right order, the solution is found very quickly.

However, predefining an order changes the algorithm into a deterministic one, and because magic does not work, we usually have no choice other than predefining a schematic order – and there we are! Only occasionally does experience help with specially structured problems. As far as the salesman is concerned, this means that there is no deterministic algorithm with a polynomial time function n^c (c = constant) that dominates $n!$ For each possible constant c there exists an n_0, so that for all n greater than n_0, $n!$ is greater than n^c.

The class of NP problems is also called 'intractable,' because for a large number of input variables, solution attempts do not arrive at a result in a reasonable time measured on a human timescale. On the other hand, existing solutions of NP problems can be verified 'quickly,' that is, in polynomial time.

A mathematical proof that the salesman problem and other related problems can have no polynomial solution is still pending. There are some heuristic methods which at least approach the optimum and are significantly faster than $O(n!)$.

This class of problems has practical applications, for example:

- drilling hundreds or thousands of holes in a circuit board with a moving laser in a minimum time,
- finding the cheapest path in a computer network,
- distributing goods in a region using a shipping agency.

1.5.2 Ω notation

The O notation defines an *upper* bound for an algorithm. Improvement of an algorithm can reduce the bound. For example, sequential search in a sorted table: $O(n)$, binary search in a sorted table: $O(\log n)$. Is there also a *lower* bound for a given algorithm? Is it possible to show that the solution of a given problem requires a certain minimum of effort?

If a problem necessitates *at least* $O(n^2)$ steps, there is no point in searching for an $O(n)$ solution.

The Ω notation describes lower bounds. For example, sequential search in a table is of the order $\Omega(n)$, because each element must be looked at at least once. $\Omega(\log n)$ is not possible. In this case, $\Omega(n) = O(n)$.

Example

Multiplication of two $n * n$ matrices:

upper bound:

$O(n^3)$ \qquad simple algorithm (three nested loops)

$O(n^{2.81})$ \qquad von Strassen 1969

$O(n^{2.376})$ \qquad Coppersmith and Winograd 1987
\qquad\qquad (quoted in Cormen *et al.* (1994))

lower bound:

$\Omega(n^2)$ \qquad at least two loops are needed, because
\qquad\qquad n^2 elements must be entered into the product matrix

1.6 Auxiliary classes and functions

This section briefly describes some tools which will be needed at a later stage.

1.6.1 Pairs

A *pair* in the sense of the STL is an encapsulation of two objects which belong together and which can be of different types. Pairs are fundamental components which will be used in later chapters. They are defined by means of a public (`struct`) template class, defined in header `<utility>`:

```
template <class T1, class T2>
struct pair
{
    T1 first;
    T2 second;
    pair(){};
    pair(const T1& a, const T2& b)
    : first(a), second(b) {}
};
```

The standard constructor causes the elements to be initiated with the standard constructors of their type. In addition to the class definition, there are some global comparison operators:

```
template <class T1, class T2>
inline bool operator==(const pair<T1, T2>& x,
                       const pair<T1, T2>& y)
```

```
{
    return x.first == y.first && x.second == y.second;
}

template <class T1, class T2>
inline bool operator<(const pair<T1, T2>& x,
                      const pair<T1, T2>& y)
{
    return x.first < y.first
        || ( !(y.first < x.first)
            && x.second < y.second);
}
```

When the first objects are equal, the return value of the < operator is determined by the comparison of the second objects. However, in order to make only minimum demands on the objects, the equality operator == is not used in the second template. It might be the case that equality of two pairs is not required in a program. Then, the above template operator==() is not applied, so that the classes T1 and T2 only have to provide the < operator.

A function facilitates the generation of pairs:

```
template <class T1, class T2>
inline pair<T1, T2> make_pair(const T1& x, const T2& y)
{
    return pair<T1, T2>(x, y);
}
```

pair objects are needed from Section 4.4.1 onward.

1.6.2 Comparison operators

The STL provides global comparison operators which make it possible that in a class only the operators == and < must be defined and yet the whole set of comparisons is available:

```
template <class T>
inline bool operator!=(const T& x, const T& y)
{
    return !(x == y);
}

template <class T>
inline bool operator>(const T& x, const T& y)
{
    return y < x;
}
```

```
template <class T>
inline bool operator<=(const T& x, const T& y)
{
    return !(y < x);
}


template <class T>
inline bool operator>=(const T& x, const T& y)
{
    return !(x < y);
}
```

Strictly speaking, it would be possible to manage with only the < operator if the following definition is contained in the STL:

```
//  not part of the STL!
template <class T>
inline bool operator==(const T& x, const T& y)
{
    return !(x < y) && !(y < x);
}
```

This kind of check is sometimes used inside the STL. Strictly speaking, the term 'equality' is no longer appropriate; one should actually use the term 'equivalence.' When comparing integer numbers with the < operator, the two terms coincide; this is, however, not generally the case, as the following example shows. In Webster's International Dictionary, accented letters are treated in the same way as the corresponding simple vowels. Thus, 'pièce de résistance' stands between 'piece by piece' and 'piece-meal.' 'pièce' and 'piece' are not equal, but equivalent with respect to sorting. Another way of carrying out comparisons is shown in Section 1.6.3.

1.6.3 Function objects

In an expression, the call of a function is replaced with the result returned by the function. The task of the function can be taken over by an object – a technique frequently employed in the algorithms of the STL. For this purpose, the function operator () is overloaded with the operator function operator()().

Then an object can be called in the same way as a function. Algorithmic objects of this kind are called *function objects* or *functors*.

Functors are objects which behave like functions but have all the properties of objects. They can be generated, passed as parameters, or have their state modified. The change of state allows a flexible application which, with functions, would be only possible via additional parameters.

Object definition (Type T)	Call	Return
`equal_to<T> X;`	`X(x, y)`	`x == y`
`not_equal_to<T> X;`	`X(x, y)`	`x != y`
`greater<T> X;`	`X(x, y)`	`x > y`
`less<T> X;`	`X(x, y)`	`x < y`
`greater_equal<T> X;`	`X(x, y)`	`x >= y`
`less_equal<T> X;`	`X(x, y)`	`x <= y`

Table 1.2   Template classes for comparison (header `<functional>`).

Comparisons

The STL provides a large number of template classes for comparisons. Objects of this class appear later under the name of comparison object. Table 1.2 shows the calls of objects as function calls, that is, `X(x,y)` is identical to `X.operator()(x,y)`.

The comparison classes are binary functions, and therefore they inherit from the `binary_function` class. The only purpose of this class is to provide uniform type names for all classes inheriting from it:

```
template<class Arg1, class Arg2, class Result>
struct binary_function
{
    typedef Arg1 first_argument_type;
    typedef Arg2 second_argument_type;
    typedef Result result_type;
};
```

For unary classes, a corresponding template `unary_function` is defined. The word `struct` saves the `public` label. Everything can be public, because the class has no data to be protected. This, for example, is the `equal_to` template for equality:

```
template<class T>
struct equal_to : binary_function<T, T, bool>
{
    bool operator()(const T& x, const T& y) const
    {
        return x == y;
    }
};
```

The aim of templates is to supply algorithms with a uniform interface. The templates rely on the corresponding operators of data type T. However, a specialized comparison class can be written for user-defined classes without having to change the algorithm. The user-defined class does not even need to have the comparison operators `==`, `<` and so on. This technique is used quite frequently; at this point, a short example will demonstrate how it functions.

A normal C array of `int` numbers is sorted once by element size using the standard comparison object `less<int>` and once by the *absolute value* of the elements, where in the second case, a user-defined comparison object `absoluteLess` is used. To show the effect more clearly, a normal C array and a modest function template `bubble_sort` are used instead of accessing the containers and algorithms of the STL.

```cpp
//  k1/a6/compare.cpp – Demonstration of comparison objects
#include<functional>        //  less<T>
#include<iostream>
#include<cstdlib>           //  abs()

struct absoluteLess
{
        bool operator()(int x, int y) const
        {
            return (abs(x) < abs(y));
        }
};
```

The following sorting routine no longer uses the < operator in the `if` condition, but the comparison object whose `operator()(...)` is called.

```cpp
template<class T, class CompareType>
void bubble_sort(T* array, int Count,
                 const CompareType& Compare)
{
    for(int i = 0; i < Count; i++)
        for(int j = i+1; j < Count; j++)
        if (Compare(array[i], array[j])) //  functor call
        {   //  exchange
            const T temp = array[i];
            array[i] = array[j];
            array[j] = temp;
        }
}

//  Auxiliary procedure for display
void Display(int *Array, int N)
{
    for(int i = 0; i < N; i++)
    {   cout.width(7);
        cout << Array[i];
    }
    cout << endl;
}

using namespace std;
```

```
int main()
{
    int Table[] = {55, -7, 3, -9, 2, -9198, -937, 1, 473};
    const int num = sizeof(Table)/sizeof(int);

    /*
    The comparison object normalCompare is of the standard class type less, which
    has been made known with #include<functional>. less compares with the
    < operator..
    */

    // Variation 1
    less<int> normalCompare;
    bubble_sort(Table, num, normalCompare);
    cout << "sorted by size:" << endl;
    Display(Table, num);
        // 473 55 3 2 1 –7 –9 –937 –9198

    /*
    Alternatively, you can do without explicit creation of an object when the constructor
    is called in the argument list.
    */

    // Variation 2
    bubble_sort(Table, num, less<int>());

    /*
    The comparison object is of the user-defined type absoluteLess which uses not only
    the < operator, but also the abs() function, and which in principle can be arbitrarily
    complex. It is a big advantage that the bubble_sort algorithm and its interface do
    not have to be changed.
    */

    cout << "sorted by absolute value:" << endl;
    bubble_sort(Table, num, absoluteLess());
    Display(Table, num);
        // –9198 –937 473 55 –9 –7 3 2 1
}   // End of example
```

The user-defined design of special comparison functions shows the great flexibility of the concept of function objects. In addition to the examples shown, appropriately written function objects can also carry data, if needed.

Arithmetic and logic operations

As in the previous section, the STL provides template classes for arithmetic and logic operations (see Table 1.3) which can be used like a function by means of the overloaded operator(). (Note that 'multiplies' was called 'times' in earlier versions of

Object definition (Type T)	Call	Return
plus<T> X;	X(x, y)	x + y
minus<T> X;	X(x, y)	x - y
multiplies<T> X;	X(x, y)	x * y
divides<T> X;	X(x, y)	x / y
modulus<T> X;	X(x, y)	x % y
negate<T> X;	X(x)	-x
logical_and<T> X;	X(x, y)	x && y
logical_or<T> X;	X(x, y)	x || y
logical_not<T> X;	X(x, y)	!x

Table 1.3   Arithmetic and logic template classes (header <functional>).

the C++ standard draft.) The advantage is again that these templates can be overwritten with specializations without having to change the interfaces of the algorithms involved.

1.6.4 Function adapters

Function adapters are nothing more than function objects which cooperate with other function objects to adapt them to different requirements. This allows us to get by with existing functors and avoid writing new ones.

not1

The function not1 takes a functor as the parameter which represents a predicate with *one* argument (thus the suffix 1) and returns a functor which converts the logical result of the predicate into its opposite. Let us assume that there exists a predicate odd with the following definition:

```
struct odd : public unary_function<int, bool>
{
    bool operator () (int x) const { return (x % 2) == 1; }
};
```

Application of not1 is shown by the following program fragment:

```
int i;
cin >> i;
if(odd()(i))
   cout << i << " is odd";
if(not1(odd())(i))
   cout << i << " is even";
```

Instead of an object declared on purpose, first a temporary object of type odd is generated whose operator () is called. In the second if instruction, not1 generates a functor whose operator () is called with the argument i. How does this work? The STL provides a class out of which not1 generates an object:

```
template <class Predicate>
class unary_negate
    : public unary_function<Predicate::argument_type, bool>
{
  protected:
    Predicate pred;
  public:
    unary_negate(const Predicate& x) : pred(x) {}
    bool operator()(const argument_type& x) const
    {
        return !pred(x);
    }
};
```

The operator () returns the negated predicate. The class inherits the type definition of argument_type from unary_function.

not2

This function works in a similar way, but it refers to predicates with *two* parameters. This can be used to reverse the sorting order of variation 2 on page 24:

```
//   Variation 2, reverse sorting order
bubble_sort(Table, num, not2(less<int>()));
```

Analogous to not1, internally a class binary_negate is used. The sorting order by *absolute value* on page 24 can be reversed with not2 only if the class inherits from binary_function for comparisons (see page 22):

```
struct absoluteLess
    : public binary_function<int, int, bool>
{  ...  //  as above
};
```

bind1st, bind2nd

These functions transform binary function objects into unary function objects by binding one of the two arguments to a value. They accept a function object with two arguments and a value x. They return a unary function object whose first or second argument is bound to the value x. For example, the known functor less (see Table 1.2) compares two values and returns true if the first value is less than the second one. If the second value is fixed, for example to 1000, a unary function object suffices which is generated by means of `binder2nd`. The `find()` algorithm described on page 6 has an overloaded variation described later (page 97) which accepts one predicate.

```
find(v.begin(), v.end(), bind2nd(less<int>(), 1000));
```

finds the first number in the `int` vector `v` which is less than 1000, and

```
find(v.begin(), v.end(), bind1st(less<int>(), 1000));
```

finds the first number in the `int` vector `v` which is not less than 1000. The functors returned by the functions `bind1st<operation, value>()` and `bind2nd<operation, value>()` are of the type `binder1st<operation, value>` and `binder2nd <operation, value>`. In an application such as the one above, the types usually do not appear explicitly (class definition in header `<functional>`).

ptr_fun

This overloaded function transforms a pointer to a function into a functor. As an argument, it has a pointer to the function which can have one or two parameters. The function returns a function object which can be called in the same way as the function. The types of function objects defined in `<functional>` are

```
pointer_to_unary_function<parameter1, result>
```

and

```
pointer_to_binary_function<parameter1, parameter2, result>
```

Frequently (but not always), these types remain hidden in the application. A short example shows its use. A pointer to a function is initialized with the sine function. Subsequently, the sine of an angle is called both via the function pointer and via a function object generated with `ptr_fun()`.

```
#include<functional>
#include<iostream>
#include<cmath>

double (*f)(double) = sin;        // initialize pointer


using namespace std;

int main()
{
   double alpha = 0.7854;
                                   // call as:
   cout << f(alpha)                // function
        << endl
        << ptr_fun(f)(alpha)       // functor
        << endl;;
}
```

1.7 Naming and other conventions

1.7.1 Notation

Sometimes, file names are used that are longer than eight characters. Some obsolete operating systems are not capable of handling these long names. For this reason, file names in the examples which are available via FTP have been shortened correspondingly, which leads to discrepancies with the text of the book which is following the current C++ standard proposal.

1.7.2 Name spaces and predefined parameters in templates

At the time of publication of this book, name spaces and predefined parameters in templates are not supported by most compilers. Declarations such as

```
namespace std {
template <class Key, class Compare = less<Key>,
        class Allocator = allocator>
class set
{
    // ...
```

are therefore simplified in the sample programs to:

```
template <class Key, class Compare>
class set
{
    // ...
```

Depending on the implementation, the parameter that was intended to be predefined can therefore appear in the declaration of objects, for example:

```
set<int, less<int> > anIntSet;
```

instead of

```
set<int> anIntSet;
```

When writing nested templates, care should be taken to write '...T> >,' that is, with a space, instead of '...T>>,' in order to prevent confusion with the shift operator. The type `Allocator` is used for allocation of memory (see page 283). If it is not specified, the allocator provided by the system is used.

1.7.3 Header files

According to the conventions of the C++ standard proposal, the new header names should be preferred (ISO/IEC, 1997). In order to achieve this behavior in the sample programs, an include directory has been added with the corresponding files which include the header files with extension .h of the current STL version by means of `#include`. This process can be omitted when the file names of the STL have been changed to the standard convention. An example:

```
//   file vector (forwarding header file)
#include<vector.h>
//   end of file vector
```

The C standard library functions are accessed as before, or by omitting the '.h' extension of the file name and prefixing the old file name with a 'c.' For example:

```
#include<string>        //   C++ string class

#include<cstring>       //   C string functions for C++
#include<string.h>      //   C string functions as before

#include<cctype>        //   ctype functions for C++
#include<ctype.h>       //   ctype functions as before
```

The new calling conventions put all C-headers into the name space `std`. For example, the standard header `<cctype>` is in the name space `std`, whereas `<ctype.h>` is in the global name space.

1.7.4 Nested templates

Currently, only a few commercially available compilers support nested templates in classes (member templates), as they are used, for example, in Section A.2 and elsewhere. They are therefore omitted in the examples.

Iterators

2

Summary: *Iterators are used by algorithms to move through containers. The simplest iterators are common pointers as shown in Section 1.3.4. This chapter describes different types of iterator and their properties in detail.*

A preliminary remark: iterators closely cooperate with containers. A parallel presentation of iterators and containers in a sequential text is however difficult and probably not very clear, and for this reason the containers of the STL are described only in the following chapter. In order to refer as far as possible only to previously explained issues, certain aspects of iterators which can only be understood with a knowledge of containers are temporarily left out. They will be considered at the end of Chapter 3.

Essential properties for all iterators are the capabilities mentioned on page 7 of advancing (++), of dereferencing (*), and of comparison (!= or ==). If the iterator is not a common pointer, but an object of an iterator class, these properties are implemented by means of the corresponding operator functions:

```
//  scheme of a simple iterator:
template<class T>
class Iterator
{
    public:
        //  constructors, destructor ....

        bool operator==(const Iterator<T>&) const;
        bool operator!=(const Iterator<T>&) const;
        Iterator<T>& operator++();              //  prefix
        Iterator<T>  operator++(int);           //  postfix
        T& operator*() const;
        T* operator->() const;
    private:
        //  association with the container ...
};
```

The operator -> allows you to use an iterator in the same way as a pointer. For a vector container, one could obviously imagine that the iterator should also have a method `operator--()`. Different reasonable and possible capabilities of iterators are discussed further below.

The corresponding implementations of the lines beginning with the comment symbol (`//`) depend on the container with which the iterator is to work. The difference with a normal pointer has already been seen in Section 1.4 which shows an iterator working with a list. The iterator remembers the element of the list to which it points in a private pointer variable `current` (see page 10). Each element of the list contains `Data` and has a variable that points to the following element.

2.1 Iterator properties

2.1.1 States

Iterators are a generalization of pointers. They allow you to work with different containers in the same way. An iterator can assume several states.

- An iterator can be generated even without being associated with a container. The association with the container is then made at a later stage. Such an iterator cannot be dereferenced. A comparable C++ pointer could, for example, have the value 0.

- An iterator can be associated with a container during generation or at a later stage. Typically – but not compulsorily – after initialization it points to the beginning of the container. The method `begin()` of a container supplies the starting position. If the container is not empty, the iterator can in this case be dereferenced. Thus, it can be used to access an element of the container. With the exception of the `end()` position (see next point) the iterator can be dereferenced for all values that can be reached with the `++` operation.

- In C++ the value of a pointer which points to a position directly *past* the last element of a C array is always defined. Similarly, the method `end()` of a container always returns an iterator with exactly this meaning, even if the container is not an array but, for example, a list. This allows you to deal with iterator objects and pointers to C++ basic data types in the same way. A comparison of a current iterator with this past-the-end value signals whether the end of a container has been reached. Obviously, an iterator which points to the position past the end of a container cannot be dereferenced.

2.1.2 Distances

In the examples on page 6 ff, the required position in the array was determined by the difference of two pointers or iterators. In C++, the difference of a subtraction of pointers is represented by the data type `ptrdiff_t` which can be seen in the header `<cstddef>`.

In a container, everything happens between `begin()` (inclusive) and `end()` (exclusive). However, the range may not be sufficient; just think of a 16-bit `int` data type for `ptrdiff_t` and a file with a million entries as the container. For this purpose, the appropriate data type for the distance between two iterators can be chosen by the user. A standard function template `distance()` then determines the distance:

```
//  previous version of the C++ standard proposal (ISO 96), see text
template<class Iterator_type, class Distance_type>
void distance(Iterator_type First, Iterator_type Second,
              Distance_type& Distance)  // int or long
{
     //  calculation
}
```

The parameter `Distance` is incremented by the calculated difference. That means, it should be set to zero before the call. The calculation for iterators that work with a vector consists only of a subtraction. If the container is a singly-linked list, the calculation will consist of a loop which counts the number of steps from the first iterator to the second. In order to advance an iterator by a given distance, the global function `advance()` can be used:

```
template<class InputIterator_type, class Distance_type>
void advance(Input_iterator& I, Distance_type N);
```

The iterator `I` is advanced by `N` steps. For iterators that can move forward and backward (bidirectional iterators) `N` may be negative.

The distance type depends on the input operator's type. Therefore, the C++ standard committee has decided to use this dependency in the `distance()` template for distance calculation (see Section 2.1.3).

2.1.3 Standard iterator and traits classes

One essential advantage of templates is the evaluation of type names at compile time. To use type names that belong to iterators in a program without having to look into the internals of the iterator, it is specified that each iterator of the C++ Standard Library makes certain type names publicly available. (This section represents a change from ISO/ANSI (1996) to ISO/IEC (1997).) The same principle also applies to containers. The `list` class on page 12 provides such type names.

Traits classes are a tool for exporting the type names of an iterator class:

```
template<class Iterator>
struct iterator_traits
{
  typedef Iterator::difference_type difference_type;
  typedef Iterator::value_type value_type;
  typedef Iterator::pointer pointer;
  typedef Iterator::reference reference;
  typedef Iterator::iterator_category iterator_category;
};
```

The question arises of why this task cannot be fulfilled directly by an iterator class itself. It can – in most cases. The algorithms of the C++ Standard Library should, however, be able to work not only on STL containers that provide type names, but also on simple C arrays. Iterators working on such arrays are, however, simply pointers, possibly to basic data types such as int. An iterator of type int* can certainly not provide any type names. To ensure that a generic algorithm can nevertheless use the usual type names, the above template is specialized for pointers:

```
// specialization for pointers
template<class T>
struct iterator_traits<T*>
{
  typedef ptrdiff_t difference_type;
  typedef T value_type;
  typedef T* pointer;
  typedef T& reference;
  typedef random_access_iterator_tag iterator_category;
};
```

The iterator category is explained from page 36 onward. With these two templates it is possible to derive the other type names needed, and the distance() function can be written differently:

```
template<class InputIterator>
iterator_traits<InputIterator>::difference_type
distance(InputIterator First, InputIterator Second)
{
    // calculation
}
```

The advantage is that only one type must be specified at the instantiation of the template. The return type is a distance type specified in the iterator_traits class. The traits classes allow definition of the data type names such as difference_type both for complex iterators and for basic data types such as int*.

How does this work in detail? The compiler reads the return type of distance() and instantiates the iterator_traits template with the corresponding iterator. Two cases must be distinguished:

- The iterator is of complex nature, for example a list iterator. Then the sought type iterator_traits<Iteratortyp>::difference_type is identical with Iteratortyp::difference_type, as results from the evaluation of the instantiated iterator_traits template. In the case of the singly-linked list of page 12 this type results in ptrdiff_t.

- The iterator is a simple pointer, for example int*. For a pointer type, no names such as difference_type can be internally defined via typedef. The specialization of the iterator_traits template for pointers now ensures that *no* access is made to names of the iterator, because the required names can be found directly in the specialization without having to pass through an iterator. Then the sought type iterator_traits<Iteratortyp>::difference_type is identical with `ptrdiff_t`, as results from the evaluation of the instantiated specialized `iterator_traits` template.

Thus, `distance()` can be described very generally, as shown above. Without the traits mechanism, there would have to be specializations for all the pointers, not only for pointers to basic data types, but also for pointers to class objects.

In order to make life easier for programmers, the C++ Standard Library specifies one standard data type for iterators from which each user-defined iterator can inherit:

```
namespace std
{
  template<class Category, class T, class Distance = ptrdiff_t,
           class Pointer = T*, class Reference = T&>
  struct iterator
  {
    typedef Distance difference_type;
    typedef T value_type;
    typedef Pointer pointer;
    typedef Reference reference;
    typedef Category iterator_category; //  see Section 2.1.4
  };
}
```

Via a `public` inheritance, these names are visible and usable in all derived classes.

2.1.4 Categories

The STL provides different iterators for the container in question. Each of these iterators can be assigned to one of the following five categories:

- input iterator
- output iterator
- forward iterator
- bidirectional iterator
- random access iterator

The categories correspond to the different capabilities of the iterators. For example, an iterator responsible for writing into a sequential file cannot move backward.

A special kind of iterator used for inserting elements into containers will be described in Section 3.5.

Input iterator

An input iterator is designed for reading a sequential stream of input data, that is, an istream. No write access to the object is possible. Thus, dereferencing does not supply an lvalue. The program fragment shows the principle of use:

```
//  'Wherefrom' is an input iterator
Wherefrom = Stream_container.begin();
while(Wherefrom != Stream_container.end())
{
    Value = *Wherefrom;
    //  further calculations with Value ...
    ++Wherefrom;
}
```

Because of the stream property of the container associated with the input iterator, it is not possible to remember a special iterator value in order to retrieve an already read object at a later stage. Input iterators are suitable only for a *single* pass.

Output iterator

An output iterator is designed for writing not only into a container, but also into a sequential stream of output data (ostream). No read access to the object via dereferencing is possible. Dereferencing results in an lvalue which should exclusively be used on the left-hand side of an assignment.

```
//  'Whereto' is an output iterator
*Whereto = Value;
++Whereto;            //  advance
```

The two instructions are usually combined to

```
*Whereto++ = Value;
```

If the output iterator works on a stream, advancing is already carried out by the assignment. Then, the ++ operation is an empty operation and exists only for reasons of syntactic uniformity (see also pages 46 and 70). Output iterators too are suitable for only *one* pass. Only one output iterator should be active on one container – thus we can do without comparison operations of two output iterators.

Forward iterator

As with the input iterator and the output iterator, the forward iterator moves forward. In contrast to the iterators mentioned above, the values of this iterator may be stored in order to retrieve an element of the container. This allows a multi-pass in one direction. A forward iterator would, for example, be suitable for a singly-linked list.

Bidirectional iterator

A bidirectional iterator can do everything that a forward iterator can do. In addition, it can move *backward*, so that it is suitable for a doubly-linked list, for example. A bidirectional iterator differs from a forward iterator by the additional methods `operator--()` (prefix) and `operator--(int)` (postfix).

Random access iterator

A random access iterator can do everything that a bidirectional iterator can do. In addition, it allows random access, as it is needed for a vector. Random access is implemented via the index operator `operator[]()`. One consequence of this is the possibility of carrying out arithmetic operations, completely analogous to the pointer arithmetic of C++.

A further consequence is the determination of an order by means of the relational operators `<`, `>`, `<=`, and `<=`. In the following program, `Position` is a random access iterator associated with `Table`, a vector container. `n1` and `n2` are variables of type `Distance_type` (see page 33).

```
//  Position is an iterator which points to
//   a location somewhere inside Table
n1 = Position - Table.begin();
cout << Table[n1] << endl;     //  is equivalent to:
cout << *Position  << endl;

if(n1 < n2)
    cout << Table[n1] <<   "lies before "
           << Table[n2] << endl;
```

In the simplest case, `Position` can be of type `int*`, and `n1` and `n2` of type `int`.

2.1.5 Reverse iterators

A reverse iterator is always possible with a bidirectional iterator. A reverse iterator moves *backward* through a container by way of the `++` operation. The start and end of a container for reverse iterators are marked with `rbegin()` (points to the last element) and `rend()` (fictitious position before the first element, an example follows on page 56). Some containers provide reverse iterators, depending on their type. These iterators are realized with the predefined class

```
template<class Iterator>
class reverse_iterator;
```

An object of this class is initialized with a bidirectional iterator or a random access iterator, depending on the type of the template parameter. Internally, a reverse iterator works with the initializing iterator and puts a wrapper with determined additional operations around it. A new interface is created for an existing iterator, so that it can adapt to different situations. For this reason, classes that transform one class into another are called *adaptors*. A bidirectional iterator can move backward with the -- operation. This property is used to move from the end of a container to its beginning by means of a reverse bidirectional iterator using the ++ operation.

The iterator adaptor `reverse_iterator` also provides the element function `base()` which returns the current position as a bidirectional iterator. `base()` is needed to allow mixed calculations with normal and reverse iterators which work on the same container:

```
container C;            //  any container type with public
                        //  predefined types for iterators

container::iterator I = C.begin();            //  start of C
container::reverse_iterator RI = C.rbegin();  //  end of C

//  .... operations with the iterators


//  calculation of distance:
container::difference_type Distance = 0;

distance(RI, I, Distance);                    //  incorrect
//  compiler error message:
//  RI and I are not of the same type

distance(RI.base(), I, Distance);             //  correct
```

There are two kinds:

- Reverse bidirectional iterator
  This iterator can do everything that a bidirectional iterator can do. The only difference is the moving direction: the ++ operation of the reverse iterator has the same effect as the -- operation of the bidirectional iterators and vice versa.

- Reverse random access iterator
  This iterator can do everything the bidirectional reverse iterator described above can do. In addition, the arithmetic operations +, -, +=, and -= allow you to jump backward and forward several positions at a time in the container. In the above example, `distance()` uses the ++ operation; with a random access iterator, however, it uses arithmetic. Thus, you can write:
  ```
  Distance = RI.base() - I;
  ```

The application of a reverse iterator is shown on page 56. Application of iterator categories in connection with containers and examples will be discussed only after the introduction of the different types of containers (Section 3.4).

2.1.6 Tag classes

Each iterator of the STL is equipped with one of the following tags which can also be employed in the users' own programs. The tags are predefined as follows:

```
//  tag classes (ISO/IEC, 1997)
struct input_iterator_tag {};

struct output_iterator_tag {};

struct forward_iterator_tag
  : public input_iterator_tag {};

struct bidirectional_iterator_tag
  : public forward_iterator_tag {};

struct random_access_iterator_tag
  : public bidirectional_iterator_tag {};
```

Note: In ISO/ANSI (1996) the relationships between classes had not yet been expressed via inheritance, so that they coexisted independently.

2.2 Stream iterators

Stream iterators are used to work directly with input and output streams. The following sections show how stream iterators are employed for reading and writing sequential files. Stream iterators use the << and >> operators known from standard input and standard output.

2.2.1 Istream iterator

The istream iterator `istream_iterator<T>` is an input iterator and uses `opera-tor>>()` for reading elements of type `T` with the well-known properties that 'white space,' that is spaces, tabs, and line feeds are ignored when in front of an element and are interpreted as separators when between two elements. Otherwise, all characters of the input stream are interpreted according to the required data type. Erroneous characters remain in the input and lead to endless loops, if no error treatment is incorporated.

During its construction and with each advance using ++, the istream iterator reads an element of type `T`. It is an input iterator with all the properties described in Section 2.1.4. At the end of a stream, the istream iterator becomes equal to the stream end iterator generated by the standard constructor `istream_iterator <T>()`. A comparison with the stream end operator is the only way of determining the end of a stream. The following very simple program reads all character strings separated by white space from a file (*istring.cpp* in the example) and outputs them line by line:

```
//  k2/istring.cpp
#include<fstream>
#include<iterator>
#include<string>
```

```
using namespace std;

int main( )
{
    //  defining and opening of input file
    ifstream Source("istring.cpp");
    istream_iterator<string, ptrdiff_t> Pos(Source), End;

    /*
    The iterator End has no association with Source because all iterators of a type which
    indicate the past-end position are considered to be equal.
    */

    if(Pos == End)
        cout << "File not found!" << endl;
    else
        while(Pos != End)
        {
            cout << *Pos << endl;
            ++Pos;
        }
}
```

 Character strings are represented by the standard data type string. At first sight, the basic data type char* might have been used as well, but there is a hitch to it: the iterator tries to read an object of type char*, but it is not possible to allocate memory to this object, and so the program will probably 'crash.' More complex types are possible, as will be shown in the next section. End is generated by the standard constructor (with no arguments), and Pos is the iterator associated with the Source stream. The first read operation is already executed during construction with the istream argument, so that the subsequent dereferencing in the while loop always results in a defined value for the character string which is then written to the standard output.

Inheriting from the istream iterator

It is possible to write an istream iterator with special properties which inherits from the istream_iterator class. An example can be found in Chapter 10. Since access to several internals is needed, some items are protected from the very beginning and are thus usable for derived classes. For this reason, an implementation is shown:

```
//  excerpt of the HP implementation of the STL
template <class T, class Distance>
class istream_iterator
    : public input_iterator<T, Distance>   //  see remark below
{
    friend bool operator==(
            const istream_iterator<T, Distance>& x,
```

```
                        const istream_iterator<T, Distance>& y);
protected:                      // access from derived classes is allowed
    istream* stream;
    T value;                    // read object

    bool end_marker;    // true, if end not yet reached
```

```
    /*
```
Naming in this citation is contradictory: end_marker becomes false when the end is reached, instead of the other way round. If the stream is all right and not empty, an element is read with read(). In the (*stream) condition, the type conversion operator void* of the ios class is called to determine the state of the stream.
```
    */
```

```
    void read()
    {
        end_marker = (*stream) ? true : false;
        if (end_marker) *stream >> value;
        end_marker = (*stream) ? true : false;
    }

public:
    istream_iterator() : stream(&cin), end_marker(false) {}

    // the constructor already reads the first element (if present)
    istream_iterator(istream& s) : stream(&s) { read(); }
    const T& operator*() const { return value; }

    istream_iterator<T, Distance>& operator++()
    {
        read();
        return *this;
    }

    istream_iterator<T, Distance> operator++(int)
    {
        istream_iterator<T, Distance> tmp = *this;
        read();
        return tmp;
    }
};
```

Two istream iterators are also equal when both point to the end of a stream, as shown by the equality operator:

```
template <class T, class Distance>
bool operator==(const istream_iterator<T, Distance>& x,
                const istream_iterator<T, Distance>& y)
{
```

```
      return x.stream == y.stream && x.end_marker == y.end_marker
        || x.end_marker == false && y.end_marker == false;
}
```

Note: The HP implementation provides an input iterator class from which the properties of the input operator are inherited. According to ISO/IEC (1997) the `istream_iterator` class would be defined in a slightly different way:

```
template <class T>
class istream_iterator
  : public iterator<input_iterator_tag, T>
{ // ...
```

The rest can remain as above, except that the second template parameter `Distance` must be deleted.

2.2.2 Ostream iterator

The ostream iterator `ostream_iterator<T>` uses `operator<<()` for writing elements. This iterator writes at each assignment of an element of type `T`. It is an output iterator with all the properties described in Section 2.1.4.

Consecutive elements are normally written with `<<` directly into the stream, one after the other and without separators. Most often, this is undesirable because the result is often unreadable. To avoid this, the ostream iterator can at its construction be equipped with a character string of type `char*` which is inserted as a separator after each element. In the example on page 45, this is `\n` which is used to generate a line feed after each output.

In contrast to the example on page 39, the data type to be read and written is to be slightly more complex than `string`. Therefore, the task is now to read all *identifiers* from a file, according to the convention of a programming language, and to write them line by line into another file. Identifiers shall be defined as follows:

- An identifier always starts with a letter or an underscore '_'.
- Each following character occurring in an identifier is either alphanumeric (that is, a letter or a digit) or an underscore.

Thus, it is evident that an identifier cannot be read with the usual `>>` operator. Instead, we need an operator which considers these syntax rules and, for example, ignores special characters. Furthermore, an identifier must be able to contain a certain number of characters. Here, the number is 100, with the assumption that longer identifiers will not occur. An identifier should be able to be output with the usual `<<` operator. With this information, we can already construct a simple class for identifiers:

```
// k2/identify/identif.h
#ifndef identif_h
#define identif_h
#include<iostream>
```

```
#include<string>
using namespace std;

class Identifier
{
  public:
    string asstring() const { return theIdentifier;}
    friend istream& operator>>(istream&, Identifier&);
    friend ostream& operator<<(ostream&, const Identifier&);
    friend bool operator==(const Identifier&, const Identifier&);
    friend bool operator<(const Identifier&, const Identifier&);
  private:
    string theIdentifier;
};
```

The method `asstring()` allows you to generate a copy of the private variable which can be read and modified without affecting the original. The comparison operators are not really needed here but, on the other hand, containers are supposed to be comparable, which assumes that the elements of a container are comparable too. The comparison operators ensure that objects of the `Identifier` class can be stored in containers.

```
inline bool operator==(const Identifier& N1,
                       const Identifier& N2)
{
    return N1.theIdentifier == N2.theIdentifier;
}

inline bool operator<(const Identifier& N1,
                      const Identifier& N2)
{
    return N1.theIdentifier < N2.theIdentifier;
}
#endif
```

In order to find the beginning of an identifier, the implementation of the input operator in the file *identif.cpp* first searches for a letter or an underscore.

```
//  k2/identify/identif.cpp
#include"identif.h"
#include<cctype>

istream& operator>>(istream& is, Identifier& N)
{
    if(!is.ipfx()) return is;

    /*
```

The prefixed input function `ipfx()` ('p' for prefix) carries out system dependent

work. In particular, it checks the input stream so that in case of error the >> operator is terminated immediately. The reasons for this are explained in Kreft and Langer (1998).
```
*/

const unsigned int maxi = 100;
char buf[maxi];                        //  buffer
int i = 0;

//  find beginning of word
buf[0] = 0;
while(is && !(isalpha(buf[0]) || '_' == buf[0]))
      is.get(buf[0]);

/*
```
When the beginning is found, all following underscores and alphanumeric characters are collected. 'White space' or a special character terminates the reading process.
```
*/

//  collect the rest
while(is &&  i < maxi
          && (isalnum(buf[i]) || '_' == buf[i]))
      is.get(buf[++i]);

/*
```
The last character read does not belong to the identifier. The *iostream* library offers the possibility of returning an unused character to the input so that it is available to a subsequent program.
```
*/

is.putback(buf[i]);     //  back into the input stream
buf[i] = char(0);

/*
```
Finally, a null byte is inserted so that buf[] can be treated in the same way as a char*, and the buffer is passed to the private variable theIdentifier.
```
*/

N.theIdentifier = buf;
is.isfx();

/*
```
If some system dependent work must be undone, isfx() ('s' for suffix) is called as a standard at the end of the operator (see Kreft and Langer (1998)).
```
*/

    return is;
}
```

Implementation of the output operator is very easy; the internal string variable of an identifier is passed to the output os:

```
ostream& operator<<(ostream& os, const Identifier& N)
{
    if(os.opfx())
    {
        os << N.theIdentifier;
        os.osfx();
    }
    return os;
}
```

For `opfx()` and `ofsx()`, the same applies as for `ipfx()` and `isfx()` (see above). There is the possibility of stripping the output operator of the `friend` property by writing

```
os << N.asstring();
```

However, this would entail an additional copy process. That is all that is needed to use stream iterators to recognize identifiers. The `main()` program which stores the list of identifiers in the file *idlist* uses the above Identifier class and is surprisingly short.

```
//  k2/identify/main.cpp
#include<iterator>
#include<fstream>
#include"identif.h"

int main( )
{
    //  defining and opening of input and output files
    ifstream Source("main.cpp");
    ofstream Target("idlist");

    istream_iterator<Identifier, ptrdiff_t> iPos(Source),
                                            End;
    //  please note the separator string '\n':
    ostream_iterator<Identifier> oPos(Target, "\n");

    if(iPos == End)
        cout << "File not found!" << endl;
    else
        while(iPos != End) *oPos++ = *iPos++;
}
```

The last line of the above program is only an abbreviated form of the following block:

```
{
    Identifier temp = *iPos;    //  dereferencing
    ++iPos;                     //  read new identifier
    *oPos = temp;               //  write temp
```

```
      ++oPos;                           //  do nothing
}
```

Looked at more closely, the `++` operation for the ostream iterator is superfluous, because it is already the assignment that calls `operator<<()`, thus triggering the write process. `++oPos` actually causes nothing. There is, however, a good reason why `operator++()` has been incorporated into the ostream iterator: the notation of the line

```
      while(iPos != End) *oPos++ = *iPos++;
```

can thus be exactly as it is used with pointers to basic data types. This C++ idiom will be discussed again in Section 3.5.

Inheriting from the ostream iterator

It is even possible to write an ostream iterator with special features which inherits from the `ostream_iterator` class. Since access to several internals is needed, some items are `protected` from the very beginning. Here, an implementation of the `ostream_iterator` is shown:

```
//  commented excerpt of the HP implementation
template <class T>
class ostream_iterator : public output_iterator
//  output_iterator: compare note on page 42
{
 protected:
     ostream* stream;
     char* Sep; //  separator for separating output elements

 public:
     ostream_iterator(ostream& s)
     : stream(&s), Sep(0)
     {}

     ostream_iterator(ostream& s, char* c)
     : stream(&s), Sep(c)
     {}

     ostream_iterator<T>& operator=(const T& value)
     {
         *stream << value;
         if (Sep) *stream << Sep; //  output separator if needed
         return *this;
     }

     //  operators only for idiomatic notation,
     //  for example = *iter++ (compare with Section 3.5)
```

```
ostream_iterator<T>& operator*() { return *this; }

ostream_iterator<T>& operator++() { return *this; }

ostream_iterator<T>& operator++(int) { return *this; }
};
```

For a derivation of this class, some knowledge of the implementation is needed because the `protected` variables must be known for a possible access.

Containers

3

Summary: *A container is an object that is used to manage other objects which in this context are called elements of the container. It deals with allocation and deallocation of memory and controls insertion and deletion of elements. The algorithms that work with containers rely on a defined interface of data types and methods which must also be adhered to by user-defined containers if proper functioning of the algorithms is to be guaranteed. The containers* vector, list, *and* deque *are described, together with their properties. At the end of the chapter, the peculiarities of cooperation between iterators and containers are discussed.*

In part, the STL containers are typical implicit data types in the sense of Section 1.2. They include vector, list, and deque. Other containers, in contrast, are abstract data types which are implemented by means of the implicit data types. These include stack, queue, and priority_queue.

   Further abstract data types are set, map, multiset, and multimap. They are implemented by means of so-called red-black trees (Cormen *et al.*, 1994). All abstract data types which do not themselves represent implicit data types can easily be recognized from the fact that they *use* appropriate implicit data types. Abstract data types are described separately in Chapter 4.

   Before the individual types of container are introduced, the data types and methods common to all containers will be discussed.

3.1 Data type interface

Each container provides a public set of data types that can be used in a program. The data type vector<int>::iterator has already been mentioned on page 9. It can be identical to a pointer type such as int*, but this is not compulsory.

   The aim of data types is to ensure that the interface to a container in a program is *unique* at compile time. This means that, for example, you can design a several megabytes size vector which is not kept in memory, but is kept as a file on hard disk. Even in this case, you could still use vector<int>::iterator as data type without any danger, but this data type would then be anything but an int pointer. The actual implementation of vector element access remains hidden to the user of the container.

   Table 3.1 shows the container data types required for user-defined containers

Data type	Meaning
X::value_type	T
X::reference	reference to container element
X::const_reference	reference to constant container element
X::iterator	type of iterator
X::const_iterator	iterator type for containers with constant elements
X::difference_type	signed integral type (see distance type, page 33)
X::size_type	unsigned integral type for size specifications

Table 3.1   Container data types.

and already provided by the containers of the STL. Let X be the data type of the container, for example vector<int>, and T be the data type of a container element, for example int. Thus, the type vector<int>::value_type is identical to int.

3.2 Container methods

Each container provides a public set of methods which can be used in a program. The methods begin() and end() have already been mentioned and used (pages 5 and 9).

Table 3.2 shows the container methods required for user-defined containers and already provided by the STL containers. X is the denomination of the container type.

Swapping two containers is possible instead of an assignment when the assigned object is no longer needed. For example:

```
const int N = 1000;
Container C(N);       // one of the types discussed below,
                      // such as vector or list
{     // start of block
    Container A(N);       // for intermediate results
        // ... here we find, for example, calculations
        // with A which use values of C
        // (therefore, C is not used directly)

    // salvage result
    C = A;          // Alternative 1 (see text)
    C.swap(A);      // Alternative 2 (see text)

}     // end of block, A is deleted
```

Alternative 1 has a cost of $O(N)$, because all N elements must be copied from A to C. Alternative 2 needs only constant time ($O(1)$), because only the management information must be exchanged. This information mainly consists of pointers to the memory areas where the data is located and size information. In the above example,

Return type method	Meaning
`X()`	standard constructor; creates empty container
`X(const X&)`	copy constructor
`~X()`	destructor; calls the destructors for all elements of the container
`iterator begin()`	beginning of the container
`const_iterator begin()`	beginning of a container with constant elements
`iterator end()`	position *after* the last element
`const_iterator end()`	`end()` for containers with constant elements
`size_type max_size()`	maximum possible container size (see text)
`size_type size()`	current size of the container (see text)
`bool empty()`	`size() == 0` or `begin() == end()`
`void swap(X&)`	swapping with argument container
`allocator_type get_allocator()`	returns reference to the allocator object used to construct the container
`X& operator=(const X&)`	assignment operator
`bool operator==(const X&)`	operator `==`
`bool operator!=(const X&)`	operator `!=`
`bool operator<(const X&)`	operator `<`
`bool operator>(const X&)`	operator `>`
`bool operator<=(const X&)`	operator `<=`
`bool operator>=(const X&)`	operator `>=`

Table 3.2   Container methods.

a good compiler would recognize that A is no longer needed and, on this basis, carry out an optimization so that Alternative 1 does not entail a run time loss either.

A further example of the `swap()` method can be found on page 55. The maximum possible size of a container, determined with `max_size()`, depends among other things on the memory model (only for MS-DOS). A `vector<int>` with a 16-bit `int` can contain at most 32 767 elements. The current size, returned by the `size()` function, results from the distance between beginning and end, as calculated by the function `distance(a.begin(), a.end(), n)` described on page 33. n is of type `size_type` and contains the required result after calling the function. Prior to this call, you must set n = 0!

In addition to the above-mentioned methods, there are the relational operators ==, !=, <, >, <=, and >=. The first two, == and !=, are based on comparison of container size and comparison of elements of type T, for which `operator==()` must be defined. The remaining four are based on a lexicographic comparison of the elements, for which `operator<()` must be defined as order relation. The relational operators are defined globally and make use of the algorithms `equal()` and `lexicographi-cal_compare()` which will be discussed later.

3.2.1   Reversible containers

Reversible containers allow iterators to traverse *backward*. Such iterators may be bidirectional and random access. For these kinds of container, the additional data types

```
X::reverse_iterator
X::const_reverse_iterator
```

and the methods

```
rbegin()
rend()
```

are provided which return a reverse iterator.

3.3   Sequences

A sequence is a container whose elements are arranged in a strictly linear way. Table 3.3 shows the methods which must be present for sequences in addition to those of Table 3.2 and which therefore exist in the STL.

Notation for intervals

It is frequently necessary to specify intervals. For this purpose, the usual mathematical interval is used, where square brackets denote intervals including the boundary values, and round parentheses denote intervals excluding the boundary values. Thus, [i, j) is an interval including i and excluding j. In Table 3.3, X is the type of a sequential container; i and j are of input iterator type. p and q are dereferenceable iterators; n is of type `size_t` and t is an element of type `X::value_type`.

The STL contains three kinds of sequential containers, namely `vector`, `list`, and `deque`. A list (`list`) should be used when frequent insertions and deletions are needed somewhere in the middle. A queue with two ends (`deque` = double ended queue) is reasonable when insertion and deletion frequently take place at either end. `vector` corresponds to an array. `deque` and `vector` allow random access to elements.

The above-mentioned operations together with their containers need only constant time. Other operations, however, such as insertion of an element into the middle of a vector or a queue, are more expensive; the average cost increases linearly with the number of already existing elements.

The sequential containers `vector`, `list`, and `deque` provided by the STL offer several other methods, listed later in Table 3.5. The methods take constant time. In addition, there are the global operators:

```
template<class T, class Container>
bool operator==(const Container& x,const Container& y);
```

Return type method	Meaning
`X(n, t)`	Creates a sequence of type `X` with `n` copies of `t`.
`X(i, j)`	Creates a sequence with the elements of the range `[i, j)` copied into the sequence.
`iterator insert(p, t)`	Copies a copy of `t` before the location `p`. The return value points to the inserted copy.
`void insert(p, n, t)`	Copies `n` copies of `t` before the location `p`.
`void insert(p, i, j)`	Copies the elements of the range `[i, j)` before the location `p`.
`iterator erase(q)`	Deletes the element pointed to by `q`. The returned iterator points to the element immediately following `q` prior to the deletion operation, provided it exists. Otherwise, `end()` is returned.
`iterator erase(q1, q2)`	Deletes the elements of the range `[q1, q2)`. The returned iterator points to the element that pointed to `q2` immediately prior to the deletion operation, provided it exists. Otherwise, `end()` is returned.
`void clear()`	Deletes all elements; corresponds to `erase(begin(), end())`.

Table 3.3 Additional methods for sequences.

Data type	Meaning
`X::pointer`	pointer to container element
`X::const_pointer`	pointer to constant container element

Table 3.4 Additional data types for `vector`, `list`, and `deque`.

```
template<class T, class Container>
bool operator<(const Container& x,const Container& y);
```

for comparison, where `Container` can be one of the types `vector`, `list` or `deque`. In addition to the data types of Table 3.1, the types of Table 3.4 are provided.

3.3.1 Vector

Now that all essential properties of a vector container have been described, let us look at some examples of its application. First, a vector with 10 places is filled with the numbers 0 to 9. At the end, the number 100 is appended, which automatically

Return type method	Meaning
`void assign(n, t = T())`	Deletes the container and subsequently inserts n elements t.
`void assign(iterator i, iterator j)`	Deletes the container and subsequently inserts the elements of the range [i, j).
`reference front()`	Supplies a reference to the first element of a container.
`const_reference front()`	Ditto for containers with constant elements.
`reference back()`	Supplies a reference to the last element of a container.
`const_reference back()`	Ditto for containers with constant elements.
`void push_back(t)`	Inserts t at the end.
`void pop_back(t)`	Deletes the last element.
`void resize(n, t = T())`	Changes the container size. n - size() elements t are inserted at the end or n - size() elements are deleted at the end, depending on whether n is less than or greater than the current size.
`reverse_iterator rbegin()`	Returns the begin iterator for backward traversal. This iterator points to the last element.
`const_reverse_iterator rbegin()`	Ditto for constant containers.
`reverse_iterator rend()`	Returns the end iterator for backward traversal.
`const_reverse_iterator rend()`	Ditto for constant containers.

Table 3.5 Additional methods for `vector`, `list`, and `deque`.

increases the container size. Subsequently, the vector is displayed in two ways: the first loop uses it as a common array; the second loop uses an iterator.

```
//  k3/vector/intvec.cpp
//  example for int vector container
#include<vector>
#include<iostream>
```

```
using namespace std;

int main()
{
    //  an int vector of 10 elements
    vector<int> intV(10);
    int i;
    for(i = 0; i < intV.size(); i++)
        intV[i] = i;                        //  fill vector, random access

    //  vector increases on demand
    intV.insert(intV.end(), 100);     //  append the number 100

    //  use as array
    for(i = 0; i < intV.size(); i++)
        cout << intV[i] << endl;
    //  use with an iterator
    vector<int>::iterator I;

    for(I = intV.begin(); I != intV.end(); ++I)
        cout << *I << endl;

    vector<int> newV(20, 0); //  all elements are 0
    cout << " newV = ";

    for(i = 0; i < newV.size(); i++)
        cout << newV[i] << ' ';

    //  swap() from Table 3.2 shows a very fast method for
    //  swapping two vectors (compare with page 50).
    newV.swap(intV);

    cout << "\n newV after swapping = ";
    for(i = 0; i < newV.size(); i++)
        cout << newV[i] << ' ';       //  old contents of intV

    cout << "\n\n intV        = ";
    for(i = 0; i < intV.size(); i++)
        cout << intV[i] << ' ';       //  old contents of newV
    cout << endl;
}
```

In the next example, the stored elements are of string type. In addition, it shows how an element is deleted which leads to a change in the number of elements. All elements following the deleted element shift by one position. This process is a time-consuming operation. Finally, a reverse_iterator is used which traverses the container backward.

```
//  k3/vector/strvec.cpp
//  example for string vector containers
#include<vector>
#include<iostream>
#include<string>

using namespace std;

int main()
{
    //  a string vector of 4 elements
    vector<string> stringVec(4);
    stringVec[0] = "First";
    stringVec[1] = "Second";
    stringVec[2] = "Third";
    stringVec[3] = "Fourth";

    //  vector increases size on demand
    stringVec.insert(stringVec.end(), string("Last"));
    cout << "size() = "
        << stringVec.size() << endl;         // 5

    //  delete the element 'Second'
    vector<string>::iterator I = stringVec.begin();
    ++I;                                     // 2nd position
    cout << "erase: "
        << *I << endl;
    stringVec.erase(I);      //  delete Second
    cout << "size() = "
        << stringVec.size() << endl;         // 4
    for(I = stringVec.begin(); I != stringVec.end(); ++I)
        cout << *I << endl;

    /*
    Output:   First
              Third
              Fourth
              Last
    */

    cout << "backwards with reverse_iterator:" << endl;
    vector<string>::reverse_iterator revI;

    for(revI = stringVec.rbegin();
        revI != stringVec.rend(); ++revI)
            cout << *revI << endl;
}
```

On average, deletion or insertion of an element at the end of a vector takes constant time, that is $O(1)$ in complexity notation (for example, pop_back()). Insertion

Return type method	Meaning
`reference operator[](n)`	Returns a reference to the nth element (usage: `a[n]`, when `a` is the container).
`const_reference operator[](n)`	Ditto for vectors with constant elements.
`reference at(n)`	Returns a reference to the nth element.
`const_reference at(n)`	Ditto for vectors with constant elements.
`void reserve(n)`	Reserves memory space, so that the available space (capacity) exceeds the currently needed space. Aim: avoiding memory allocation operation during vector use.
`size_type capacity()`	Returns the capacity value (see `reserve()`). `size()` is always less than or equal to `capacity()`.

Table 3.6   Additional vector methods.

or deletion of an element somewhere in the middle takes a time proportional to the number of elements that have to be shifted, thus, $O(n)$ for n vector elements.

It should be noted that iterators previously pointing to elements of the vector become invalid when the elements in question are shifted by the insertion or deletion. This also applies when the available space of the vector becomes insufficient for `insert()` and new space is allocated. The reason for this is that after allocation of new, larger memory space all elements are copied into the new space and therefore all old positions are no longer valid.

In addition to the methods of Tables 3.2 to 3.5, `vector` provides the methods of Table 3.6.

3.3.2 List

This example refers to the program on page 42 for the determination of identifiers contained in a file. It makes use of the `Identifier` class described there, with the difference that the identifiers are not written into a file, but into a list which is subsequently displayed:

```
//  k3/list/id_main.cpp
#include<fstream>
#include<list>
#include"identif.h"

using namespace std;
```

```
int main( )
{
    // define and open input file
    ifstream Source("id_main.cpp");

    list<Identifier> Identifier_list;

    istream_iterator<Identifier, ptrdiff_t> iPos(Source),
                                            end;

    if(iPos == end)
        cout << "File not found!" << endl;

    else
        while(iPos != end)
            // insert identifier and read next one
            Identifier_list.push_back(*iPos++);

    // output
    list<Identifier>::iterator I = Identifier_list.begin();
    while(I != Identifier_list.end())
        cout << *I++ << endl;
}
```

The structure of the `main()` programs resembles the one on page 45. This resemblance facilitates learning how to use iterators and containers. In contrast to the vector, `insert()` and `erase()` do not invalidate iterators that point to elements of the list, with the exception of an iterator that points to an element to be deleted.

In addition to the methods of Tables 3.2 to 3.5, `list` provides the methods of Table 3.7. Each operation takes constant time ($O(1)$) if not otherwise specified. The predicates mentioned in the table are simply function objects (description on page 21). They determine whether a statement about an element is true or false.

One could, for example, imagine a function object `P` for `Identifier` objects which returns whether the identifier begins with an upper case letter. `remove_if(P)` would then delete all elements of the list that have an upper case initial.

For two of the methods of Table 3.7, namely `merge()` and `splice()`, sample applications are shown.

Merging of sorted lists

Two small sorted lists are to be merged into one big sorted list. After the end of the process, the calling list contains all elements of the two lists, whereas the called list is empty. `merge()` is stable; thus, the relative order of the elements of a list is maintained.

Return type method	Meaning
`void merge(list&)`	Merges two sorted lists.
`void merge(list&, Compare_object)`	Merges two sorted lists, using a `Compare_object` for the comparison of elements.
`void push_front(const T& t)`	Inserts an element at the beginning.
`void pop_front()`	Deletes the first element.
`void remove(const T& t)`	Removes all elements that are equal to the passed element `t`.
`void remove_if( Predicate P)`	Removes all elements to which the predicate applies.
`void reverse()`	Reverts the order of elements in the list (time complexity $O(n)$).
`void sort()`	Sorts the elements in the list. Time complexity is $O(n \log n)$. The sorting criterion is the < operator defined for the elements.
`void sort( Compare_object)`	as `sort()`, but with the sorting criterion of the Comparison object (see page 22).
`void splice(iterator pos, list& x)`	Inserts the contents of list `x` before `pos`. Afterwards, `x` is empty.
`void splice(iterator p, list&x, iterator i)`	Inserts element `*i` of `x` before `p` and removes `*i` from `x`.
`void splice(iterator pos, list& x, iterator first, iterator last)`	Inserts elements in the range `[first, last)` of `x` before `pos` and removes them from `x`. Calling the same object (that is, `&x == this`), takes constant time, otherwise, the cost is of the order $O(n)$. `pos` must not lie in the range `[first, last)`.
`void unique()`	Deletes identical consecutive elements except for the first one (cost $O(n)$). Application to a sorted list leads to the effect that no element occurs more than once.
`void unique( binaryPredicate)`	Ditto, only that instead of the identity criterion another binary predicate is used.

Table 3.7 Additional methods for lists.

```
//  k3/list/merge.cpp
#include<list>

void displayIntList(list<int> & L)    // auxiliary function
{
    list<int>::iterator I = L.begin();
    while(I != L.end())
        cout << *I++ << ' ';
    cout << " size() ="
        << L.size() << endl;
}

using namespace std;

int main( )
{
    list<int> L1, L2;

    //  fill lists with sorted numbers
    for(int i = 0; i < 10; i++)
    {
        L1.push_back(2*i);          //  even numbers
        L2.push_back(2*i+1);        //  odd numbers
    }

    displayIntList(L1); //  0 2 4 6 8 10 12 14 16 18 size() =10
    displayIntList(L2); //  1 3 5 7 9 11 13 15 17 19 size() =10

    L1.merge(L2);                   //  merge
    displayIntList(L1);
    //  0 1 2 3 4 5 6 7 8 9 10 11 12 13 14 15 16 17 18 19 size() =20
    displayIntList(L2); //  size() =0
}
```

The example first outputs a list of even numbers and a list of odd numbers. After the merge() operation, the first list contains all the numbers; the second list is empty.

Splicing of lists

The term 'splicing' originates from the nautical cabling technique and denotes the fastening together or uniting of several ropes by tucking several strands of rope or cable into each other. Here, we talk about uniting lists. Of the possibilities listed in Table 3.7, we only look at how to transfer a section of a list into another list. From the previous example, only the line containing the merge() operation is substituted with the following program fragment:

```
list<int>::iterator I = L2.begin();
advance(I, 4);                           //  4 steps
L1.splice(L1.begin(), L2, I, L2.end());
```

State of the lists before `splice()`:
L1: *0 2 4 6 8 10 12 14 16 18*
L2: *1 3 5 7 9 11 13 15 17 19*

State of the lists after `splice()`:
L1: *9 11 13 15 17 19 0 2 4 6 8 10 12 14 16 18*
L2: *1 3 5 7*

All elements of list `L2` from position 4 (counting starts with 0) onward up to the end of the list are transferred to the beginning of list `L1`. Afterwards, list `L2` contains only the first four elements, whereas list `L1` has grown by six elements at the beginning.

3.3.3 Deque

Deque is an abbreviation for *double ended queue*. Like a vector, this sequence allows random access iterators and, exactly like a list, it allows insertion and deletion at the beginning or the end in constant time. Insertions and deletions somewhere in the middle, however, are quite costly ($O(n)$), because many elements must be shifted. A deque might be seen as being internally organized as an arrangement of several memory blocks, where memory management is hidden in a similar way to `vector`. During insertion at the beginning or the end, a new block of memory is added whenever available space is no longer sufficient.

In addition to the methods of Tables 3.2 to 3.5, `deque` provides the methods of Table 3.8.

Return type method	Meaning
`reference operator[](n)`	Returns a reference to the nth element (usage: `a[n]`, when `a` is the container).
`const_reference opera-tor[](n)`	Ditto for deques with constant elements.
`reference at(n)`	Returns a reference to the nth element.
`const_reference at(n)`	Ditto for deques with constant elements.
`void push_front(const T& t)`	Inserts an element at the beginning.
`void pop_front()`	Deletes the first element.

Table 3.8 Additional deque methods.

3.3.4 showSequence

A remark to start with: showSequence() is not an algorithm of the STL, but a sequence display tool written for the examples in this book. The function is defined as follows:

```
// Template for the display of sequences (file include/showseq)
#ifndef showseq
#define showseq
#include<iostream>

template<class T>
void showSequence(T& s, char* sep = " ",
                        ostream& where = cout)
{
   T::iterator iter = s.begin();
   while(iter != s.end())
      where << *iter++ << sep;
   where << endl;
}
#endif
```

If nothing different is specified, output is written to cout. The sequence is output completely, that is, from begin() to (but excluding) end(). The sep character string separates the individual elements. It defaults to a space if nothing else is specified in the function call. With these definitions, you can simply write

```
showSequence(v);
```

in your program to display an int vector v, instead of

```
vector<int>::iterator iter = v.begin();
while(iter != v.end()) cout << *iter++ << " ";
cout << endl;
```

The function is neither designed for nor suited to simple C arrays. Its advantage is that because of the shorter notation, programs become more readable. The function template is read into memory with #include<showseq>. Inclusion of #include<iostream> is done by *showseq* and is therefore no longer needed in programs using showSequence().

3.4 Iterator categories and containers

In this section, the different iterator categories which are associated to the containers are evaluated, for example in order to select the most effective algorithm possible at compile time. The previous version of the C++ standard proposal (ISO/ANSI, 1996) defined the classes listed here. The traits concept of ISO/IEC (1997) described on page 33 has now made them superfluous. As the new concept is not yet supported by the currently available compilers, both versions are explained. For the same reason, the sample programs in this book are still based on ISO/ANSI (1996).

```
//  Iterator classes (after ISO/ANSI (1996))
template <class T, class Distance>
    struct input_iterator {};

struct output_iterator {};

template <class T, class Distance>
    struct forward_iterator {};

template <class T, class Distance>
    struct bidirectional_iterator {};

template <class T, class Distance>
    struct random_access_iterator{};
```

The `output_iterator` is not a template, because neither a value type nor a distance type is defined for it. The classes have no data, since the only aim is to use the names in order to determine at compile time where compatibilities exist or to select the most efficient algorithm. The class definitions greatly facilitate the determination of an iterator type by means of the overloaded global function `iterator_category()` which returns an object of the corresponding type. Only the most specific type is returned: a random access operator is also a bidirectional operator, but not vice versa. Thus, the type determination of an iterator associated with a vector container returns a `random_access_iterator_tag` object (see Section 2.1.6).

```
//  Excerpt of the HP implementation of the STL
template <class T, class Distance>
inline input_iterator_tag
iterator_category(const input_iterator<T, Distance>&)
{
    return input_iterator_tag();
}

//  no template
inline output_iterator_tag
iterator_category(const output_iterator&)
{
    return output_iterator_tag();
}
```

Equivalent overloaded functions exist for the other iterator tags. They are built on the same scheme and are therefore not shown. These functions are used at compile time to determine the compatibility of containers and algorithms.

This function no longer exists in ISO/IEC (1997), because each function call can be substituted by

```
iterator_traits<Iterator>::iterator_category()
```

that is, by a call to the standard constructor of the type in question. Downward compatibility can be achieved by means of the template

```
template <class Iter>
inline iterator_traits<Iter>::iterator_category
iterator_category(const Iter&)
{
    return iterator_traits<Iter>::iterator_category();
}
```

The following example shows how at compile time the correct function for the display of the iterator type is selected from a set of overloaded functions:

```
//  k3/iterator/ityp.cpp        determination of the iterator type
#include<string>
#include<fstream>
#include<vector>
#include<iterator>

using namespace std;

//  overloaded functions
void whichIterator(const input_iterator_tag&)
{
    cout << "Input iterator!" << endl;
}

void whichIterator(const output_iterator_tag&)
{
    cout << "Output iterator!" << endl;
}

void whichIterator(const forward_iterator_tag&)
{
    cout << "Forward iterator!" << endl;
}

void whichIterator(const random_access_iterator_tag&)
{
    cout << "Random access iterator!" << endl;
}

//  application
int main( )
{
    //  define a file object for reading
    //  (actual file is not required here)
    ifstream Source;
```

```
    // an istream_iterator is an input iterator
    istream_iterator<string, ptrdiff_t> IPos(Source);

    // display of iterator type
    whichIterator(iterator_category(IPos));

    // define a file object for writing
    ofstream Destination;

    // an ostream_iterator is an output iterator
    ostream_iterator<string> OPos(Destination);

    // display of iterator type
    whichIterator(iterator_category(OPos));

    vector<int> v(10);
    int *ip;                          // random access iterator
    // display of iterator type
    whichIterator(iterator_category(ip));
}
```

A further example shows how to write an overloaded function whose selected implementation depends on the iterator type. The task is to output the last n elements of a container by means of the function showLastElements(). It is assumed that at least bidirectional iterators can work on the container. Thus, it is sufficient to equip the function with an iterator to the end of the container and the required number.

```
//  k3/iterator/iappl.cpp
#include<iostream>
#include<list>
#include<vector>
#include<iterator>
using namespace std;

// calling implementation
template<class Iterator, class Distance>
void showLastElements(Iterator last, Distance n)
{
    showLastElements(last, n, iterator_category(last));
}
```

The Distance type is needed because, depending on container type and call, the number passed can be of type int or of type long. This function now calls the corresponding overloaded variation, where the selection at compile time is carried out by the parameter iterator_category(last) whose type corresponds to an iterator tag:

```
//  first overloaded function
template<class Iterator, class Distance>
void showLastElements(Iterator last, Distance n,
                      bidirectional_iterator_tag)
```

```
{
    Iterator temp = last;
    advance(temp, -n);
    while(temp != last)
    {
        cout << *temp << ' ';
        ++temp;
    }
    cout << endl;
}
```

The bidirectional iterator does not allow random access and therefore there is no iterator arithmetic. Only the operators ++ and -- are allowed for moving. Therefore, advance() is used to go back n steps and then display the remaining elements. A random access iterator allows arithmetic, which makes the implementation of this case slightly easier:

```
//  second overloaded function
template<class Iterator, class Distance>
void showLastElements(Iterator last, Distance n,
                      random_access_iterator_tag)
{
    while(n) cout << *(last - n--) << ' ';
    cout << endl;
}

using namespace std;

int main( )
{
    int i;
    list<int> L;                        //  list
    for(i=0; i < 10; i++) L.push_back(i);

    //  call of 1st implementation
    showLastElements(L.end(), 5L);    //  5 long

    vector<int> v(10);                  //  vector
    for(i = 0; i < 10; i++) v[i] = i;

    //  call of 2nd implementation
    showLastElements(v.end(), 5);     //  5 int
}
```

This scheme – providing a function as an interface which then calls one of the overloaded functions with the implementation – allows you to use completely different implementations with one and the same function call. This allows you, in a properly designed program, to change a container type without having to modify the rest of the program.

3.4.1 Derivation of value and distance types

The STL is based on the fact that algorithms use iterators to work with containers. However, this also means that inside an algorithm the container and its properties are not known, and that all the required information must be contained in the iterators. In analogy to the `iterator_category()` function just described, ISO/ANSI (1996) defines functions `distance_type()` for determination of the distance type and `value_type()` for determination of the value type. Both functions return a *pointer* to the corresponding type.

This pointer is exclusively used for generating the correct, type-dependent program code from the template! How do `distance_type()` and `value_type()` function? Let us look at a sample implementation:

```
template <class T, class Distance>
inline Distance*
distance_type(const bidirectional_iterator<T, Distance>&)
{
    return (Distance*)(0);
}

template <class T, class Distance>
inline T*
value_type(const bidirectional_iterator<T, Distance>&)
{
    return (T*)(0);
}
```

The return value is simply a null pointer matching the iterator. The implementations are predefined for all iterator categories.

A null pointer is returned, corresponding to the iterator type. In ISO/ANSI (1996) the implementations are predefined for all iterator categories.

In ISO/IEC (1997) there are no functions of this kind because function calls can be replaced by

```
(iterator_traits<Iterator>::difference_type*)(0) // resp.
(iterator_traits<Iterator>::value_type*)(0)
```

that is, by null pointers of the corresponding type. The templates

```
template <class Iter>
inline iterator_traits<Iter>::difference_type*
distance_type(const Iter&)
{
    return (iterator_traits<Iter>::difference_type*)(0);
}

template <class Iter>
inline iterator_traits<Iter>::value_type*
value_type(const Iter&)
```

```
{
    return (iterator_traits<Iter>::value_type*)(0);
}
```

provide downward compatibility between the standard versions.

It makes no sense to return an object of type

```
{ iterator_traits<Iter>::value_type}
```

instead of a null pointer because the only objective is to recognize the type. For this purpose it is not necessary to construct a possibly big object. It may also be that a standard constructor does not exist.

A short example follows to show how value and distance types can be derived. Let us assume two different containers, a list and a vector, in which the element order is to be reversed. The function revert() is only passed the iterators to the beginning and the end of the corresponding containers.

```
//  k3/iterator/valdist.cpp
//  Determination of value and distance types
#include<showseq>
#include<list>
#include<vector>
#include<iterator>

using namespace std;

template<class BidirectionalIterator>
void revert(BidirectionalIterator first,
            BidirectionalIterator last)
{
    revert(first, last, value_type(first),
           distance_type(first));
}
```

Reversing the order means that one element must be intermediately stored. To do this, its type must be known. Following the well-proven scheme, the function calls a suitable implementation for the iterator type, with the C++ template mechanism deducing the data types T and Distance on the basis of the passed pointers:

```
template<class BidirectionalIterator, class T,
         class Distance>
void revert(BidirectionalIterator first,
            BidirectionalIterator last,
            T*, Distance*)
{
    //  use of the distance type to calculate
    //  the number of exchanges
    //  Distance n = 0;    // ISO/ANSI (1996), Distance = distance type
    //  distance(first, last, n);
```

```
Distance n = distance(first, last);  //  ISO/IEC (1997)
--n;

while(n > 0)
{
    T temp = *first;        //  T = value type
    *first++ = *--last;
    *last = temp;
    n -= 2;
}
}
```

At first sight, it would appear that the algorithm could do without the distance type when comparing iterators and stop when `first` becomes $\geq$ `last`. However, this assumption holds only when a $>$ relation is defined for the iterator type. For a vector, where two pointers point to a continuous memory area, this is no problem. It is, however, impossible for containers of a different kind, such as lists or binary trees. To conclude, here is the corresponding main program:

```
int main()
{
    int i;
    list<int> L;
    for(i=0; i < 10; i++) L.push_back(i);
    revert(L.begin(), L.end());
    showSequence(L);

    vector<double> V(10);
    for(i = 0; i < 10; i++) V[i] = i/10.;
    revert(V.begin(), V.end());
    showSequence(V);
}
```

3.4.2 Inheriting iterator properties

When user-defined iterators are built, they should conform to those of the STL. Now, instead of redefining `iterator_category()`, `distance_type()`, and `value_type()` on purpose, it is easier to inherit properties from the predefined iterator classes. An iterator supposed to work on a structure of `double` elements could be defined as follows:

```
//  user-defined bidirectional iterator, basis ISO/ANSI (1996)
class MyIterator : public bidirectional_iterator<double, int>
{
    //  program code for operator++(), and so on
}
```

Here, `int` represents the distance type. If a container contains such a number of elements that `int` is not sufficient, `long` must be employed. If you want to keep to the naming conventions for a container type `C`, you must write:

```
class MyIterator : public
    bidirectional_iterator<C::value_type, C::difference_type>
{
    // program code for operator++(), and so on
}
```

This looks slightly different when based on ISO/IEC (1997), as already mentioned on page 42:

```
// user-defined bidirectional iterator, basis: ISO/IEC (1997)
// using int as distance type
class MyIterator
: public iterator<bidirectional_iterator_tag, int>
{
    // program code for operator++(), and so on
}
```

Here too `int` may be substituted by a suitable difference type, if needed.

3.5 Iterators for insertion into containers

The idiom shown on page 46

```
while(first != last) *result++ = *first++;
```

copies an input range into an output range, where `result` and `first` in Section 2.2.2 represent output and input iterators for streams. An output stream normally has more than sufficient space for all copied elements. The same idiomatic notation can also be used for the copying of containers; the previous contents of the target container are overwritten:

```
container Source(100), Target(100);
// fill Source with values here

container::iterator first  = Source.begin(),
                    last   = Source.end(),
                    result = Target.begin();

// copying of the elements
while(first != last) *result++ = *first++;
```

There can, however, be a problem: this scheme fails when the `Target` container is *smaller* than the `Source` container, because at some time `result` will no longer be defined. Perhaps the old contents of `Target` should not also be overwritten, but should remain intact and the new contents should just be added.

For these purposes, predefined iterators exist which allow insertion. For consistency with the existing naming conventions, we will call them insert iterators. Insert iterators are output iterators.

The insert iterators provide the operators `operator*()` and `operator++()` in both prefix and postfix version, together with `operator=()`. All operators return a reference to the iterator. The first two have no other function. They exist only for keeping the usual notation `*result++ = *last++`:

```
// Implementation of some operators (excerpt)
template <class container>
class insert_iterator : public output_iterator
{
  public:
    insert_iterator<container>& operator*() { return *this;}
    insert_iterator<container>& operator++() { return *this;}
    insert_iterator<container>& operator++(int) { return *this;}
// ... and so on
```

Only the assignment operator calls an element function of the container, which is dependent on the kind of container. Now, let us look at the expression `*result++ = *last++` in detail, remembering that the order of evaluation is from left to right. `*last` is the value to be inserted. The call of the first two operators yields a reference to the iterator itself, so that `result` can be substituted successively:

```
result.operator*().operator++(int).operator=(*last++);
      result.operator++(int).operator=(*last++);
            result.operator=(*last++);
```

The compiler optimizes the first two calls, so that the task of insertion only remains with the assignment operator . The three different predefined insert iterators described in the next sections differ exactly on this point.

back_insert_iterator

A back insert iterator inserts new elements into a container from the end, making use of the element function `push_back()` of the container, called by the assignment operator:

```
// Implementation of an assignment operator
back_insert_iterator<container>& operator=(
                    const container::value_type& value)
{
    container.push_back(value);
    return *this;
}
```

The following example shows the application of a back insert iterator in which the numbers 1 and 2 are appended to a vector:

```
//  k3/iterator/binsert.cpp
//  Insert iterators : back insert
#include<showseq>
#include<vector>
#include<iterator>

using namespace std;

int main()
{
    vector<int> aVector(5, 0);          // 5 zeros
    cout << "aVector.size() = "
        << aVector.size() << endl; // 5
    showSequence(aVector);              // 0 0 0 0 0

    back_insert_iterator<vector<int> >
                    aBackInserter(aVector);

    //  insertion by means of the operations *, ++, =
    int i = 1;
    while(i < 3)
        *aBackInserter++ = i++;

    cout << "aVector.size() = "
        << aVector.size() << endl;   // 7

    showSequence(aVector);              // 0 0 0 0 0 1 2
}
```

The predefined function `back_inserter()` returns a back insert iterator and facilitates passing iterators to functions. Let us assume a function `copyadd()` which copies the contents of one container into another or adds it when the iterator used is an insert iterator:

```
template <class InputIterator, class OutputIterator>
OutputIterator copyadd(InputIterator first,
                    InputIterator last,
                    OutputIterator result)
{
    while (first != last)
        *result++ = *first++;
    return result;
}
```

The above program can be integrated with the following lines in which this function is passed the iterator created with `back_inserter()`:

```
// copying with function back_inserter()
vector<int> aVector2;                   // size is 0
```

```
copyadd(aVector.begin(), aVector.end(),
                         back_inserter(aVector2));

cout << "aVector2.size() = "
     << aVector2.size() << endl; // 7

showSequence(aVector2);              // 0000012
```

front_insert_iterator

A front insert iterator inserts new elements into a container from the beginning, making use of the element function push_front() of the container, called by the assignment operator. Thus, it is very similar to the back insert iterator. In the following example, list is used instead of vector, because push_front is not defined for vectors.

```
//   k3/iterator/finsert.cpp
//   Insert iterators: front inserter
#include<showseq>
#include<list>
#include<iterator>

using namespace std;

int main()
{
    list<int> aList(5, 0);        // 5 zeros

    cout << "aList.size() = "
         << aList.size() << endl;

    showSequence(aList);
    front_insert_iterator<list<int> >
                         aFrontInserter(aList);
    //  insertion by means of the operations *, ++, =
    int i = 1;
    while(i < 3)
          *aFrontInserter++ = i++;
    cout << "aList.size() = "
         << aList.size() << endl;

    showSequence(aList);
}
```

The copyadd() function, not shown here, works exactly as with the back insert iterator.

insert_iterator

Now, something may have to be inserted not just at the beginning or at the end, but at an arbitrary position in the container. The insert iterator has been designed for this purpose. Since it can also insert at the beginning and at the end, it can also be used instead of the back and front insert iterators already described. It must be passed only the insertion point. For this purpose, the insert iterator uses the element function `insert()` of the container, called by the assignment operator, whose implementation is shown here:

```
//  Implementation of the assignment operator (commented excerpt of the HP STL)
insert_iterator<container>& operator=(
                const container::value_type& value)
{
    //  iter is a private variable of the insert_iterator object
    iter = container.insert(iter, value);
    ++iter;
    return *this;
}
```

The private variable `container` is a reference to the container, which is passed to the constructor together with the insertion position, as shown in the following example. The insertion position is stored in the private variable `iter`.

```
//  k3/iterator/insert.cpp
//  Insert iterator
#include<showseq>
#include<vector>
#include<iterator>

using namespace std;

int main()
{
    vector<int> aVector(5, 0);          //  5 zeros

    cout << "aVector.size() = "
         << aVector.size() << endl;     //  5
    showSequence(aVector);              //  0 0 0 0 0

    //  insertion by means of the operations *, ++, =
    insert_iterator<vector<int> >
        aBeginInserter(aVector, aVector.begin());

    int i = 1;
    while(i < 3) *aBeginInserter++ = i++;
    //  vector: 1 2 0 0 0 0 0
    //  size() is now 7
```

```
insert_iterator<vector<int> >
    aMiddleInserter(aVector, aVector.begin() +
                        aVector.size()/2);

while(i < 6) *aMiddleInserter++   = i++;
//  vector: 1 2 0 3 4 5 0 0 0 0
//  size() is now 10

insert_iterator<vector<int> >
    anEndInserter(aVector, aVector.end());
while(i < 9) *anEndInserter++    = i++;

cout << "aVector.size() = "
    << aVector.size() << endl;  //  13
showSequence(aVector);          //  1 2 0 3 4 5 0 0 0 0 6 7 8
}
```

Here, the insert iterator is used to insert elements at the beginning, at the end and, in the middle. It should be noted that an insert iterator destroys references to the container when, for reasons of space, the container is moved to a different memory location! Applied to the above example, this means that the definitions of the insert operators *cannot* be concentrated at the top shortly after main() at *one* point: the begin() and end() iterators and the size size() would be invalid for the second iterator immediately after execution of the first one.

As above, it is not specifically necessary to write an insert iterator. It is sufficient to call the predefined function inserter() in the parameter list because the function returns an insert iterator.

```
//  Copying with function inserter()
//  here: beginning at the beginning
vector<int> aVector2;                   //  empty vector

copyadd(aVector.begin(), aVector.end(),
        inserter(aVector2, aVector2.begin()));

cout << "aVector2.size() = "
    << aVector2.size() << endl; //  13

showSequence(aVector2);                 //  1 2 0 3 4 5 0 0 0 0 6 7 8
```

Abstract data types $\boxed{4}$

Summary: Abstract data types and the implicit data types used for their realization have already been generally discussed in Section 1.2. This chapter first deals with the abstract data types stack, queue, and priority_queue which are provided as template classes by the STL. Subsequently, the sorted associative containers set, map, multiset, and multimap are considered.

A template class of the kind presented here is also called a *container adaptor* because it adapts an interface. This means that adaptors insert an interface level with changed functionality between the user and the implicit data types. Thus, when you use a stack object, you work via stack methods with the underlying container which can, for example, be a vector.

The container used as an implicit data type is contained as an object in the class of an abstract data type (aggregation). The abstract data type makes use of the methods of the container. This principle is called *delegation*.

4.1 Stack

A stack is a container which allows insertion, retrieving, and deletion only at one end. Objects inserted first are removed last. As an implicit data type, all sequential container classes are allowed which support the operations back(), push_back(), and pop_back(), as shown in the following excerpt:

```
namespace std {
  template <class T,
            class Container = deque<T> >        // default
  class stack
  {
    public:
      typedef typename Container::value_type value_type;
      typedef typename Container::size_type size_type;
      typedef typename Container container_type;

    protected:
      Container c;
```

```
public:
    explicit stack(const Container& = Container());

    bool empty()                    const  { return c.empty();}
    size_type size()                const  { return c.size(); }
    value_type& top()                      { return c.back(); }
    const value_type& top() const          { return c.back(); }
    void push(const value_type& x) { c.push_back(x);  }
    void pop()                      { c.pop_back();    }
};

template <class T, class Container>
bool operator==(const stack<T,Container>& x,
                const stack<T,Container>& y)
{
    return x.c == y.c;
}

template <class T, class Container>
bool operator<(const stack<T,Container>& x,
               const stack<T,Container>& y)
{
    return x.c < y.c;
}
```

In particular, you can also choose vector or list instead of the standard value deque. Thus, a stack<int, vector<int> > is a stack for int values implemented by means of a vector. An example of the application of stacks follows in Section 4.2.

4.2 Queue

A queue allows you to insert objects at one end and to remove them from the opposite end. The objects at both ends of the queue can be read without being removed. Both list and deque are suitable data types for implementation. The class queue provides the following interface:

```
template<class T, class Container = deque<T> >
class queue
{
  public:
    explicit queue(const Container& = Container());

    typedef typename Container::value_type value_type;
    typedef typename Container::size_type size_type;
    typedef typename Container container_type;

    bool empty()                    const;
```

```
size_type size()                    const;
value_type& front();                    //  read value in front
const value_type& front() const;    //  read value in front
value_type& back();                     //  read value at end
const value_type& back()  const;    //  read value at end
void push(const value_type& x);     //  append x
void pop();                             //  delete first element
};
```

Of course, the underlying implementation is very similar to that of the stack. The global operators `==` and `<` exist as well. Both `queue::value_type` and `queue::size_type` are derived from the type (`deque` or `list`) used for the container. The following short program is intended to show the practical application of queue and stack as simply as possible. More complicated problems will follow later.

```
//  k4/div_adt.cpp
#include<stack>
#include<queue>
#include<deque>
#include<list>
#include<vector>

using namespace std;

int main()
{
    queue<int, list<int> > aQueue;

    int numbers[] = {1, 5, 6, 0, 9, 1, 8, 7, 2};
    const int count = sizeof(numbers)/sizeof(int);

    cout << "Put numbers into the queue:" << endl;

    for(int i = 0; i < count; i++)
    {
        cout.width(6); cout << numbers[i];
        aQueue.push(numbers[i]);
    }

    stack<int> aStack;

    cout << "\n\n Read numbers from the queue (same "
            "order)\n and put them into the stack:"
         << endl;

    while(!aQueue.empty())
    {
        int Z = aQueue.front();  //  read value
```

```
        cout.width(6); cout << Z;
        aQueue.pop();                    // delete value
        aStack.push(Z);
    }
// ... (to be continued)
```

This little program puts a sequence of int numbers into a queue, reads them back out, and puts them on a stack. The stack is built with a deque (default), whereas the queue uses a list (list).

4.3 **Priority queue**

A priority queue always returns the element with the highest priority. The priority criterion must be specified when creating the queue. In the simplest case, it is the greatest (or smallest) number in the queue. The criterion is characterized by a class of suitable function objects for comparison (see Section 1.6.3).

In a priority queue you could, for example, store pairs consisting of references to print jobs and associated priorities. For simplicity, only int elements are used in the example. The continuation of the program of the previous section shows the application, in which the priority queue internally uses a vector and employs the standard comparison type greater:

```
// continued from Section 4.2

    priority_queue<int, vector<int>, greater<int> > aPrioQ;
    // greater: small elements first (= high priority)
    // less: large elements first

    cout << "\n\n Read numbers from the stack "
            "(reverse order!)\n"
            " and put them into the priority queue:" << endl;

    while(!aStack.empty())
    {
        int Z = aStack.top();        // read value
        cout.width(6); cout << Z;    // display
        aStack.pop();                // delete value
        aPrioQ.push(Z);
    }

    cout << "\n\n Read numbers from the priority queue "
            "(sorted order!)" << endl;

    while(!aPrioQ.empty())
    {
        int Z = aPrioQ.top();        // read value
        cout.width(6); cout << Z;    // display
```

```
        aPrioQ.pop();                    //  delete value
    }
}
```

Because of the internal representation of the priority queue as a binary heap for efficiency reasons (see Section 5.7), only implicit data types with random access iterators are suited, for example deque and vector. priority_queue provides the following interfaces, where Container and Compare denote the data types for the implicit container and the comparison type:

```
template<class T, class Container = vector<T>,
        class Compare = less<Container::value_type> >
class priority_queue
{
  public:
    typedef Container::value_type value_type;
    typedef Container::size_type size_type;
    typedef typename Container container_type;

    bool empty()            const;
    size_type size()        const;
    const value_type& top() const;
    void push(const value_type& x);
    void pop();
```

The meaning of the above methods corresponds to that of stack and queue; the constructor, however, looks slightly different:

```
explicit priority_queue(const Compare& x = Compare(),
                        const Container& = Container());
```

The constructor requires a Compare object. If none is passed, an object generated by the standard constructor of the Compare class is passed. In the sample program above, this is greater<int>().

```
priority_queue(InputIterator first, InputIterator last,
               const Compare& x = Compare(),
               const Container& = Container());
```

This constructor takes input iterators as the argument, in order to create a priority queue for a large range in one go. This is more efficient than a series of push() operations. In our sample program on page 80, a further priority queue could be created by means of the instruction

```
priority_queue<int, vector<int>, greater<int> >
        anOtherPrioQ(numbers, numbers+count);
```

and at the same time be initialized with the whole number array. The name of the array numbers is to be taken as a constant pointer, as is usual in C++.

Global operators == and < do not exist because the comparison does not seem reasonable and would be expensive in terms of run time behavior. In Section 10.2, a priority queue is used to accelerate sorting processes on sequential files.

4.4 Sorted associative containers

An associative container allows fast access to data by means of a key which need not coincide with the data. For example, the name and address of an employee could be accessed via a personnel number used as a key. In sets and multisets, the data itself is used as key, whereas in maps and multimaps, key and data are different. The STL provides four types of associative containers:

- set
  The keys coincide with the data. There are no elements with the same key in the set, that is, a key occurs either once or it does not occur at all.

- multiset
  The keys coincide with the data. There may be identical keys (elements) in the set, that is, a key can occur not at all, once, or any number of times.

- map
  The keys do not coincide with the data. For example, the key could be a number (personnel number) by means of which the data (address, salary, ...) can be accessed. Keys can be any kind of objects. In a dictionary, for example, the key could be an English word which is used to determine a foreign language word (the data). map maps a set of keys to a set of associated data. The elements of a map container are pairs of keys and data. They describe a binary relation, that is, a relation between elements of two sets.

  The set of possible keys is called the 'definition range' of the map, the set of associated data is called the 'value range.' The map type is characterized by a unique map, because one key is associated with exactly *one* datum.

  There are no identical keys, that is, a key either does not occur at all or occurs only once.

- multimap
  A multimap object has the properties described under map, with one exception: there may be identical keys. This means that a key can occur not at all, once or any number of times. Unambiguousness is therefore no longer given.

The STL containers store the keys *sorted*, although this is not required by the actual task described in the above points. This is just an implementation detail that allows you to store these containers in a very compact way as balanced binary trees (red-black trees). Because of the sorting, access to the elements is very fast and the tree grows only by the strictly required amount. An alternative, namely hashing, requires an initial assignment of memory, but is even faster in accessing elements (an average of $O(1)$ with sufficient space instead of $O(\log N)$).

This alternative was not incorporated into the STL, since after a certain date all major modifications or extensions were no longer accepted in order not to jeopardize the time scale for standardization of the programming language and its library. Because of their efficiency, hashed associative containers will be described in Chapter 7.

4.4.1 Set

A set is a collection of distinguishable objects with common properties. $N = \{0, 1, 2, 3, ...\}$, for example, denotes the set of natural numbers. Since the elements are distinguishable, there can be no two identical elements in one set. All sets used in computer programs are finite.

The class set supports mapping of sets in the computer. Although the elements of a set in the mathematical sense are not subject to any order, they are nevertheless internally represented in ordered form to facilitate access. The ordering criterion is specified at the creation of a set. If it is not specified, less<T> is used by default.

For sets, the STL provides the class template set. With regard to the typical operations with sets, such as intersection and union, set is subject to several restrictions which, however, are remedied by the extensions described in Chapter 6.

In addition to the data types specified in Table 3.1 and the methods in Table 3.2 and Section 3.2, a class set< Key, Compare> provides the public interface described in Tables 4.1 to 4.3. Here, Key is the type of those elements that also have the function of keys, and Compare is the type of the comparison object.

Data type	Meaning
key_type	Key
key_compare	Compare. **Standard:** less<Key>
value_compare	Compare. **Standard:** less<Key>

Table 4.1 Set data types.

Constructor	Meaning
set()	Standard constructor: creates an empty container, with Compare() used as comparison object.
set(c)	Constructor: creates an empty container, with c used as comparison object.
set(i, j, c)	Constructor: creates an empty container, into which subsequently the elements of the iterator range [i, j) are inserted by means of the comparison object c. The cost is $N \log N$ with N as the number of inserted elements.
set(i, j)	As set(i, j, c), but with Compare() as comparison object.

Table 4.2 Set constructors.

Return type method	Meaning	Complexity
key_compare key_comp()	Returns a copy of the comparison object used for the construction of the set.	1
value_compare value_comp()	As key_comp() (difference only in map).	1
pair<iterator,bool> insert(t)	Inserts the element t, provided that an element with the corresponding key does not yet exist. The bool component indicates whether the insertion has taken place; the iterator component points to the inserted element or to the element with the same key as t.	$\log G$
iterator insert(p,t)	As insert(t), with the iterator p being a hint as to where the search for inserting should begin. The returned iterator points to the inserted element or the element with the same key as t.	$\log G$
void insert(i,j)	Inserts the elements of the iterator range [i, j).	$N \log(G + N)$
size_type erase(k)	Deletes all elements with a key equal to k. The number of deleted elements is returned.	$N + \log G$
void erase(q)	Deletes the element pointed to by the iterator q.	1
void erase(p, q)	Deletes all elements in the iterator range [p, q).	$N + \log G$
void clear()	Deletes all elements.	$N + \log G$
iterator find(k)	Returns an iterator to an element with the key k, provided it exists. Otherwise, end() is returned.	$\log G$
size_type count(k)	Returns the number of elements with key k.	$N + \log G$
iterator lower_bound(k)	Points to the first element whose key is not less than k.	$\log G$
iterator upper_bound(k)	Returns an iterator to the first element whose key is greater than k.	$\log G$
pair<iterator, iterator> equal_range(k)	Returns a pair of iterators between which the keys are equal k.	$\log G$

Table 4.3 Set methods.

In this case, `key_compare` and `value_compare` are identical and are included only for completeness. The difference occurs only later in Section 4.4.3 in the `map` class.

The right-hand column of Table 4.3 indicates the complexity, where N refers to the number of inserted, deleted, or counted elements. G stands for the current size of the container returned by `size()`.

The meaning of some methods can only be fully understood in connection with multisets (see below). For example, `equal_range()`, which for a `set` object a is equivalent to the call `make_pair( a.lower_bound(k), a.upper_bound(k))`, supplies only a pair of directly consecutive iterators when applied to a `set`.

The `count()` method can yield only 0 or 1. It is included only for compatibility with multisets (`multiset`). All methods that return an iterator or a pair of iterators return constant iterators for constant sets. Methods for constant sets are not specially listed in Table 4.3.

The following example shows the application of a set of type `set`. More complex operations, such as union and intersection will be discussed in Section 5.6 and Chapter 6.

```
//  k4/setm.cpp    Example for sets
#include<set>
#include<showseq>

using namespace std;

int main()
{
    int i;
    set<int> Set;   //  comparison object: less<int>()

    for(i = 0; i < 10; i++) Set.insert(i);
    for(i = 0; i < 10; i++) Set.insert(i); //  no effect
    showSequence(Set);                     //  0 1 2 3 4 5 6 7 8 9

    /*
```
The display shows that the elements of the set really occur exactly once. In the next part of the program, elements are deleted. In the first variation, first the element is sought in order to delete it with the found iterator. In the second variation, deletion is carried out via the specified key.
```
    */

    cout << "Deletion by iterator\n"
            "Delete which element? (0..9)" ;
    cin >> i;
    set<int>::iterator iter = Set.find(i);
    if(iter == Set.end())
        cout << i << " not found!\n";
    else
    {
```

```
        cout << "The element " << i              // 1
            << " exists" << Set.count(i) << " times." << endl;
        Set.erase(iter);
        cout << i << " deleted!\n";
        cout << "The element " << i              // 0
            << " exists" << Set.count(i) << " times." << endl;
    }
    showSequence(Set);

    /*
```

The `count()` method yields either 0 or 1. Thus, it is an indicator as to whether an element is present in the set.

```
    */

    cout << "Deletion by value\n"
            "Delete which element? (0..9)" ;
    cin >> i;
    int Count = Set.erase(i);
    if(Count == 0)
        cout << i << " not found!\n";
    showSequence(Set);

    /*
```

A further set `NumberSet` is not initialized with a loop, but by specifying the range to be inserted in the constructor. Suitable iterators for `int` values are pointers of `int*` type. The name of a C array can be interpreted as a constant pointer to the beginning of the array. When the number of array elements is added to this pointer, the result is a pointer that points to the position after the last array element. Both pointers can be used as iterators for initialization of a set:

```
    */

    cout << "call constructor with iterator range\n";

    // 2 and 1 twice!
    int Array[] = { 1, 2, 2, 3, 4, 9, 13, 1, 0, 5};
    Count = sizeof(Array)/sizeof(Array[0]);

    set<int> NumberSet(Array, Array + Count);
    showSequence(NumberSet);      // 0 1 2 3 4 5 9 13
}
```

In this example it can also be seen that the occurring elements are displayed only once although duplicates exist in the original array.

4.4.2 Multiset

A multiset behaves like a set with the exception that not just one, but arbitrarily many identical elements may be present. Table 4.4 shows `insert()` as the only method

Return type method	Meaning	Complexity
`iterator insert(t)`	Inserts the element `t` independently of whether an element with the same key already exists. The iterator points to the newly inserted element.	$\log G$

Table 4.4   Multiset: difference from set.

which behaves differently from its counterpart in the set class and has a different return type.

4.4.3 Map

Exactly like a `set`, a `map` is an associative container, in which, however, unlike `set`, keys and associated data are different. Here, the difference between `key_compare` and `value_compare` mentioned on page 85 takes effect. In the declaration of a set container, the types of key and possibly comparison objects must be specified; in `map`, the data type is needed as well:

```
map<int, string, greater<int> > aMap;
```

The definition is a mapping of `int` numbers onto `string` objects, with the numbers internally sorted in descending order. As with `set`, sorting is not a property of the map, but of internal storage. The type of the comparison object can be left out: `map<int, string> aMap` is then the same as `map<int, string, less<int> > aMap`.

The elements of a map container are pairs: the type `value_type` is identical to `key_type` in `set` or `multiset`, whereas `map::value_type` is equivalent to `pair< Key, T>`, with `Key` being the type of key and `T` the type of data.

The `map` class essentially provides constructors with the same parameters and methods with the same names and parameters as the `set` class. The meaning is equivalent; it is sufficient to remember that pairs are stored instead of single values. There are only two exceptions. The method

```
value_compare value_comp();
```

differs in its meaning from the one in `set`. It returns a function object which can be used for comparison of objects of type `value_type` (that is, pairs). This function object compares two pairs on the basis of their keys and the comparison object used for the construction of the `map`. The class `value_compare` is declared inside the class `map`. For example, let us assume two pairs and a map with the following definitions:

```
pair<int, string> p(9921, "algorithms"),
                  q(2726, "data structures");
```

Now, if there is a map `M` which during construction was associated the comparison object `CK` for the comparison of keys, then the call

```
bool x= M.value_comp()(p,q);
```

is identical to

```
bool x= CK(p.first, q.first);
```

that is, the comparison of the keys stored in first. The second exception is the index operator provided in map, which also allows you to access the data via the key as an index. The key must not necessarily be a number:

```
// int key
cout << AddressMap[6];          // output of a name

// string key
cout << DictionaryMap["hello"]; // 'Hallo'
```

 If during access the key does not yet exist, it is included into the map, inserting an object generated with the standard constructor in place of the data! Therefore, before reading with the index operator, check whether the required element exists. Otherwise, the map will inadvertently be filled with objects generated by the standard constructor.

In the following example, some names are associated personnel numbers of the long type. These numbers are so big that it would not make sense to employ them as an index of an array. After entering a personnel number, the program outputs the corresponding name.

In order to make the program more readable, the data type for mapping names to numbers and the data type for a value pair are renamed by means of typedef.

```
// k4/map.cpp: Example for map
#include<map>
#include<string>
using namespace std;

// two typedefs for abbreviations
// comparison object: less<long>()
typedef map<long, string> MapType;
typedef MapType::value_type ValuePair;

int main()
{
    MapType Map;

    Map.insert(ValuePair(836361136, "Andrew"));
    Map.insert(ValuePair(274635328, "Berni"));
    Map.insert(ValuePair(260736622, "John"));
    Map.insert(ValuePair(720002287, "Karen"));
    Map.insert(ValuePair(138373498, "Thomas"));
    Map.insert(ValuePair(135353630, "William"));
    // insertion of Xaviera is not executed, because
```

```
//  the key already exists.
Map.insert(ValuePair(720002287, "Xaviera"));

/*
Owing to the underlying implementation, the output of the names is sorted by num-
bers:
*/

cout << "Output:\n";
MapType::iterator iter = Map.begin();
while(iter != Map.end())
{
        cout << (*iter).first << ':'        //  number
               << (*iter).second            //  name
               << endl;
        ++iter;
}

cout << "Output of the name after entering the number\n"
        << "Number: ";
long Number;
cin >> Number;
iter = Map.find(Number);       //  O(log N), see text

if(iter != Map.end())
     cout << (*iter).second << ' '  //  O(1)
            << Map[Number]       //  O(log N)
            << endl;
else cout << "Not found!" << endl;
}
```

The name is sought by way of the number. This process is of complexity $O(\log N)$, where N is the number of entries. If the entry is found, it can be output directly by dereferencing the iterator.

Another way to access a map element is via the index operator. Here, it can be clearly seen that the index can be an arbitrarily large number which has nothing to do with the number of actual entries – this is completely different from the usual array.

The access `Map[Number]` has the same complexity as `find()`, and we could do without `find()` in the above example if we could be sure that only numbers that actually exist are entered.

If the index operator is called with a non-existing number, it stores this number in the map and uses the standard constructor for generating the data (see the exercises). This ensures that the index operator never returns an invalid reference. In our case, an empty string would be entered. In order to prevent this, `find()` is called beforehand.

Exercises

4.1 For a map `m`, data of type `T` and a key `k`, the call `m[k]` is semantically equivalent to

```
(*((m.insert(make_pair(k, T())))).first)).second
```

because an entry is made for a non-existing key. Analyze the expression, in both the case when the key `k` is contained in `m`, and when it is not.

4.2 Is there a difference if `value_type` is written instead of `make_pair` in the previous exercise?

4.4.4 Multimap

`multimap` differs from `map` in the same way as `multiset` differs from `set`: multiple entries of elements with identical keys are possible, for example, the name Xaviera in the sample program of the previous section. Correspondingly, the function `insert(value_type)` does not return a pair `pair<iterator, bool>`, but only an iterator which points to the newly inserted element (compare with `set`/`multiset`).

Part II
Algorithms

Standard algorithms $\boxed{5}$

Summary: Previous chapters described the basic effects of algorithms on containers. This chapter is a catalog or reference for algorithms.

Note: A thorough reading of two or three sections of this chapter to learn the structure and a quick leafing through the rest will be sufficient to give rapid access to a suitable algorithm with sample applications. Only in Part III does the combination of algorithms and containers reveal new aspects.

All the algorithms presented in this chapter are completely separated from the special implementation of the containers on which they work. They only know iterators which can be used to access the data structures in containers. The iterators must satisfy only a few criteria (see Chapter 2). For this reason, iterators can be both complex objects and simple pointers. Some algorithms bear the same names as container methods. However, because of the different way in which they are used, no confusion will occur.

The complete separation can, however, also have disadvantages: a very generic find() algorithm will have to search a container from beginning to end. The complexity is $O(N)$, where N is the number of elements of the container. If the container structure is known, find() can be much faster. For example, the complexity of search in a sorted set container is only $O(\log N)$. Therefore, there are several algorithms which under the same name appear both as a generic algorithm and as a member function of a container. Where the situation allows, the made-to-measure member function is to be preferred.

5.1 Copying algorithms

For reasons of speed, some algorithms exist in two variations: the first works directly on the container, the second copies the container. The second variation is always sensible when a copy process is required, for example to keep the original data, and when, with regard to complexity, the algorithm itself is no more expensive than the copy process. Let us look at the different cases:

1. A copy B is to be made of container A, removing all elements from the copy which satisfy a given condition, for example all clients with less than 50,000 dollars of turnover. The following alternatives exist:

(a) copy A to B and remove all unwanted elements from B, or

(b) copy all elements from A to B, but only if they satisfy a given criterion.

Both alternatives are of complexity $O(n)$. It is, however, obvious that the second alternative is faster and therefore a copying variation of the algorithm makes sense.

2. A *sorted* copy B is to be generated of container A. Here too, two possibilities exist:

(a) copy A to B and sort B, or

(b) take all elements of A and insert them sorted into B.

The second possibility is no better than the first one. The sorting process is at least of complexity $O(N \log N)$, thus definitely greater than copying ($O(N)$). Thus, a variation of a sorting algorithm which at the same time copies is simply superfluous. If a copy is required, the first variation can be chosen without any loss of speed.

In the following sections, the copying variations are mentioned, provided they exist. All algorithms which as well as their proper task also generate a copy of a container bear the suffix _copy in their names.

5.2 Algorithms with predicates

'Predicate' means a function object (see Section 1.6.3) which is passed to an algorithm and returns a value of type bool when it is applied to a dereferenced iterator. The dereferenced iterator is simply a reference to an object stored in the container.

The function object is to determine whether this object has a given property. Only if this question is answered with true is the algorithm applied to this object. A general scheme for this is:

```
template <class InputIterator, class Predicate>
void algorithm(InputIterator first,
               InputIterator last,
               Predicate pred)
{
    while (first != last)
    {
        if(pred(*first))              //  does predicate apply?
        {
            show_it(*first);          //  ... or another function
        }
        ++first;
    }
}
```

The Predicate class must not alter an object. An example is given on page 97.

Some algorithms that use predicates have a suffix `_if` in their names, others do not. A feature common to all of them is that they expect a predicate in the parameter list.

5.2.1 Algorithms with binary predicates

A binary predicate requires two arguments. This allows you to formulate a condition for two objects in the container, for example a comparison. The algorithm might contain the following kernel:

```
if(binary_pred(*first, *second))        //  does the predicate apply?
{
    do_something_with(*first, *second);
    //  ...
```

In this sense, you can also use objects of the classes of Table 1.2 as binary predicates. The second parameter of a binary predicate, however, need not be an iterator:

```
template <class InputIterator,
          class binaryPredicate,
          class T>
void another_algorithm(InputIterator first,
                       InputIterator last,
                       binaryPredicate bpred,
                       T aValue)

{
    while (first != last)
    {
        if(bpred(*first, aValue))
        {
            show_it(*first);
        }
        ++first;
    }
}
```

5.3 Nonmutating sequence operations

The algorithms described in this section work on sequences, but do not alter them. With one exception, all algorithms are of complexity $O(N)$, where N is the number of elements in the sequence. The exception is the `search` algorithm.

5.3.1 for_each

The `for_each` algorithm causes a function to be executed on each element of a container. The definition is so short and simple that it is shown in its entirety:

```
template <class InputIterator, class Function>
Function for_each(InputIterator first,
                  InputIterator last, Function f)
{
    while (first != last)
        f(*first++);
    return f;
}
```

A possible return value of the function `f` is ignored. In the following program, the function is the display of an `int` value which, together with the `for_each` algorithm, writes a vector on the standard output.

The class `Function` in the above definition is a placeholder which could as well be the type of a function object. The `Increment` class for incrementing an `int` value is employed in this way.

```
#include<algorithm>
#include<vector>
#include<iostream>
using namespace std;
void display(int x)                    //  function
{
    cout << x << ' ';
}
class Increment                        //  functor class
{
    public:
        Increment(int i = 1) : howmuch(i) {}
        void operator()(int& x) { x += howmuch;}
    private:
        int howmuch;
};
int main()
{
    vector<int> v(5, 0);   //  vector of 5 zeros
    for_each(v.begin(), v.end(), display);    //  0 0 0 0 0
    cout << endl;
    //  with Increment constructor
    for_each(v.begin(), v.end(), Increment(2));
    for_each(v.begin(), v.end(), display);    //  2 2 2 2 2
    cout << endl;
```

```
//   with Increment object
Increment anIncrement(7);
for_each(v.begin(), v.end(), anIncrement);
for_each(v.begin(), v.end(), display);   //  9 9 9 9 9
}
```

In the example, the return value of `for_each()`, the function object, is not used. It is feasible to transfer information from `for_each()` to the caller, for example the number of calls, via a change in the state of the object.

5.3.2 find and find_if

There are two kinds of `find()` algorithm: with and without a compulsory predicate (as `find_if()`). It seeks the position in a container, let us call it C, at which a given element can be found. The result is an iterator which either points to the position found or is equal to `C.end()`. The prototypes are:

```
template <class ForwardIterator, class T>
ForwardIterator find(ForwardIterator first,
                 ForwardIterator last,
                 const T& value);

template <class ForwardIterator, class Predicate>
ForwardIterator find_if(ForwardIterator first,
                 ForwardIterator last,
                 Predicate pred);
```

The way the `find()` algorithm functions is extensively discussed in Section 1.3.4, with corresponding examples on pages 6ff. Therefore, we will look at only one example for `find_if()`, that is, a `find()` with the predicate. In a sequence of numbers, the first odd number is sought, with the criterion 'odd' checked by means of a function object.

```
//   k5/find_if.cpp
#include<algorithm>
#include<vector>
#include<iostream>
using namespace std;

void display(int x) {  cout << x << ' ';}

class odd
{
    public:
        //  odd argument yields true
        bool operator()(int x) { return x % 2;}
};
```

```
int main()
{
    vector<int> v(8);

    for(int i = 0; i < v.size(); i++)
        v[i] = 2*i;                          //  all even
    v[5] = 99;                               //  an odd number

    //  display
    for_each(v.begin(), v.end(), display);
    cout << endl;

    //  search for odd number
    vector<int>::iterator iter
        = find_if(v.begin(), v.end(), odd());

    if(iter != v.end())
    {
        cout << "The first odd number ("
            << *iter
            << ") was found at position "
            << (iter - v.begin())
            << "." << endl;
    }
    else cout << "No odd number found." << endl;
}
```

5.3.3 find_end

This algorithm finds a subsequence inside a sequence. Neither this nor the following algorithm (`find_first_of()`) is contained in the original version of the STL (Stepanov and Lee, 1995; Musser and Saini, 1996), but both have been added to the C++ standard draft. The prototypes are:

```
template<class ForwardIterator1, class ForwardIterator2>
ForwardIterator1 find_end( ForwardIterator1 first1,
                           ForwardIterator1 last1,
                           ForwardIterator2 first2,
                           ForwardIterator2 last2);

template<class ForwardIterator1, class ForwardIterator2>
ForwardIterator1 find_end( ForwardIterator1 first1,
                           ForwardIterator1 last1,
                           ForwardIterator2 first2,
                           ForwardIterator2 last2,
                           BinaryPredicate pred);
```

The interval (([first1, last1])) is the range to be searched; the interval (([first2, last2])) describes the sequence to be sought. The return value is the last iterator in the search range that points to the beginning of the subsequence. If the subsequence is not found, the algorithm returns last1. If the returned iterator is named i,

```
*(i+n) == *(first2+n)
```

or

```
pred(*(i+n), *(first2+n)) == true
```

according to the prototype, apply for all n in the range 0 to (last2-first2). The complexity is $O(N_2 * (N_1 - N_2))$, when N_1 and N_2 are the lengths of the search range and the subsequence to be sought.

5.3.4 find_first_of

The algorithm finds an element in a subsequence within a sequence. The prototypes are:

```
template<class ForwardIterator1, class ForwardIterator2>
ForwardIterator1 find_first_of(ForwardIterator1 first1,
                               ForwardIterator1 last1,
                               ForwardIterator2 first2,
                               ForwardIterator2 last2);

template<class ForwardIterator1, class ForwardIterator2>
ForwardIterator1 find_first_of(ForwardIterator1 first1,
                               ForwardIterator1 last1,
                               ForwardIterator2 first2,
                               ForwardIterator2 last2,
                               BinaryPredicate pred);
```

The interval (([first1, last1])) is the search range; the interval (([first2, last2])) describes a range of elements to be sought. The return value is the first iterator i in the search range which points to an element which is also present in the second range. Assuming that an iterator j points to the element in the second range, then

```
*i == *j
```

or

```
pred(*i, *j) == true
```

apply, according to the prototype. If no element of the first range is found in the second range, the algorithm returns last1. The complexity is $O(N_1 * N_2)$, when N_1 and N_2 are the range lengths.

5.3.5 adjacent_find

Two identical, directly adjacent elements are found with `adjacent_find()`. Here too, two overloaded variations exist – one without and one with binary predicate. The first variation compares the elements by means of the equality operator `==`, the second one uses the predicate. The prototypes are:

```
template <class ForwardIterator>
ForwardIterator adjacent_find(ForwardIterator first,
                              ForwardIterator last);


template <class ForwardIterator, class BinaryPredicate>
ForwardIterator adjacent_find(ForwardIterator first,
                              ForwardIterator last,
                              BinaryPredicate binary_pred);
```

The returned iterator points to the first of the two elements, provided that a corresponding pair is found. The first example shows how to find two identical adjacent elements:

```
//  k5/afind.cpp
#include<algorithm>
#include<vector>
#include<iostream>
using namespace std;

void display(int x) { cout << x << ' ';}

int main()
{
    vector<int> v(8);

    for(int i = 0; i < v.size(); i++)
        v[i] = 2*i;                   //  even
    v[5] = 99;                        //  two identical adjacent elements
    v[6] = 99;

    //  display
    for_each(v.begin(), v.end(), display);
    cout << endl;

    //  find identical neighbors
    vector<int>::iterator iter
        = adjacent_find(v.begin(), v.end());

    if(iter != v.end())
    {
        cout << "The first identical adjacent numbers ("
```

```
                    << *iter
                    << ") were found at position "
                    << (iter - v.begin())
                    << "." << endl;
        }
        else
            cout << "No identical adjacent numbers found."
                << endl;
}
```

The second example shows the application of a completely different – in the end arbitrary – criterion. A sequence is checked to see whether the second of two adjacent elements is twice as large as the first one:

```
//  k5/a1find.cpp
#include<algorithm>
#include<vector>
#include<iostream>
using namespace std;

void display(int x) {  cout << x << ' ';}

class doubled
{
    public:
        bool operator()(int a, int b) { return (b == 2*a);}
};

int main()
{
    vector<int> v(8);

    for(int i = 0; i < v.size(); i++)
        v[i] = i*i;
    v[6] = 2 * v[5];          //  twice as large successor

    //  display
    for_each(v.begin(), v.end(), display);
    cout << endl;

    //  search for twice as large successor
    vector<int>::iterator iter
        = adjacent_find(v.begin(), v.end(), doubled());

    if(iter != v.end())
    {
        cout << "The first number ("
            << *iter
            << ") with a twice as large successor"
```

```
                          " was found at position "
                    << (iter - v.begin())
                    << "." << endl;
        }
        else cout << "No number with twice as large "
                     "successor found." << endl;
    }
```

The technique of employing a function object reveals itself as very useful and powerful. In `operator()()`, arbitrarily complex conditions can be formulated without having to change the `main()` program.

5.3.6 **count**

This algorithm adds to the number n the number of the elements which are equal to a given value `value` or the number of the elements which satisfy a given predicate. The prototypes

```
// ISO/ANSI (1996)
template <class InputIterator, class T, class Size>
void count(InputIterator first, InputIterator last,
           const T& value, Size& n);

template <class InputIterator, class Predicate, class Size>
void count_if(InputIterator first, InputIterator last,
              Predicate pred, Size& n);
```

show that the number n of elements is passed by reference. If, prior to the application, n is set to 0, the result is the number of elements satisfying the required criterion.

After introducing the traits concept in ISO/IEC (1997), the algorithms have been redefined so that the number is passed back to the caller by a return statement in the algorithm.

```
template <class InputIterator, class T>
iterator_traits<InputIterator>::difference_type
count(InputIterator first, InputIterator last, const T& value);

template <class InputIterator, class Predicate>
iterator_traits<InputIterator>::difference_type
count_if(InputIterator first, InputIterator last,
         Predicate pred);
```

The program fragment shows the application, with reference to the vector v of the previous examples.

```
int Count = 0;
count(v.begin(), v.end(), 99, Count);
cout << "There exist " << Count
```

```
              << " elements with the value 99."
              << endl;
```

At its construction, the function object of type `myComparison` receives the value with which the comparison is to be made. Here, `count_if()` enters into the action:

```
// #include... and so on

class myComparison
{
    public:
        myComparison(int i): withwhat(i) {}
        bool operator()(int x) { return x == withwhat;}
    private:
        int withwhat;
};

int main()
{
    vector<int> v(100);
    // initialize v here

    int Count = 0;
    count_if(v.begin(), v.end(), myComparison(99), Count);
    cout << "There exist " << Count
            << " elements with the value 99."
            << endl;
}
```

5.3.7 mismatch

`mismatch()` checks two containers for matching contents, with one variation using a binary predicate. The prototypes are:

```
template <class InputIterator1, class InputIterator2>
pair<InputIterator1, InputIterator2> mismatch(
            InputIterator1 first1,
            InputIterator1 last1,
            InputIterator2 first2);

template <class InputIterator1, class InputIterator2,
        class BinaryPredicate>
pair<InputIterator1, InputIterator2> mismatch(
            InputIterator1 first1,
            InputIterator1 last1,
            InputIterator2 first2,
            BinaryPredicate binary_pred);
```

The algorithm returns a pair of iterators which point to the first position of mismatch in the corresponding containers. If both containers match, the first iterator of the returned pair is equal to `last1`. The following example shows that the containers do not have to be of the same type: here, a `vector` and a `set` are compared. Because of the sorted storage in the `set`, the vector must be sorted as well:

```cpp
//  k5/mismatch.cpp
#include<algorithm>
#include<vector>
#include<set>
#include<showseq>

using namespace std;

int main()
{
    vector<int> v(8);

    for(int i = 0; i < v.size(); i++)
        v[i] = 2*i;                      //  sorted sequence

    set<int> s(v.begin(), v.end());  //  initialize set with v
    v[3] = 7;                        //  insert mismatch

    showSequence(v);                     //  display
    showSequence(s);

    //  comparison for match with iterator pair where
    pair<vector<int>::iterator, set<int>::iterator>
        where = mismatch(v.begin(), v.end(), s.begin());

    if(where.first == v.end())
        cout << "Match found." << endl;
    else
      cout << "The first mismatch ("
           << *where.first << " != "
           << *where.second
           << ") was found at position "
           << (where.first - v.begin())
           << "." << endl;
}
```

In the `set`, no index-like position is defined; therefore an expression of the kind (`where.second - s.begin()`) is invalid. It is true that `where.second` points to the position of the mismatch in `s`, but the arithmetic is not permitted. If you really need the relative number with reference to the first element in `s`, you can use `distance()`.

The second example checks character sequences, with the simple `mismatch()` finding the first mismatch, whereas `mismatch()` with binary predicate ignores mismatches in upper case and lower case spelling.

```
//   k5/mismat_b.cpp
#include<algorithm>
#include<vector>
#include<iostream>
#include<cctype>

using namespace std;

class myCharCompare //   tolerates upper/lower case spelling
{
    public:
      bool operator()(char x, char y)
      {
          //   convert to lower case if needed
          x = tolower(x);
          y = tolower(y);
          return x == y;
      }
};

int main()
{
    char Text1[] = "Algorithms and Data Structures";
    char Text2[] = "Algorithms and data Struktures"; //  2 errors

    //  copy texts into vector (−1 because of null byte)
    vector<char> v1(Text1, Text1 + sizeof(Text1)-1);
    vector<char> v2(Text2, Text2 + sizeof(Text2)-1);

    //  compare with iterator pair where
    pair<vector<char>::iterator, vector<char>::iterator>
        where = mismatch(v1.begin(), v1.end(), v2.begin());

    if(where.first != v1.end())
    {
        cout << Text1 << endl << Text2 << endl;
        cout.width(1 + where.first - v1.begin());

        cout << "^";
        cout << "  first mismatch" << endl;
    }

    //  compare with predicate
    where = mismatch(v1.begin(), v1.end(), v2.begin(),
                myCharCompare());

    if(where.first != v1.end())
    {
        cout << Text1 << endl << Text2 << endl;
```

```
            cout.width(1 + where.first - v1.begin());
            cout << "^";
            cout << "  first mismatch at\n"
                    "tolerance of upper/lower case spelling"
                 << endl;
        }
    }
```

The specification of output width in connection with the ^ character is used to mark the position visually on screen.

5.3.8 equal

equal() checks two containers for matching contents, with one variation using a binary predicate. Unlike mismatch(), however, no position is indicated. As can be seen from the return type bool, it checks only whether the containers match or not. The prototypes are:

```
template <class InputIterator1, class InputIterator2>
bool equal(InputIterator1 first1,
           InputIterator1 last1,
           InputIterator2 first2);

template <class InputIterator1, class InputIterator2,
          class BinaryPredicate>
bool equal(InputIterator1 first1,
           InputIterator1 last1,
           InputIterator2 first2,
           BinaryPredicate binary_pred);
```

When you compare equal() with mismatch(), you will see a strong similarity: depending on whether mismatch() yields a match or not, equal() must return the value true or false (see Exercises 5.1 and 5.2). An application within the program of the previous example might look as follows:

```
if(equal(v1.begin(), v1.end(), v2.begin()))
    cout << "equal character strings" << endl;
else
    cout << "unequal character strings" << endl;

// remember the negation:
if(!equal(v1.begin(), v1.end(), v2.begin(),
    myCharCompare()))
        cout << "un";
cout << "equal character strings at "
        "tolerance of upper/lower case spelling " << endl;
```

The negation saves some writing effort in the program.

Exercises

5.1   What would the implementation of `equal()` look like, if it were to use the `mismatch()` algorithm?

5.2   What would the implementation of `equal()` with a binary predicate look like, if it were to use `mismatch()` with a binary predicate?

5.3.9 search

The `search()` algorithm searches a sequence of size N to see whether a second sequence of size G is contained in it. In the worst case, the complexity is $O(NG)$; on average, however, the behavior is better. The return value is an iterator to the position within the first sequence at which the second sequence starts, provided it is contained in the first one. Otherwise, an iterator to the `last1` position of the first sequence is returned. The prototypes are:

```
template <class ForwardIterator1, class ForwardIterator2>
ForwardIterator1 search(ForwardIterator1 first1,
                        ForwardIterator1 last1,
                        ForwardIterator2 first2,
                        ForwardIterator2 last2);

template <class ForwardIterator1, class ForwardIterator2,
          class BinaryPredicate>
ForwardIterator1 search(ForwardIterator1 first1,
                        ForwardIterator1 last1,
                        ForwardIterator2 first2,
                        ForwardIterator2 last2,
                        BinaryPredicate binary_pred);
```

In the example, a sequence of numbers is searched for, inside another sequence of numbers. The binary predicate compares the absolute values of the numbers, ignoring the signs.

```
// k5/search.cpp
#include<algorithm>
#include<vector>
#include<iostream>
#include<cstdlib>

using namespace std;

class AbsIntCompare // ignore signs
{
    public:
      bool operator()(int x, int  y)
      {
          return abs(x) == abs(y);
```

```
        }
};

int main()
{
    int i;
    vector<int> v1(12);
    for(i = 0; i < v1.size(); i++)
        v1[i] = i;          //  0 1 2 3 4 5 6 7 8 9 10 11 12

    vector<int> v2(4);
    for(i = 0; i < v2.size(); i++)
        v2[i] = i + 5;      //  5 6 7 8
```

```
    // search for substructure v2 in v1
    vector<int>::iterator
        where = search(v1.begin(), v1.end(),
                    v2.begin(), v2.end());
```

```
    // if the sequence v2 does not begin with 5, but with a number ≥ 10,
    // the else branch of the if condition is executed.
```

```
    if(where != v1.end())
    {
        cout << "  v2 is contained in v1 from position "
            << (where - v1.begin())
            << " onward." << endl;
    }
    else
        cout << "  v2 is not contained in v1."
            << endl;
```

```
    // put negative numbers into v2
    for(i = 0; i < v2.size(); i++)
        v2[i] = -(i + 5);  // –5 –6 –7 –8
```

```
    // search for substructure v2 in v1, ignore signs
    where = search(v1.begin(), v1.end(),
                v2.begin(), v2.end(),
                AbsIntCompare());
```

```
    if(where != v1.end())
    {
        cout << "  v2 is contained in v1 from position "
            << (where - v1.begin())
            << " onward (signs are ignored)."
            << endl;
    }
    else
        cout << "  v2 is not contained in v1."
```

```
                    << endl;
    }
```

Here, with the changed criterion, it is found that v2 is contained in v1.

5.3.10 search_n

The search_n() algorithm searches a sequence for a sequence of equal values. The prototypes are:

```
template <class ForwardIterator, class Size, class T>
ForwardIterator search_n(ForwardIterator first,
                         ForwardIterator last,
                         Size count,
                         const T& value);

template <class ForwardIterator, class Size, class T,
          class BinaryPredicate>
ForwardIterator search_n(ForwardIterator first,
                         ForwardIterator last,
                         Size count,
                         const T& value,
                         BinaryPredicate binary_pred);
```

The first function returns the iterator to the start of the first sequence with at least count values that are equal to value. If such a sequence is not found, the function returns last. The second function does not check for equality but evaluates the binary predicate. In case of success, (X) binary_pred(X, value) must hold for at least count consecutive values.

5.4 Mutating sequence operations

If not specified otherwise, the complexity of all algorithms in this section is $O(N)$, where N is the number of moved or altered elements of the sequence.

5.4.1 iota

This algorithm is part of the HP reference implementation, but not of the C++ standard draft. It is shown here, because it can from time to time be employed in practice.

Iota is the ninth letter of the Greek alphabet (ι). The corresponding English word 'iota' means 'a very small quantity' or 'an infinitesimal amount.' However, the name has not been chosen for this reason, but is taken from the ι operator of the APL programming language. As an 'Index generator,' the APL instruction ι n supplies a vector with an ascending sequence of the numbers 1 to n. The function itself is rather simple, as can be seen from the definition:

```
//  include/iota
template <class ForwardIterator, class T>
```

```
void iota(ForwardIterator first, ForwardIterator last, T value)
{
    while (first != last) *first++ = value++;
}
```

All elements in the interval [first, last) of a sequence are assigned a value, with the value being increased by one at each iteration. The type T for the value can also be a pointer type, so that addresses are incremented. iota() is going to be employed in the example in Section 5.4.2. In the following text it is assumed that iota is not part of the header <algorithm> (as it is in the HP implementation) but is contained in an extra header <iota>.

5.4.2 copy

The copy() algorithm copies the elements of a source range into the target range; copying can start at the beginning or at the end of the ranges (with copy_backward()). If the target range is not to be overwritten, but the copied elements are to be inserted, an insert iterator is chosen as the output iterator, as shown on page 72. Exceptionally, in order to make the functioning clearer, the complete definitions are shown instead of the prototypes:

```
template <class InputIterator, class OutputIterator>
OutputIterator copy(InputIterator first,
                    InputIterator last,
                    OutputIterator result)
{
    while (first != last) *result++ = *first++;
    return result;
}

template <class BidirectionalIterator1,
          class BidirectionalIterator2>
BidirectionalIterator2 copy_backward(
                    BidirectionalIterator1 first,
                    BidirectionalIterator1 last,
                    BidirectionalIterator2 result)
{
    while (first != last) *--result = *--last;
    return result;
}
```

Here too, as usual in the C++ Standard Template Library, last does not denote the position of the last element, but the position after the last element. As Figure 5.1 shows, three cases must be considered:

(a) The ranges are completely separated from each other. The ranges can lie in the same or in different containers. result points to the beginning of the target

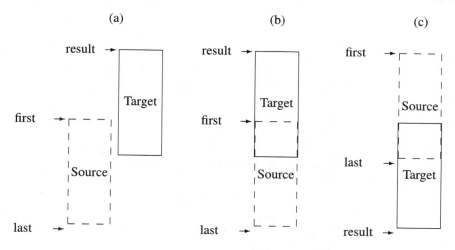

Figure 5.1   Copying without and with range overlapping.

range. copy() copies the source range starting with *first. The return value is result + (last - first), that is, the position after the last element of the target range.

(b) The ranges overlap in such a way that the target range begins *before* the source range. result points to the beginning of the target range. copy() copies the source range beginning with *first. As with (a), the position after the last element of the target range is returned.

(c) The ranges overlap in such a way that the target range begins somewhere in the *middle* of the source range. In order not to destroy the data, copying must start from the end. result points to the position directly after the *end* of the target range. copy_backward() copies the source range by first copying *(--last) to the position --result. Here, result - (last - first) is returned, that is, the position of the last copied element in the target range.

The behavior of the copying algorithms is undefined when result lies in the interval [first, last). The application of copy() and copy_backward() is shown in the following example:

```
//  k5/cpy.cpp
#include<algorithm>
#include<vector>
#include<showseq>
#include<iota>

using namespace std;

int main()
```

```
{
    vector<int> v1(7),
                v2(7, 0);                       //  7 zeros
    iota(v1.begin(), v1.end(),0);               //  result:

    showSequence(v1);      //  0 1 2 3 4 5 6
    showSequence(v2);      //  0 0 0 0 0 0 0

    /*
```
In the copy process from v1 to v2 itself, the beginning of the target range is marked
by v2.begin().
```
    */

    //  copy v1 to v2
    copy(v1.begin(), v1.end(), v2.begin());
    showSequence(v2);      //  0 1 2 3 4 5 6

    /*
```
In order to show the variety of the iterator principle, the algorithm copy() is used
with a special iterator instead of the algorithm for_each() algorithm. This iterator
is defined as an ostream iterator (see Exercise 5.3) which can display int numbers on
the standard output. The copy() algorithm has no difficulties with this (in practice, it
doesn't give a hoot!).
```
    */

    //  copy v1 to cout, separator *
    ostream_iterator<int> Output(cout, "*");
    copy(v1.begin(), v1.end(), Output);         //  0*1*2*3*4*5*6*
    cout << endl;

    /*
```
Now, a range inside v1 is copied to a different position which lies *inside* v1. The
range is chosen such that source and target ranges overlap. The first four numbers are
copied, so that case (c) of Figure 5.1 applies.
```
    */

    //  overlapping ranges:
    vector<int>::iterator last = v1.begin();
    advance(last, 4);                           //  4 steps forward
    copy_backward(v1.begin(), last, v1.end());
    copy(v1.begin(), v1.end(), Output);         //  0*1*2*0*1*2*3*
}
```

Exercise

5.3 In the sample program, an ostream_iterator was used. What would its implementation look like? Hints can be found in Section 2.2.2.

5.4.3 swap

The swap() algorithm exchanges elements of containers. It occurs in three variations:

- swap() swaps two individual elements. The two elements can be in the same or in different containers.

```
template <class T>
void swap(T& a, T& b);
```

- iter_swap() takes two iterators and swaps the associated elements. The two iterators can belong to the same or to different containers.

```
template <class ForwardIterator1, class ForwardIterator2>
void iter_swap(ForwardIterator1 a, ForwardIterator2 b);
```

- swap_ranges() swaps two ranges.

```
template <class ForwardIterator1, class ForwardIterator2>
ForwardIterator2 swap_ranges(ForwardIterator1 first1,
                             ForwardIterator1 last1,
                             ForwardIterator2 first2);
```

first1 points to the beginning of the first range, last1 to the position after the last element of the first range. The beginning of the second range is given by first2. The number of elements to be swapped is given by the size of the first range. The ranges can lie in the same container, but they must not overlap. swap_ranges() returns an iterator to the end of the second range.

All three variations are employed in the next example where, for simplicity, all movements take place in the same container – which, in general, is not necessarily the case. At the end of each swapping action, the result is displayed on standard output.

```
//  k5/swap.cpp
#include<algorithm>
#include<vector>
#include<showseq>
#include<iota>

using namespace std;

int main()
{
    vector<int> v(17);
    iota(v.begin(), v.end(), 10);
    showSequence(v);
        //  10 11 12 13 14 15 16 17 18 19 20 21 22 23 24 25 26

    cout << "Swap elements v[3] and v[5]:\n";
    swap(v[3], v[5]);                        //  swap
```

```
        showSequence(v);
         //  10 11 12 15 14 13 16 17 18 19 20 21 22 23 24 25 26

        cout << "swap first and last elements"
                " via iterator:\n";
        vector<int>::iterator first = v.begin(),
                              last = v.end();
        last--;

        iter_swap(first, last);              // swap
        showSequence(v);
         //  26 11 12 15 14 13 16 17 18 19 20 21 22 23 24 25 10

        int oneThird = v.size()/3;
        cout << "swap about the first and last thirds "
             << "(" << oneThird << " Positions):\n";
        last = v.begin();
        advance(last, oneThird);          // end of first third
        vector<int>::iterator target = v.end();
        advance(target, -oneThird);               // beginning of second third

        swap_ranges(first, last, target);  // swap
        showSequence(v);
         //  22 23 24 25 10 13 16 17 18 19 20 21 26 11 12 15 14
    }
```

5.4.4 transform

When the task is not only to copy something, but also to transform it at the same time, then transform() is the right algorithm. The transformation can concern only one element or two elements at a time. Correspondingly, there are two overloaded versions:

```
template <class InputIterator, class OutputIterator,
        class UnaryOperation>
OutputIterator transform(InputIterator first,
                         InputIterator last,
                         OutputIterator result,
                         UnaryOperation op);
```

Here, the operation op is applied to each element in the range first to last exclusive, and the result is copied into the range beginning with result. result may be identical to first; in this case, the original elements are substituted by the transformed ones. The return value is an iterator to the position after the end of the target range.

```
template <class InputIterator1, class InputIterator2,
        class OutputIterator, class BinaryOperation>
```

```
OutputIterator transform(InputIterator1 first1,
                         InputIterator1 last1,
                         InputIterator2 first2,
                         OutputIterator result,
                         BinaryOperation bin_op);
```

In the second version, two ranges are taken into account. The first is the interval [first1, last1), the second the interval [first2, first2 + last1 - first1), that is, the second range has exactly the same size as the first. The bin_op operation takes one element from each of the two ranges and stores their result in result. result may be identical to first1 or first2; in this case, the original elements are substituted with the transformed ones. The return value is an iterator to the position after the end of the target range.

The example shows two vectors of names. The elements of one vector are changed into upper case letters. The elements of the third vector originate from the elements of the first two vectors joined by 'and.'

```cpp
//  k5/transfrm.cpp
#include<algorithm>
#include<showseq>
#include<string>
#include<vector>

using namespace std;

string uppercase(string s)        //  unary operation as function
{
    for(int i = 0; i < s.length(); i++)
        if(s[i] >= 'a' && s[i] <= 'z')
            s[i] -= 'a'-'A';
    return s;
}

class join                        //  binary operation as functor
{
    public:
        string operator()(const string& a, const string& b)
        {
            return a + " and " + b;
        }
};

int main()
{
    vector<string> Gals(3), Guys(3),
                   Couples(3);    //  there must be enough space
    Gals[0] = "Annabella";
    Gals[1] = "Scheherazade";
```

```
        Gals[2] = "Xaviera";

        Guys[0]  = "Bogey";
        Guys[1]  = "Amadeus";
        Guys[2]  = "Wladimir";

        transform(Guys.begin(), Guys.end(),
                  Guys.begin(),    // Target == Source
                  uppercase);

        transform(Gals.begin(), Gals.end(),
                  Guys.begin(), Couples.begin(),
                  join());

        showSequence(Couples, "\n");
    }
```

Output of the program is:

Annabella and BOGEY
Scheherazade and AMADEUS
Xaviera and WLADIMIR

The example shows different variations:

- The unary transformation `uppercase()` is implemented as a function, the binary one as a functor. This also works the other way round.
- The application of `uppercase()` with the `transform()` algorithm uses the same container to store the results, whereas the binary transformation `join()` stores the results in a different container `Couples`.

5.4.5 replace

The `replace()` algorithm replaces each occurrence of value `old_value` with `new_value` sequentially. Alternatively, a condition-controlled replacement with a unary predicate is possible with `replace_if()`:

```
template <class ForwardIterator, class T>
void replace(ForwardIterator first,
             ForwardIterator last,
             const T& old_value,
             const T& new_value);

template <class ForwardIterator, class Predicate, class T>
void replace_if(ForwardIterator first,
                ForwardIterator last,
                Predicate pred,
                const T& new_value);
```

Now, for the first time, we can see the copying variations of algorithms discussed in Section 5.1:

```
template <class InputIterator, class OutputIterator, class T>
OutputIterator replace_copy(InputIterator first,
                            InputIterator last,
                            OutputIterator result,
                            const T& old_value,
                            const T& new_value);

template <class Iterator, class OutputIterator,
         class Predicate, class T>
OutputIterator replace_copy_if(Iterator first,
                               Iterator last,
                               OutputIterator result,
                               Predicate pred,
                               const T& new_value);
```

The copying variations differ in their names by an added _copy. In the following example, all four cases are presented because up to now there has not been one sample program with a copying variation.

```
//  k5/replace.cpp
#include<algorithm>
#include<showseq>
#include<string>
#include<vector>

using namespace std;

//  unary predicate as functor
class Citrusfruit
{
    public:

        bool operator()(const string& a)
        {
            return  a == "lemon"
                 || a == "orange"
                 || a == "lime";
        }
};

int main()
{
    vector<string> Fruitbasket(3), Crate(3);

    Fruitbasket[0] = "apple";
    Fruitbasket[1] = "orange";
```

```
Fruitbasket[2] = "lemon";
showSequence(Fruitbasket); // apple orange lemon

cout << "replace: "
        "replace apple with quince:\n";
replace(Fruitbasket.begin(), Fruitbasket.end(),
        string("apple"), string("quince"));
showSequence(Fruitbasket); // quince orange lemon

cout << "replace_if: "
        "replace citrus fruits with plums:\n";
replace_if(Fruitbasket.begin(), Fruitbasket.end(),
        Citrusfruit(), string("plum"));
showSequence(Fruitbasket); // quince plum plum

cout << "replace_copy: "
        "copy and replace the plums "
        "with limes:\n";
replace_copy(Fruitbasket.begin(), Fruitbasket.end(),
        Crate.begin(), string("plum"), string("lime"));
showSequence(Crate);      // quince lime lime

cout << "replace_copy_if: copy and replace "
        "the citrus fruits with tomatoes:\n";
replace_copy_if(Crate.begin(), Crate.end(),
        Fruitbasket.begin(), Citrusfruit(), string("tomato"));
showSequence(Fruitbasket); // quince tomato tomato
}
```

Since the scheme is always the same, from now on the _copy variations of the algorithms will be considered only as prototypes, but not as examples.

5.4.6 fill

When a sequence is to be completely or partly initialized with the same values, the fill() or fill_n() algorithms will help:

```
template <class ForwardIterator, class T>
void fill(ForwardIterator first, ForwardIterator last,
        const T& value);

template <class OutputIterator, class Size, class T>
OutputIterator fill_n(OutputIterator first, Size n,
                    const T& value);
```

Both are as simple as iota() and easy to apply:

```
// k5/fill.cpp
#include<algorithm>
#include<vector>
```

```
#include<showseq>

using namespace std;

int main()
{
    vector<double> v(8);
    //  initialize all values with 9.23
    fill(v.begin(), v.end(), 9.23);

    showSequence(v);

    /*
    fill_n() expects the specification of the number of elements in the sequence which
    are to be initialized with a value and returns an iterator to the end of the range. Here,
    the first half of the sequence is changed:
    */

    //  initialize the first half with 1.01
    vector<double>::iterator iter =
        fill_n(v.begin(), v.size()/2, 1.01);

    showSequence(v);
    cout << "iter is in position = "
        << (iter - v.begin())
        << ", *iter = " << *iter << endl;
}
```

5.4.7 generate

A generator in the `generate()` algorithm is a function object or a function which is called without parameters and whose results are assigned one by one to the elements of the sequence. As with `fill()`, there is a variation which expects an iterator pair, and a variation which needs the starting iterator and a number of pieces:

```
template <class ForwardIterator, class Generator>
void generate(ForwardIterator first, ForwardIterator last,
              Generator gen);

template <class OutputIterator, class Size,
          class Generator>
OutputIterator generate_n(OutputIterator first, Size n,
                          Generator gen);
```

The example shows both variations, with the generator occurring in two versions as well. The first generator is a function object and generates random numbers, the second one is a function for generating powers of two.

```
//  include/myrandom
#ifndef myrandom_h
#define myrandom_h

#include<cstdlib>    //  rand() and RAND_MAX

class Random
{
    public:
      Random(int b): Range(b) {}
      //  returns an int random number between 0 and Range -1
      int operator()()
      {
          return (int)(((double)rand()*(Range))/(RAND_MAX+1.0));
      }
    private:
      int Range;
};
#endif
```

The random function object uses the standard function `rand()` from *cstdlib* (that is, *stdlib.h* in the old notation) which generates a value between 0 and RAND_MAX which is subsequently normalized to the required range. For further use, the random number generator is packed into an include file and stored in the include directory.

```
//  k5/generate.cpp
#include<algorithm>                     //  main program
#include<vector>
#include<showseq>
#include<myrandom>                       //  (see above)


int PowerOfTwo()     //  double value, but begin with 1
{
    static int Value = 1;
    return (Value *= 2)/2;
}

using namespace std;

int main()
{
    vector<double> v(12);

    Random whatAChance(1000);
    generate(v.begin(), v.end(), whatAChance);
    showSequence(v); //  10 3 335 33 355 217 536 195 700 949 274 444
```

```
generate_n(v.begin(), 10, PowerOfTwo);  // only 10 out of 12!
showSequence(v); // 1 2 4 8 16 32 64 128 256 512 274 444
}
```

5.4.8 remove

The algorithm removes all elements from a sequence which are equal to a value value or which satisfy a predicate pred. Here, the prototypes are listed including the copying variations:

```
template <class ForwardIterator, class T>
ForwardIterator remove(ForwardIterator first,
                       ForwardIterator last,
                       const T& value);

template <class ForwardIterator, class Predicate>
ForwardIterator remove_if(ForwardIterator first,
                          ForwardIterator last,
                          Predicate pred);

template <class InputIterator, class OutputIterator, class T>
OutputIterator remove_copy(InputIterator first,
                           InputIterator last,
                           OutputIterator result,
                           const T& value);

template <class InputIterator, class OutputIterator,
          class Predicate>
OutputIterator remove_copy_if(InputIterator first,
                              InputIterator last,
                              OutputIterator result,
                              Predicate pred);
```

'Removing an element' in practice means that all subsequent elements shift one position to the left. When only one element is removed, the last element is duplicated, because a copy of it is assigned to the preceding position. remove() returns an iterator to the now shortened end of the sequence.

It should be noted that the total length of the sequence does not change! No rearrangement of the memory space is carried out. The range between the returned iterator and end() only contains meaningless elements.

```
//  k5/remove.cpp
#include<iostream>
#include<algorithm>
#include<vector>
#include<string>
#include<iota>
```

```cpp
bool Vowel(char c)
{
    char vowel[] = "aeiouAEIOU";
    for(int i = 0; i < sizeof(vowel); i++)
        if(c == vowel[i]) return true;
    return false;
}

using namespace std;

int main()
{
    vector<char> v(26);
    // generate alphabet in lower case letters:
    iota(v.begin(), v.end(), 'a');
    ostream_iterator<char> Output(cout, "");
    copy(v.begin(), v.end(), Output);
    cout << endl;

    /*
```

Here, the sequence is not displayed by means of showSequence(), because not all values between begin() and end() are to be shown, but only the significant ones (iterator last).

```cpp
    */
    cout << "remove 't': ";
    vector<char>::iterator last =
        remove(v.begin(), v.end(), char('t'));

    // last = new end after shifting
    // v.end() remains unchanged
    copy(v.begin(), last, Output);
        // abcdefghijklmnopqrsuvwxyz      (t is missing)
    cout << endl;

    last = remove_if(v.begin(), last, Vowel);
    cout << "only consonants left: ";
    copy(v.begin(), last, Output);
        // bcdfghjklmnpqrsvwxyz
    cout << endl;

    cout << "complete sequence up to end() with "
            " meaningless rest elements: ";
    copy(v.begin(), v.end(), Output);
        // bcdfghjklmnpqrsvwxyzvwxyzz
    cout << endl;
}
```

5.4.9 **unique**

The `unique()` algorithm deletes identical consecutive elements except one and is already known as the element function of containers (Table 3.7). In addition, it is provided as a global function with an additional copying variation:

```
template <class ForwardIterator>
ForwardIterator unique(ForwardIterator first,
                       ForwardIterator last);

template <class ForwardIterator, class BinaryPredicate>
ForwardIterator unique(ForwardIterator first,
                       ForwardIterator last,
                       BinaryPredicate binary_pred);

template <class InputIterator, class OutputIterator>
OutputIterator unique_copy(InputIterator first,
                           InputIterator last,
                           OutputIterator result);

template <class InputIterator, class OutputIterator,
          class BinaryPredicate>
OutputIterator unique_copy(InputIterator first,
                           InputIterator last,
                           OutputIterator result,
                           BinaryPredicate binary_pred);
```

A simple example shows the first two variations. As with `remove()`, shortening the sequence through deletion of the identical adjacent elements does not affect the total length of the sequence. Therefore, here too an iterator to the logical end of the sequence is returned, which is different from the physical end given by `end()`.

```
//  k5/unique.cpp
#include<iostream>
#include<algorithm>
#include<vector>

using namespace std;

int main()
{
    vector<int> v(20);
    //  sequence with identical adjacent elements
    for(int i = 0; i < v.size(); i++)
        v[i] = i/3;

    ostream_iterator<int> Output(cout, " ");
    copy(v.begin(), v.end(), Output);
                              //  0 0 0 1 1 1 2 2 2 3 3 3 4 4 4 5 5 5 6 6
    cout << endl;
```

```
        vector<int>::iterator last =
            unique(v.begin(), v.end());
        copy(v.begin(), last, Output); // 0 1 2 3 4 5 6
    }
```

5.4.10 reverse

reverse() reverses the order of elements in a sequence: the first shall be last – and vice versa. Since the first element is swapped with the last, the second with the last but one, and so on, a bidirectional iterator is required which can process the sequence starting with the end.

```
template <class BidirectionalIterator>
void reverse(BidirectionalIterator first,
             BidirectionalIterator last);

template <class BidirectionalIterator, class OutputIterator>
OutputIterator reverse_copy(BidirectionalIterator first,
                            BidirectionalIterator last,
                            OutputIterator result);
```

The example reverses a character sequence which represents a nonperfect palindrome and a sequence of numbers.

```
//  k5/reverse.cpp
#include<algorithm>
#include<showseq>
#include<vector>
#include<iota>

using namespace std;

int main()
{
    char s[] = "Madam";
    vector<char> vc(s, s + sizeof(s)-1); // −1 because of null byte
    showSequence(vc);     // Madam

    reverse(vc.begin(), vc.end());
    showSequence(vc);     // madaM

    vector<int> vi(10);
    iota(vi.begin(), vi.end(), 10);
    showSequence(vi);     // 10 11 12 13 14 15 16 17 18 19

    reverse(vi.begin(), vi.end());
    showSequence(vi);     // 19 18 17 16 15 14 13 12 11 10
}
```

5.4.11 **rotate**

This algorithm shifts the elements of a sequence to the left in such a way that those that fall out at the beginning are inserted back at the end.

```
template <class ForwardIterator>
void rotate(ForwardIterator first,
            ForwardIterator middle,
            ForwardIterator last);

template <class ForwardIterator, class OutputIterator>
OutputIterator rotate_copy(ForwardIterator first,
                           ForwardIterator middle,
                           ForwardIterator last,
                           OutputIterator result);
```

The reference document (Stepanov and Lee, 1995) states in an 'immediately obvious' way, that for each non-negative integer i < last - first, an element is moved from position (first + i) into position (first + (i + (last - middle)) % (last - first)). In other words: first and last as usual specify the range in which the rotation is to take place. The middle iterator points to the element which is to be located at the beginning of the sequence, after the rotation.

The example shows a series of rotations by one element each and a series of rotations by two positions each.

```
//  k5/rotate.cpp
#include<showseq>
#include<algorithm>
#include<vector>
#include<iota>

using namespace std;

int main()
{
    vector<int> v(10);
    iota(v.begin(), v.end(), 0);

    for(int shift = 1; shift < 3; shift++)
    {
        cout << "Rotation by " << shift << endl;
        for(int i = 0; i < v.size()/shift; i++)
        {
            showSequence(v);
            rotate(v.begin(), v.begin() + shift, v.end());
        }
    }
}
```

The program displays:

Rotation by 1
0 1 2 3 4 5 6 7 8 9
1 2 3 4 5 6 7 8 9 0
2 3 4 5 6 7 8 9 0 1
...
9 0 1 2 3 4 5 6 7 8

Rotation by 2
0 1 2 3 4 5 6 7 8 9
2 3 4 5 6 7 8 9 0 1
4 5 6 7 8 9 0 1 2 3
...
8 9 0 1 2 3 4 5 6 7

Exercise

5.4 Write an algorithm

```
template <class ForwardIterator, class Distance>
void rotate_steps(ForwardIterator first,
                  ForwardIterator last,
                  Distance steps);
```

making use of `rotate()` which, apart from the iterators for the range, expects the number of rotations `steps`. A negative value of `steps` will rotate the sequence by `steps` positions to the left, a positive value to the right. The value of `steps` can be greater than the length of the sequence. A possible application could be:

```
vector<int> v(10);
iota(v.begin(), v.end(), 0);
showSequence(v);

cout << "Rotation by -11 (left)" << endl;
rotate_steps(v.begin(), v.end(), -11);
showSequence(v);

cout << "Rotation by +1 (right)" << endl;
rotate_steps(v.begin(), v.end(), 1);
showSequence(v);
```

The result would be a sequence shifted by 1 (= 11 modulo 10) to the left, cancelled by the subsequent shift to the right.

5.4.12 random_shuffle

This algorithm is used for random shuffling of the order of elements in a sequence that provides random access iterators, for example vector or deque. It exists in two variations:

```
template <class RandomAccessIterator>
void random_shuffle(RandomAccessIterator first,
                    RandomAccessIterator last);

template <class RandomAccessIterator,
          class RandomCountGenerator>
void random_shuffle(RandomAccessIterator first,
                    RandomAccessIterator last,
                    RandomNumberGenerator& rand);
```

The shuffling of the order will be uniformly distributed; this obviously depends on the random number generator used. The first variation uses an internal random number function, that is, not one specified in ISO/IEC (1997).

It is expected that the random number generator or the random function will take a positive argument n of the distance type of the random access iterator used and return a value between 0 and $(n-1)$.

For a change, a second random number generator named RAND is specified in the example, which has the advantages of being very simple and independent from system functions. The disadvantage is its short period. But in many cases, this is irrelevant.

```
//  include/rand.h
#ifndef rand_h
#define rand_h

class RAND
{
    public:
      RAND() : r(1) {}
      int operator()(int X)
      //  returns an int pseudo random number between 0 and X-1
      //  period: 2048
      {
          r = (125 * r) % 8192;
          return int(double(r)/8192.0*(X));
      }
    private:
      long int r;
};
#endif
```

This simple random number generator may be used more often by including *rand.h* via `#include`. The two random number generators presented up to now differ not only in their algorithms, but also in their application:

- `RAND` is used when the call needs as function object an argument X. A value between 0 and (X – 1) is returned. The construction of a `RAND` object does not requires parameters.

- `Random` (see page 120) does not need a parameter at all. However, during construction of a `Random` object, a number X must be specified which defines the range of possible random numbers (0 to X – 1).

Depending on the purpose, one or the other variation may be chosen. More sophisticated random number generators can be found in the literature (for example, Knuth (1994) and Sedgewick (1992)). For the examples in this book, the two variations above are sufficient.

```cpp
//  k5/rshuffle.cpp
//  Example for random_shuffle()
#include<algorithm>
#include<vector>
#include<showseq>
#include<iota>
#include"rand.h"

using namespace std;

int main()
{
    vector<int> v(12);
    iota(v.begin(), v.end(), 0);     // 0 1 2 3 4 5 6 7 8 9 10 11

    random_shuffle(v.begin(), v.end());
    showSequence(v);                 // 4 8 5 11 7 1 3 9 6 2 10 0

    random_shuffle(v.begin(), v.end(), RAND());
    showSequence(v);                 // 8 1 2 6 11 0 5 4 10 3 9 7
}
```

5.4.13 partition

A sequence can be split with `partition()` into two ranges such that all elements that satisfy a given criterion `pred` lie before all those that do not. The return value is an iterator which points to the beginning of the second range. All elements lying before this iterator satisfy the predicate. A typical application of such a partition can be found in the well-known quicksort algorithm.

The second variation, `stable_partition()`, guarantees in addition that the relative order of the elements within one range is maintained. From a function point of view, this second variation means that the first variation is normally not needed at all. With limited memory, however, the second variation takes slightly longer to run ($O(N \log N)$ instead of $O(N)$, $N = last - first$), so the STL provides both variations. The prototypes are:

```
template <class BidirectionalIterator, class Predicate>
BidirectionalIterator partition(BidirectionalIterator first,
                                BidirectionalIterator last,
                                Predicate pred);

template <class ForwardIterator, class Predicate>
ForwardIterator stable_partition(ForwardIterator first,
                                 ForwardIterator last,
                                 Predicate pred);
```

In the example, a randomly ordered sequence is partitioned into positive and negative numbers. Both simple and stable partitions are shown:

```
//  k5/partitio.cpp
#include<algorithm>
#include<vector>
#include<showseq>
#include<iota>
#include"rand.h"        //  see page 127

bool negative(int x) { return x < 0;}

using namespace std;

int main()
{
    vector<int> v(12);
    iota(v.begin(), v.end(), -6);
    random_shuffle(v.begin(), v.end(), RAND());

    vector<int> unstable = v,
                stable = v;

    partition(unstable.begin(), unstable.end(), negative);
    stable_partition(stable.begin(), stable.end(), negative);

    cout << "Partition into negative and positive elements\n";
    cout << "sequence          :";
    showSequence(v);           // -5 -1 3 2 -3 5 -4 -6 4 0 1 -2

    cout << "stable partition  :";
    showSequence(stable);      // -5 -1 -3 -4 -6 -2 3 2 5 4 0 1

    cout << "unstable partition :";
    //  the negative elements are no longer
```

```
    //  in their original order
    showSequence(unstable); //  -5 -1 -2 -6 -3 -4 5 2 4 0 1 3
}

//  declared in tempbuf.ht
//  definition for stable_partition()
char __stl_temp_buffer[__stl_buffer_size];
```

The last line depends on the STL implementation used:

Public domain HP reference implementation

The last line allocates a memory area for `stable_partition`. The reason for the separate allocation of global memory is because the template files are read in the same way as header files and therefore do not contain implementations of data areas. An alternative to this process is the compilation of the file *stl/include/tempbuf.cpp* belonging to the STL and linking the generated object file.

C++ standard

In an implementation that follows the standard draft, the memory area definition can be omitted, because a function `get_temporary_buffer()` is provided, which allocates temporary memory and can be used by `stable_partition()`.

5.5 Sorting, merging, and related operations

All algorithms described in this section have two variations. One compares elements with the `<` operator, the other uses a function object which shall be called `comp`. Instead of the function object, a function can be used as well.

The function call with the parameters `A` and `B` or the call `comp(A, B)` of the function object yields `true`, if `A < B` applies with regard to the required ordering relation.

5.5.1 sort

The `sort()` algorithm sorts between the iterators `first` and `last`. It is suitable only for containers with random access iterators, such as `vector` or `deque`. Random access to elements of a list is not possible; therefore, the member function `list::sort()` must be employed for lists of type `list`.

```
template <class RandomAccessIterator>
void sort(RandomAccessIterator first, RandomAccessIterator last);

template <class RandomAccessIterator, class Compare>
void sort(RandomAccessIterator first, RandomAccessIterator last,
          Compare comp);
```

Sorting is not stable, that is, different elements which have the same sorting key may not have the same position in relation to each other in the sorted sequence that they had in the unsorted sequence. The average cost is $O(N \log N)$ with $N =$ `last` - `first`. No cost estimate is given for the worst case behavior. If the worst case behavior is relevant, however, it is recommended that you use `stable_sort()`.

By looking into the implementation we can see the basic reason for this: `sort()` uses quicksort, which in the worst case has a complexity of $O(N^2)$, depending on the data and the internal partitioning.

```
template <class RandomAccessIterator>
void stable_sort(RandomAccessIterator first,
                 RandomAccessIterator last);

template <class RandomAccessIterator, class Compare>
void stable_sort(RandomAccessIterator first,
                 RandomAccessIterator last,
                 Compare comp);
```

Even in the worst case, the complexity of `stable_sort()` is $O(N \log N)$, if enough memory is available. Otherwise, the cost is at most $O(N(\log N)^2)$. Internally, a merge sort algorithm is used (more about this on page 140), whose time consumption is on average a constant factor of 1.4 higher than that of quicksort. The time increase of 40% is compensated by the excellent worst case behavior and the stability of `stable_sort()`.

The example shows both variations. The random number generator is taken from the previous example. The use of a function instead of the < operator is also shown; the ordering criterion in this case is the *integer* part of a `double` number. This leads to elements with the same key but with different values, which are used to show the non-stability of `sort()`.

```
//  k5/sort.cpp
#include<algorithm>
#include<vector>
#include<showseq>
#include"rand.h"       //  see page 127

bool integer_less(double x, double y)
{   return long(x) < long(y);}

//  In the same way as partition(), stable_sort(),
//  depending on the implementation (see page 130)
//  needs a temporary buffer (declaration in tempbuf.h)
char __stl_temp_buffer[__stl_buffer_size];

using namespace std;

int main()
{
    vector<double> v(17);
    RAND aChance;
```

```
//   initialize vector with random values, with
//   many values having the same integer part:

int i;
for(i = 0; i < v.size(); i++)
{
    v[i] =  aChance(3)
            + double(aChance(100)/1000.0);
}

random_shuffle(v.begin(), v.end(), RAND());

vector<double> unstable = v,        // auxiliary vectors
                  stable = v;

cout << "Sequence                :\n";
showSequence(v);
```
    // *1.032 1.081 0.042 0.069 0.016 2.065 0.03 0.09*
    // *2.022 1.07 0.086 0.073 0.045 1.042 1.077 2.097 1.098*

```
//   sorting with < operator:
stable_sort(stable.begin(), stable.end());
cout << "\n no difference, because double number "
        "is used as key\n";
cout << "stable sorting    :\n";
showSequence(stable);
```
    // *0.016 0.03 0.042 0.045 0.069 0.073 0.086 0.09*
    // *1.032 1.042 1.07 1.077 1.081 1.098 2.022 2.065 2.097*

```
sort(unstable.begin(), unstable.end());
cout << "unstable sorting :\n";
showSequence(unstable);
```
    // *0.016 0.03 0.042 0.045 0.069 0.073 0.086 0.09*
    // *1.032 1.042 1.07 1.077 1.081 1.098 2.022 2.065 2.097*

```
//   sorting with function instead of < operator:
unstable = v;
stable = v;
cout << "\n differences, because only the int part "
        "is used as key\n";

stable_sort(stable.begin(), stable.end(),integer_less);
cout << "stable sorting (integer key)   :\n";
showSequence(stable);
```
    // *0.042 0.069 0.016 0.03 0.09 0.086 0.073 0.045*
    // *1.032 1.081 1.07 1.042 1.077 1.098 2.065 2.022 2.097*

```
sort(unstable.begin(), unstable.end(), integer_less);
cout << "unstable sorting (integer key):\n";
showSequence(unstable);
```

```
//   0.042 0.069 0.016 0.03 0.09 0.045 0.073 0.086
//   1.098 1.077 1.042 1.07 1.081 1.032 2.022 2.065 2.097
}
```

partial_sort

Partial sorting brings the M smallest elements to the front, the rest remains unsorted. The algorithm, however, does not require the number M, but an iterator `middle` to the corresponding position, so that M = `middle - first` applies. The prototypes are:

```
template <class RandomAccessIterator>
void partial_sort(RandomAccessIterator first,
                  RandomAccessIterator middle,
                  RandomAccessIterator last);

template <class RandomAccessIterator, class Compare>
void partial_sort(RandomAccessIterator first,
                  RandomAccessIterator middle,
                  RandomAccessIterator last,
                  Compare comp);
```

The complexity is approximately $O(N \log M)$. The program excerpt for a vector v shows the partial sorting. In the result, all elements in the first half are smaller than those in the second half. Furthermore, in the first half the elements are sorted, in the second half they are not.

```
showSequence(v);
partial_sort(v.begin(), v.begin() + v.size()/2,  v.end());
cout << "half sorted:\n";
showSequence(v);
```

Both variations exist in a copying version, where `result_first` and `result_last` refer to the target container. The number of sorted elements results from the smaller of the two differences `result_last - result_first` and `last - first`.

```
template <class InputIterator, class RandomAccessIterator>
RandomAccessIterator partial_sort_copy(
                  InputIterator first,
                  InputIterator last,
                  RandomAccessIterator result_first,
                  RandomAccessIterator result_last);

template <class InputIterator, class RandomAccessIterator,
          class Compare>
RandomAccessIterator partial_sort_copy(
                  InputIterator first,
                  InputIterator last,
                  RandomAccessIterator result_first,
```

```
                    RandomAccessIterator result_last,
                    Compare comp);
```

The returned random access iterator points to the end of the described range, that is, to `result_last` or `result_first + (last - first)`, whichever value is smaller.

Exercise

5.5 Complete the sample program from page 132 with instructions that compare the vectors `stable[]` and `unstable[]` and display all element pairs of `v[]` or `stable[]` for which the stability criterion was violated.

5.5.2 nth_element

The nth largest or nth smallest element of a sequence of random access iterators can be found by means of `nth_element()`.

```
template <class RandomAccessIterator>
void nth_element(RandomAccessIterator first,
                 RandomAccessIterator nth,
                 RandomAccessIterator last);

template <class RandomAccessIterator, class Compare>
void nth_element(RandomAccessIterator first,
                 RandomAccessIterator nth,
                 RandomAccessIterator last,
                 Compare comp);
```

The iterator `nth` is set to the required position, for example, the beginning of the container. After a call of `nth_element()`, the smallest element has been placed in this position. Thus, the order of elements in the container is *changed*. If before the call `nth` points, for example, to the position `v.begin() + 6`, then, after the call, this position contains the seventh smallest element.

After the call of the algorithm, only elements that are smaller than or equal to (`*nth`) and all elements to the right of it stand to the left of `nth`.

The average time of the algorithm is linear ($O(N)$). In the present implementation, the time is $O(N^2)$ in the worst but rare case when a partition mechanism similar to quicksort is used.

```
// k5/nth.cpp     Example for nth_element
#include<algorithm>
#include<deque>
#include<showseq>
#include<myrandom>

using namespace std;
```

```
int main()
{
    deque<int> d(15);
    generate(d.begin(), d.end(), Random(1000));
    showSequence(d);
        //  10 3 335 33 355 217 536 195 700 949 274 444 108 698 564

    deque<int>::iterator nth = d.begin();
    nth_element(d.begin(), nth, d.end());

    cout << "smallest element:"
         << (*nth)                          //  3
         << endl;

    /*
```
The standard comparison object greater causes the sequence to be reversed. In this case, the greatest element is at the first position:
```
    */

    nth = d.begin();
    nth_element(d.begin(), nth, d.end(), greater<int>());

    cout << "greatest element  :"
         << (*nth)                          //  949
         << endl;

    /*
```
With the < operator, the greatest element is at the end:
```
    */

    nth = d.end();
    nth--;                  //  now points to the last element
    nth_element(d.begin(), nth, d.end());

    cout << "greatest element  :"
         << (*nth)                          //  949
         << endl;

    //  assumption for median value: d.size() is odd
    nth = d.begin() + d.size()/2;
    nth_element(d.begin(), nth, d.end());

    cout << "Median value       :"
         << (*nth)                          //  335
         << endl;
}
```

5.5.3 Binary search

All algorithms in this section are variations of a binary search. The way binary search functions was briefly explained on page 17. When it is possible to access a sorted sequence of n elements randomly with a random access iterator, a binary search is very fast. A maximum of $1 + \log_2 n$ accesses are needed to find the element or to determine that it does not exist.

If random access is not possible, for example in a list where you have to travel from one element to the other in order to find a given one, access time is of the order $O(n)$.

The STL provides four algorithms used in connection with searching and inserting in sorted sequences, which are very similar to each other:

binary_search

```
template <class ForwardIterator, class T>
bool binary_search(ForwardIterator first, ForwardIterator last,
                   const T& value);


template <class ForwardIterator, class T, class Compare>
bool binary_search(ForwardIterator first, ForwardIterator last,
                   const T& value,
                   Compare comp);
```

This is the binary search proper. Here and in the following three algorithms (or six, when you include the Compare variations), the forward iterator can be substituted with a random access iterator, provided the container allows it. The function returns true if the value is found.

Only the < operator is used, evaluating, in the first variation, the (!(*i < value) && !(value < *i)) relation (compare with operator==() on page 21). i is an iterator in the range [first, last). In the second variation (!comp(*i, value) && !comp(value, *i)) is evaluated accordingly. An example is shown after the next three algorithms.

lower_bound

This algorithm finds the first position where a value value can be inserted without violating the ordering. The returned iterator, let us call it i, points to this position, so that insertion with insert(i, value) is possible without any further search processes. For all iterators j in the range [first, i) it holds that *j < value or comp(*j, value) == true. The prototypes are:

```
template <class ForwardIterator, class T>
ForwardIterator lower_bound(ForwardIterator first,
                            ForwardIterator last,
                            const T& value);


template <class ForwardIterator, class T, class Compare>
ForwardIterator lower_bound(ForwardIterator first,
                            ForwardIterator last,
```

```
                const T& value,
                Compare comp);
```

upper_bound

This algorithm finds the *last* position where a value value can be inserted without violating the ordering. The returned iterator i points to this position, so that rapid insertion is possible with insert(i, value). The prototypes are:

```
template <class ForwardIterator, class T>
ForwardIterator upper_bound(ForwardIterator first,
                            ForwardIterator last,
                            const T& value);

template <class ForwardIterator, class T, class Compare>
ForwardIterator upper_bound(ForwardIterator first,
                            ForwardIterator last,
                            const T& value,
                            Compare comp);
```

equal_range

This algorithm determines the largest subrange within which a value value can be inserted at an arbitrary position without violating the ordering. Thus, with regard to ordering, this range contains identical values. The elements p.first and p.second of the returned iterator pair, here p, limit the range. For each iterator k which satisfies the condition p.first $\leq$ k $<$ p.second, rapid insertion is possible with insert(k, value). The prototypes are:

```
template <class ForwardIterator, class T>
pair<ForwardIterator, ForwardIterator>
equal_range(ForwardIterator first,
            ForwardIterator last,
            const T& value);

template <class ForwardIterator, class T, class Compare>
pair<ForwardIterator, ForwardIterator>
equal_range(ForwardIterator first, ForwardIterator last,
            const T& value, Compare comp);
```

The algorithms described above are now shown with the aid of a sample program. Because of its similarity with lower_bound(), upper_bound() is not included. You must ensure that the container is sorted, since all algorithms in this section make this assumption.

```
// k5/bsearch.cpp
// Example for binary_search and related algorithms
```

```
#include<algorithm>
#include<list>
#include<string>
#include<showseq>

using namespace std;

int main()
{
    list<string> Places;
    Places.push_front("Bremen");
    Places.push_front("Paris");
    Places.push_front("Milan");
    Places.push_front("Hamburg");
    Places.sort();                          //  important precondition
    showSequence(Places);

    string Town;
    cout << "Search/insert which town? ";
    cin >> Town;

    if(binary_search(Places.begin(), Places.end(), Town))
        cout << Town << " exists\n";
    else
        cout << Town << " does not yet exist\n";

    //  insertion at the correct position
    cout << Town << " is inserted:\n";
    list<string>::iterator i =
        lower_bound(Places.begin(), Places.end(), Town);
    Places.insert(i, Town);
    showSequence(Places);

    //  range of identical values
    pair<list<string>::iterator, list<string>::iterator>
     p = equal_range(Places.begin(), Places.end(), Town);

    //  The two iterators of the pair p limit the range
    //  in which Town occurs:
    //  ISO96
    //  list<string>::difference_type n = 0;
    //  distance(p.first, p.second, n);
    //  ISO97
    list<string>::difference_type n =
            distance(p.first, p.second);
    cout << Town << " is contained " << n
            << " times in the list\n";
}
```

5.5.4 **Merging**

Merging is a method for combining two sorted sequences into one. Step by step, the first elements of both sequences are compared, and the smaller (or the greater, depending on the ordering criterion) element is placed in the output sequence. The prototypes are:

```
template <class InputIterator1, class InputIterator2,
        class OutputIterator>
OutputIterator merge(InputIterator1 first1,
                InputIterator1 last1,
                InputIterator2 first2,
                InputIterator2 last2,
                OutputIterator result);

template <class InputIterator1, class InputIterator2,
        class OutputIterator, class Compare>
OutputIterator merge(InputIterator1 first1,
                InputIterator1 last1,
                InputIterator2 first2,
                InputIterator2 last2,
                OutputIterator result,
                Compare comp);
```

merge() assumes an existing output sequence. When one of the two input sequences is exhausted, the remainder of the other one is copied into the output sequence. A brief example will illustrate this:

```
//  k5/merge0.cpp
#include<algorithm>
#include<showseq>
#include<vector>
#include<iota>

using namespace std;

int main()
{
    vector<int> v1(6);                      // sequence 1
    iota(v1.begin(), v1.end(), 0);          // initialize
    showSequence(v1);                       // display

    vector<int> v2(10);                     // sequence 2
    iota(v2.begin(), v2.end(), 0);          // initialize
    showSequence(v2);                       // display

    vector<int> result(v1.size()+v2.size()); // sequence 3

    merge(v1.begin(), v1.end(),             // merge
```

```
                    v2.begin(), v2.end(),
                    result.begin());
        showSequence(result);              // display
    }
```

The result of the program is

```
0 1 2 3 4 5                    (v1)
0 1 2 3 4 5 6 7 8 9            (v2)
0 0 1 1 2 2 3 3 4 4 5 5 6 7 8 9   (result)
```

Thanks to its structure, merging allows very fast sorting with a complexity of $O(N \log N)$ following the recursive scheme:

1. Split list into two halves.
2. If the halves have more than one element, sort both halves with *this procedure* (recursion).
3. Merge both halves into result list.

Obviously, a nonrecursive variation is possible. Sorting is stable. The disadvantage is the additional storage space for the result. For comparison with the above scheme, the merge sort algorithm is now formulated with the means provided by the STL:

```
// k5/msort.cpp      Simple example for mergesort()
#include<algorithm>
#include<showseq>
#include<vector>
#include<myrandom>

using namespace std;


// Template for deriving the distance type (compare with page 67 and the note below)
template<class InputIterator, class OutputIterator>
void mergesort(InputIterator first,
               InputIterator last,
               OutputIterator result)
{
    mergesort(first, last, result, distance_type(first));
}

template<class InputIterator, class OutputIterator,
         class Distance>
void mergesort(InputIterator first,
               InputIterator last,
               OutputIterator result,
               Distance*)
{
    Distance n = 0;
    distance(first, last, n);
```

```
        Distance Half = n/2;
        InputIterator Middle = first;
        advance(Middle, Half);

        if(Half > 1)                // sort left half, if needed
            mergesort(first, Middle, result);   // recursion

        if(n - Half > 1)            // sort right half if needed
        {
            OutputIterator result2 = result;
            advance(result2, Half);
            mergesort(Middle, last, result2);   // recursion
        }

        // merge both halves and copy back the result
        OutputIterator End =
              merge(first, Middle, Middle, last, result);
        copy(result, End, first);
    }

int main()
{
    vector<int> v(20), buffer(20);
    Random whatAChance(1000);

    generate(v.begin(), v.end(), whatAChance);
    showSequence(v);       // random numbers

    // sort and display
    mergesort(v.begin(), v.end(), buffer.begin());
    showSequence(v);       // sorted Sequence
}
```

The last two lines of the function can be combined into one, as can often be found in the implementation of the STL, although this will make it more difficult to read:

```
// Merge both halves and copy back the result
copy(result, merge(first, Middle, Middle, last, result), first);
```

Note: In ISO/IEC (1997) the template for derivation of the distance type is no longer necessary because `Distance` can be determined from the iterator type. `mergesort()` can then be written as follows:

```
template<class InputIterator, class OutputIterator>
void mergesort(InputIterator first,
               InputIterator last,
               OutputIterator result)
{
```

```
iterator_traits<InputIterator>::difference_type
      n      = distance(first, last),
      Half   = n/2;
// ... the rest as above
```

The advantage of the algorithm described above over `stable_sort()` is that not just containers working with random access iterators can be sorted. Bidirectional iterators are sufficient, so that `v` in the above program can also be a list. It can be filled with `push_front()`. The only condition is that a list `buffer` exists which has at least as many elements as `v`. Only a few changes are needed in `main()`; `mergesort()` remains unchanged:

```
//  Excerpt from k5/msortl.cpp
int main()          //  with list instead of vector
{
    list<int> v;
    for(int i = 0; i < 20; i++)
        v.push_front(0);               //  create space
    Random whatAChance(1000);
    generate(v.begin(), v.end(), whatAChance);
    showSequence(v);      //  random numbers

    list<int> buffer = v;
    mergesort(v.begin(), v.end(), buffer.begin());
    showSequence(v);      //  sorted sequence
}
```

The 'merge sort' technique is used in a slightly different form when very large files are to be sorted which do not fit into memory, but mass storage can also be used (see Chapter 10).

Merging in place

When sequences are to be merged in place, a buffer must be used. The `inplace_merge()` function merges sequences in such a way that the result replaces the input sequences. The prototypes are:

```
template <class BidirectionalIterator>
void inplace_merge(BidirectionalIterator first,
                   BidirectionalIterator middle,
                   BidirectionalIterator last);

template <class BidirectionalIterator, class Compare>
void inplace_merge(BidirectionalIterator first,
                   BidirectionalIterator middle,
                   BidirectionalIterator last,
                   Compare comp);
```

The buffer provided is dependent on the implementation (see page 130).

```
//  k5/merge1.cpp
#include<algorithm>
#include<showseq>
#include<vector>

using namespace std;

//  implementation dependent (see page 130):
//  definition of the buffer for inplace_merge()
char __stl_temp_buffer[__stl_buffer_size];

int main()
{
    vector<int> v(16);                      //  even number
    int middle = v.size()/2;
    for(int i = 0; i < middle; i++)
    {
        v[i]          = 2*i;                //  even
        v[middle + i] = 2*i + 1;            //  odd
    }
    showSequence(v);
    inplace_merge(v.begin(), v.begin() + middle, v.end());
    showSequence(v);
}
```

Here, the first half of a vector is filled with even numbers, the second half with odd numbers. After the merge, the same vector contains all numbers without explicitly having to specify a result range:

0 2 4 6 8 10 12 14 1 3 5 7 9 11 13 15   before
0 1 2 3 4 5 6 7 8 9 10 11 12 13 14 15   after

5.6 Set operations on sorted structures

This section describes the basic set operations, such as union, intersection, and so on, on *sorted* structures. In the STL, the set class is based on sorted structures (see Section 4.4.1). The complexity of the algorithms is $O(N_1 + N_2)$, where N_1 and N_2 denote the number of elements of the sets involved.

The algorithms presented here, which use output iterators, are suitable for set operations only to a limited extent, as explained in Section 5.6.6.

5.6.1 **includes**

The function `includes` determines whether each element of a second sorted structure S_2 is contained in the first structure S_1. Thus, it checks whether the second structure is a subset of the first one. The return value is `true`, if $S_2 \subseteq S_1$ holds, otherwise it is `false`. The prototypes are:

```
template <class InputIterator1, class InputIterator2>
bool includes(InputIterator1 first1, InputIterator1 last1,
              InputIterator2 first2, InputIterator2 last2);

template <class InputIterator1, class InputIterator2,
          class Compare>
bool includes(InputIterator1 first1, InputIterator1 last1,
              InputIterator2 first2, InputIterator2 last2,
              Compare comp);
```

The following example initializes some `set` objects as sorted structures. You could also take simple vectors, provided they are sorted. Since the example is referred to again in subsequent sections, it contains more than is strictly needed for `includes()`.

```
//  Excerpt from k5/setalgo.cpp
#include <algorithm>
#include<set>
#include<showseq>

using namespace std;

int main ()
{
    int v1[] = {1, 2, 3, 4};
    int v2[] = {0, 1, 2, 3, 4, 5, 7, 99, 13};
    int v3[] = {-2, 5, 12, 7, 33};

    //  initialize sets with the vector contents
    //  default comparison object: less<int>()
    //  (implicit automatic sorting)

    set<int> s1(v1, v1 + 4);
    set<int> s2(v2, v2 + 8);
    set<int> s3(v3, v3 + 5);

    if(includes(s2.begin(), s2.end(), s1.begin(), s1.end()))
    {
        showSequence(s1);             // 1 2 3 4
        cout << " is a subset of ";
        showSequence(s2);             // 0 1 2 3 4 5 7 99
    }
```

5.6.2 **set_union**

The function set_union builds a sorted structure which contains all the elements that occur in at least one of two other sorted structures S_1 and S_2. Thus, the union of both structures is formed:

$$S = S_1 \cup S_2$$

The precondition is that the receiving structure provides enough space, or that it is empty and an insert iterator is used as the output iterator (see Section 5.6.6). The prototypes are:

```
template <class InputIterator1, class InputIterator2,
          class OutputIterator>
OutputIterator set_union(InputIterator1 first1,
                         InputIterator1 last1,
                         InputIterator2 first2,
                         InputIterator2 last2,
                         OutputIterator result);

template <class InputIterator1, class InputIterator2,
          class OutputIterator, class Compare>
OutputIterator set_union(InputIterator1 first1,
                         InputIterator1 last1,
                         InputIterator2 first2,
                         InputIterator2 last2,
                         OutputIterator result,
                         Compare comp);
```

At the beginning, the result set Result (see below) is empty. In the following example, the output iterator must be an insert iterator. For this purpose, the function inserter(), which is described on page 74, is included in the parameter list. It returns an insert iterator. The sole use of Result.begin() as the output iterator leads to errors. The reasons for this can be found in Section 5.6.6.

```
set<int> Result;              // empty set (s1, s2, s3 as above)

set_union(s1.begin(), s1.end(),
          s3.begin(), s3.end(),
          inserter(Result, Result.begin()));

showSequence(s1);                        // 1 2 3 4
cout << "  united with ";
showSequence(s3);                        // –2 5 7 12 33
cout << " yields ";
showSequence(Result);                    // –2 1 2 3 4 5 7 12 33
```

5.6.3 set_intersection

The function `set_intersection` builds a sorted structure which contains all the elements that occur in both of two other sorted structures S_1 and S_2. Thus, the intersection of both structures is formed:

$$S = S_1 \cap S_2$$

The conditions described in Section 5.6.6 apply. The prototypes are:

```
template <class InputIterator1, class InputIterator2,
         class OutputIterator>
OutputIterator set_intersection(InputIterator1 first1,
                                InputIterator1 last1,
                                InputIterator2 first2,
                                InputIterator2 last2,
                                OutputIterator result);

template <class InputIterator1, class InputIterator2,
         class OutputIterator, class Compare>
OutputIterator set_intersection(InputIterator1 first1,
                                InputIterator1 last1,
                                InputIterator2 first2,
                                InputIterator2 last2,
                                OutputIterator result,
                                Compare comp);
```

In order to delete the old results, `clear()` is called. Otherwise, they would be displayed again.

```
Result.clear();                    // empty the set

set_intersection(s2.begin(), s2.end(),
                 s3.begin(), s3.end(),
              inserter(Result, Result.begin())));

showSequence(s2);                  // 0 1 2 3 4 5 7 99
cout << " intersected with ";
showSequence(s3);                  // –2 5 7 12 33
cout << " yields ";
showSequence(Result);              // 5 7
```

5.6.4 set_difference

The function `set_difference` builds a sorted structure which contains all the elements that occur in the first sorted structure S_1, but not in the second sorted structure S_2. Thus, the difference $S_1 - S_2$ of both structures is formed, which is also written as $S_1 \setminus S_2$. The conditions described in Section 5.6.6 apply. The prototypes are:

```
template <class InputIterator1, class InputIterator2,
         class OutputIterator>
```

```
OutputIterator set_difference(InputIterator1 first1,
                              InputIterator1 last1,
                              InputIterator2 first2,
                              InputIterator2 last2,
                              OutputIterator result);

template <class InputIterator1, class InputIterator2,
          class OutputIterator, class Compare>
OutputIterator set_difference(InputIterator1 first1,
                              InputIterator1 last1,
                              InputIterator2 first2,
                              InputIterator2 last2,
                              OutputIterator result,
                              Compare comp);
```

The example follows the above pattern:

```
Result.clear();
set_difference(s2.begin(), s2.end(),
               s1.begin(), s1.end(),
             inserter(Result, Result.begin()));

showSequence(s2);                // 0 1 2 3 4 5 7 9 9
cout << " minus ";
showSequence(s1);                // 1 2 3 4
cout << " yields ";
showSequence(Result);            // 0 5 7 9 9
```

5.6.5 *set_symmetric_difference*

The function `set_symmetric_difference` builds a sorted structure which contains all the elements that occur either in the first structure S_1 or in a second sorted structure S_2, but not in both. Thus, the symmetric difference of both structures is formed, which is also called 'exclusive-or.' The symmetric difference can be expressed using the previously introduced operations:

$$S = (S_1 - S_2) \cup (S_2 - S_1)$$

or

$$S = (S_1 \cup S_2) - (S_2 \cap S_1)$$

The conditions described in Section 5.6.6 apply. The prototypes are:

```
template <class InputIterator1, class InputIterator2,
          class OutputIterator>
OutputIterator set_symmetric_difference(
                     InputIterator1 first1,
                     InputIterator1 last1,
                     InputIterator2 first2,
```

```
                         InputIterator2 last2,
                         OutputIterator result);

   template <class InputIterator1, class InputIterator2,
             class OutputIterator, class Compare>
   OutputIterator set_symmetric_difference(
                         InputIterator1 first1,
                         InputIterator1 last1,
                         InputIterator2 first2,
                         InputIterator2 last2,
                         OutputIterator result,
                         Compare comp);
```

The last example of this kind shows the symmetric difference:

```
Result.clear();

set_symmetric_difference(s2.begin(), s2.end(),
                         s3.begin(), s3.end(),
            inserter(Result, Result.begin())));

showSequence(s2);                    //  0 1 2 3 4 5 7 99
cout << "  exclusive or ";
showSequence(s3);                    //  –2 5 7 12 33
cout << "yields ";
showSequence(Result);                //  –2 0 1 2 3 4 12 33 99
```

5.6.6 Conditions and limitations

It was mentioned on page 143 that the algorithms introduced in this section are only to a certain extent suitable for set operations. The reason is that the output iterator must refer to a container that already has enough space. When there is insufficient space, using an insert iterator does not always make sense.

Let us consider the following example in which the intersection of two sorted structures v1 and v2 is to be found and stored in a result vector result. We have three possible cases:

1. result provides enough space for the result.
2. result lacks space.
3. result lacks space at the beginning, but an insert iterator is used.

```
//  Case 1: everything OK
#include<algorithm>
#include<vector>
#include<showseq>
#include<iterator>    //  for case 3
```

```
int main ()
{
    vector<int> v1(4);
    vector<int> v2(5);
    vector<int> result(4,0);

    v1[0] = 2; v1[1] = 4; v1[2] = 9; v1[3] = 13;
    v2[0] = 1; v2[1] = 2; v2[2] = 9; v2[3] = 13; v2[4] = 43;

    vector<int>::iterator last =
        set_intersection (v1.begin(), v1.end(),
                          v2.begin(), v2.end(),
                          result.begin());
    showSequence(result);                       // 2 9 13 0

    cout << "only the interesting range: \n";
    vector<int>::iterator temp = result.begin();
    while(temp != last)
        cout << *temp++ << ' ';                 // 2 9 13
    cout << endl;
```

The `last` iterator indicates the position after the last element displayed, so that the output can be limited to the interesting range.

```
//  Case 2: result1 is too small:
    vector<int> result1(1,0);
    last = set_intersection (v1.begin(), v1.end(),
                            v2.begin(), v2.end(),
                            result1.begin());

    cout << "interesting range: \n";
    temp = result1.begin();
    while(temp != last)
        cout << *temp++ << ' ';                 // 2 9 13  Error!
    cout << endl;
    cout << "!! result1.size() = "
         << result1.size()                      // 1
         << endl;
```

Here, the result range is too small, so that *the memory area following the result vector is overwritten*. This basic mistake cannot be picked up by using a vector with index check (see Section 9.1), because only pointers are used. Also, the attempt to generate space by using an insert iterator does not lead to a satisfying result:

```
//  Case 3: result2 is too small, but an insert iterator is used
    vector<int> result2(1,0);
    back_insert_iterator<vector<int> > where(result2);
    set_intersection (v1.begin(), v1.end(),
                      v2.begin(), v2.end(),
```

```
                                    where);
            showSequence(result2);                        // 0 2 9 13
```

The insert iterator appends the elements at the end without considering whether there is still enough space – it simply does not know any better. Given these three cases, it is evident that set operations on sorted structures make sense only under certain conditions:

- Standard containers from Chapter 3: `vector`, `list`, `deque`

  – The result container provides enough space. The disadvantage is that after the end of the result sequence, there are still old values in the container if the space is more than sufficient.

  – The output iterator `where` must not be identical with `v1.begin()` or `v2.begin()`.

  – The result container is empty. In this case, an insert iterator is to be used as the output iterator.

- Associative containers from Section 4.4: `set`, `map`
  An insert iterator has to be used in any case. The contents of an element must not be changed directly, that is, via a reference to the element. This would be the behavior of a non-inserting output iterator, and the ordering within the container and therefore its integrity would be violated.

Thus, some serious thinking has to be done. If the result container is not empty, but also does not provide sufficient space, there is no elegant solution. The reason for this 'flaw' lies in the requirement that the algorithms must also be able to work on simple C-like arrays without being changed. The best thing would be to concentrate only on the result without caring about available space in containers and iterators to be employed. Chapter 6 introduces set operations without the above restrictions.

5.7 Heap algorithms

The priority queue described in Section 4.3 is based on a binary heap. Before we describe the heap algorithms of the STL, let us define the most important features of a heap:

- The N elements of a heap lie in a continuous array on the positions 0 to $N - 1$. It is assumed that random access is possible.

- The kind of arrangement of the elements in the array corresponds to a complete binary tree in which all levels are occupied by elements. The only possible exception is the lowest level in which all elements appear on the left-hand side. Figure 5.2 shows the array representation of a heap H of 14 elements, where the circled numbers represent the array indices (*not* the element values). Thus, the element $H[0]$ is always the root, and each element $H[j], (j > 0)$ has a parent node $H[(j - 1)/2]$.

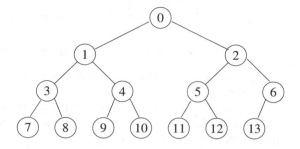

Figure 5.2   Array representation of a heap (number = array index).

- Each element $H[j]$ is assigned a priority which is greater than or equal to the priority of the child nodes $H[2j + 1]$ and $H[2j + 2]$. For simplicity, we assume that here and in the following discussion large numbers mean high priorities. This could, however, well be the other way round, or completely different criteria might determine the priority. Figure 5.3 shows examples of *element values* of a heap: $H[0]$ equals 99, and so on.

Please note that the heap is not completely sorted; we are interested only in the priority relation between parent nodes and corresponding child nodes.

An array H of N elements is a heap if and only if $H[(j - 1)/2] \geq H[j]$ holds for $1 \leq j < N$. This means automatically that $H[0]$ is the greatest element. A priority queue simply removes the topmost element of a heap; subsequently, the heap is restructured, that is, the next greatest element moves to the top. With reference to Figures 5.2 and 5.3, this would be element number 2 with the value 56.

The STL provides four heap algorithms which can be applied to all containers that can be accessed with random access iterators:

- push_heap() adds an element to an existing heap.
- pop_heap() removes the element with the highest priority.

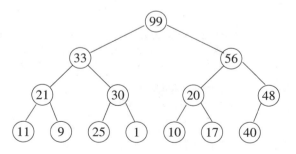

Figure 5.3   Array representation of a heap (number = element value).

- `make_heap()` arranges all elements in a range in such a way that the range represents a heap.
- `sort_heap()` converts a heap into a sorted sequence.

As usual in the STL, these algorithms do not have to know any details about the containers. They are merely passed two iterators that mark the range to be processed. `less<T>` is predefined as the priority criterion, but a different criterion might be required. Therefore, there is an overloaded variation for each algorithm which allows passing of a comparison object.

5.7.1 make_heap

`make_heap()` ensures that the heap condition applies to all elements inside a range. The prototypes are:

```
template <class RandomAccessIterator>
void make_heap(RandomAccessIterator first,
               RandomAccessIterator last);

template <class RandomAccessIterator, class Compare>
void make_heap(RandomAccessIterator first,
               RandomAccessIterator last,
               Compare comp);
```

The complexity is proportional to the number of elements between `first` and `last`. An example shows the application to a vector as container:

```
//  k5/heap.cpp
#include<algorithm>
#include<showseq>
#include<vector>
#include<iota>

using namespace std;

int main()
{
    vector<int> v(12);              //  container for heap
    iota(v.begin(), v.end(), 0); //  enter 0 .. 11
    showSequence(v); //  0 1 2 3 4 5 6 7 8 9 10 11

    //  create valid heap
    make_heap(v.begin(), v.end());
    showSequence(v); //  11 10 6 8 9 5 0 7 3 1 4 2
}
```

5.7.2 pop_heap

The function `pop_heap()` removes one element from a heap. The range `[first, last)` is to be considered a valid heap. The prototypes are:

```
template <class RandomAccessIterator>
void pop_heap(RandomAccessIterator first,
              RandomAccessIterator last);

template <class RandomAccessIterator, class Compare>
void pop_heap(RandomAccessIterator first,
              RandomAccessIterator last,
              Compare comp);
```

The 'removal' consists only in the fact that the value with the highest priority which stands at position `first` is swapped with a value at position (`last` −1). Subsequently, the range [`first`, `last-1`) is converted into a heap. The complexity of `pop_heap()` is $O(\log(last - first))$. The previous example is continued:

```
//   display and remove the two numbers
//   with the highest priority:
vector<int>::iterator last = v.end();
cout << *v.begin() << endl;          //  11
pop_heap(v.begin(), last--);

cout << *v.begin() << endl;          //  10
pop_heap(v.begin(), last--);
```

It should be noted that the end of the heap is no longer indicated by `v.end()`, but by the iterator `last`. The range between these two values is undefined with regard to the heap properties of `v`.

5.7.3 push_heap

The function `push_heap()` adds an element to an existing heap. As the prototypes show, the function is passed only two iterators and, if needed, a comparison object. The element to be added does not appear:

```
template <class RandomAccessIterator>
void push_heap(RandomAccessIterator first,
               RandomAccessIterator last);

template <class RandomAccessIterator, class Compare>
void push_heap(RandomAccessIterator first,
               RandomAccessIterator last,
               Compare comp);
```

The precondition must apply that the range [`first`, `last-1`) is a valid heap. `push_heap()` does not care about the value to be added. Therefore, the value to be added to the heap is *previously* entered at its position (`last`). The subsequent call of `push_heap(first, last)` ensures that after the call, the range [`first`, `last`) is a heap. The handling of this function is somewhat long-winded, but it is only intended as an auxiliary function and it is very fast. The complexity of `push_heap()`

is $O(\log(last - first))$. At this point, two numbers are added to the sample heap, as described above:

```
// enter an 'important number' (99)
*last-1 = 99;
push_heap(v.begin(), ++last);

// enter an 'unimportant number' (-1)
*last-1 = -1;
push_heap(v.begin(), ++last);

// display of the complete heap
// (no complete ordering, only heap condition!)
showSequence(v);    // 99 9 6 7 8 5 0 2 3 14 – 1
```

During insertion, care must be taken that `last` does not run past `v.end()`. Because during removal the value with the highest priority is always placed on top, the output is sorted:

```
// display of all numbers by priority:
while(last != v.begin())
{
    cout << *v.begin() << ' ';
    pop_heap(v.begin(), --last);
}
cout << endl;        // 99 9 8 7 6 5 4 3 2 1 0 –1
```

5.7.4 sort_heap

`sort_heap()` converts a heap into a sorted sequence. The sorting is not stable; the complexity is $O(N \log N)$, when N is the number of elements to be sorted. The prototypes are:

```
template <class RandomAccessIterator>
void sort_heap(RandomAccessIterator first,
               RandomAccessIterator last);

template <class RandomAccessIterator, class Compare>
void sort_heap(RandomAccessIterator first,
               RandomAccessIterator last,
               Compare comp);
```

The sequence is sorted in *ascending* order. This means that the elements of high priority are placed *at the end* of the sequence:

```
// generate new valid heap of all elements
make_heap(v.begin(), v.end());

// and sort
sort_heap(v.begin(), v.end());
```

```
//  display of the completely sorted sequence
showSequence(v);    //  –10 1 2 3 4 5 6 7 8 9 99
```

We will encounter further heap algorithms in Section 11.2.

5.8 Minimum and maximum

The inline templates `min()` and `max()` return the smaller or the greater of two elements, respectively. In case of equality, the first element is returned. The prototypes are:

```
template <class T>
const T& min(const T& a, const T& b);

template <class T, class Compare>
const T& min(const T& a, const T& b, Compare comp);

template <class T>
const T& max(const T& a, const T& b);

template <class T, class Compare>
const T& max(const T& a, const T& b, Compare comp);
```

The templates `min_element()` and `max_element()` return an iterator to the smallest (or greatest) element of an interval `[first, last)`. In case of equality of the iterators, the first one is returned. The complexity is linear. The prototypes are:

```
template <class ForwardIterator>
ForwardIterator min_element(ForwardIterator first,
                            ForwardIterator last);

template <class ForwardIterator, class Compare>
ForwardIterator min_element(ForwardIterator first,
                            ForwardIterator last,
                            Compare comp);

template <class ForwardIterator>
ForwardIterator max_element(ForwardIterator first,
                            ForwardIterator last);

template <class ForwardIterator, class Compare>
ForwardIterator max_element(ForwardIterator first,
                            ForwardIterator last,
                            Compare comp);
```

5.9 Lexicographical comparison

The lexicographical comparison is used to compare two sequences which can even be of different lengths. The function returns `true` when the first sequence is lexicographically smaller. Both sequences are compared element by element, until the algorithm encounters two different elements. If the element of the first sequence is smaller than the corresponding element of the second sequence, `true` is returned.

If one of the two sequences has been completely searched before a different element is found, the shorter sequence is considered to be smaller. The prototypes are:

```
template <class InputIterator1, class InputIterator2>
bool lexicographical_compare(InputIterator1 first1,
                             InputIterator1 last1,
                             InputIterator2 first2,
                             InputIterator2 last2);

template <class InputIterator1, class InputIterator2,
          class Compare>
bool lexicographical_compare(InputIterator1 first1,
                             InputIterator1 last1,
                             InputIterator2 first2,
                             InputIterator2 last2,
                             Compare comp);
```

This allows alphabetical sorting of character strings, as shown in the example:

```
//  k5/lexicmp.cpp
#include<algorithm>
#include<iostream>

char text1[] = "Arthur";
int length1  = sizeof(text1);
char text2[] = "Vera";
int length2  = sizeof(text2);

using namespace std;

int main ()
{
  if(lexicographical_compare(
          text1, text1 + length1,
          text2, text2 + length2))
    cout << text1 << " comes before " << text2 << endl;
  else
    cout << text2 << " comes before " << text1 << endl;

  if(lexicographical_compare(
          text1, text1 + length1,
          text2, text2 + length2,
          greater<char>()))        // reverse sorting order
    cout << text1 << " comes after " << text2 << endl;
  else
```

```
    cout << text2 << " comes after " << text1 << endl;
}
```

The simple `char` arrays are chosen on purpose. We ignore that objects of the `string` class can be compared in this way by means of the `<` operator. Lexicographical sorting of the kind found in a phone book requires slightly more effort, because, for example, umlauts and accented letters are considered to be equivalent to the corresponding unaccented letters.

5.10 **Permutations**

A permutation originated from a sequence by exchanging two elements (0, 2, 1) is also a permutation originated from (0, 1, 2). For a sequence of N elements, there exist $N! = N(N-1)(N-2)...2 \cdot 1$ permutations, that is $3 \cdot 2 \cdot 1 = 6$ in the above example:

(0, 1, 2), (0, 2, 1), (1, 0, 2), (1, 2, 0), (2, 0, 1), (2, 1, 0)

You can imagine the set of all $N!$ permutations of a sequence in an ordered form as above, with the ordering created either by means of the `<` operator or with a comparison object `comp`.

The ordering defines a unique sequence, so that the next or the previous permutation is uniquely determined. The sequence is regarded as cyclic, that is, the permutation following (2, 1, 0) is (0, 1, 2). The algorithms `prev_permutation()` and `nextprev_permutation()` convert a sequence into the previous or next permutation, respectively:

```
template <class BidirectionalIterator>
bool prev_permutation(BidirectionalIterator first,
                      BidirectionalIterator last);

template <class BidirectionalIterator,
          class Compare>
bool prev_permutation(BidirectionalIterator first,
                      BidirectionalIterator last
                      Compare comp);

template <class BidirectionalIterator>
bool next_permutation(BidirectionalIterator first,
                      BidirectionalIterator last);

template <class BidirectionalIterator,
          class Compare>
bool next_permutation(BidirectionalIterator first,
                      BidirectionalIterator last
                      Compare comp);
```

When a permutation is found, the return value is `true`. Otherwise, it is the end of a cycle. Then, `false` is returned and the sequence is converted into the smallest possible one (with `next_permutation()`) or the greatest possible one (with `prev_permutation()`), according to the sorting criterion. For example:

```
//  k5/permute.cpp
#include<algorithm>
#include<showseq>
#include<vector>
#include<iota>

long factorial(unsigned n)
{
    long fac = 1;
    while(n > 1) fac *= n--;
    return fac;
}

using namespace std;

int main()
{
    vector<int> v(4);
    iota(v.begin(), v.end(), 0);      //  0 1 2 3
    long fac = factorial(v.size());

    for(int i = 0; i < fac; i++)
    {
        if(!prev_permutation(v.begin(), v.end()))
          cout << "Start of cycle:\n";
        showSequence(v);
    }
}
```

This example first produces the message 'Start of cycle,' because the initialization of the vector with (0, 1, 2, 3) does not allow determination of a *previous* permutation without exceeding the cycle. Therefore, the greatest sequence after sorting is produced next, namely (3, 2, 1, 0). The 'Start of cycle' message could be prevented by substituting `prev_permutation()` with `next_permutation()` in the example, or alternatively by passing a comparison object `greater<int>()` as the third parameter.

5.11 Numeric algorithms

In the context of standardization, these algorithms have been transferred into the numeric library. However, in the HP reference implementation, access to these algorithms is still possible via

`#include<algorithm>` **or** `#include<algo.h>`

whereas after the C++ standard draft

```
#include<numeric>
```

is needed.

5.11.1 **accumulate**

This algorithm adds all values $*i$ of an iterator i from first to last to an initial value. If, instead of the addition, another operation is to be used, there are overloaded variations which are passed this operation as the last parameter. The prototypes are:

```
template<class InputIterator, class T>
T accumulate(InputIterator first,
             InputIterator last,
             T init);

template<class InputIterator, class T,
         class binaryOperation>
T accumulate(InputIterator first,
             InputIterator last,
             T init,
             binaryOperation binOp);
```

The following example calculates the sum and the product of all elements of a vector. In these cases, 0 or 1 have to be used as initial values for init. Since in the example the vector is initialized with the sequence of natural numbers, the product equals the factorial of 10. The functor multiplies is described on page 24.

```
// k5/accumulate.cpp
#include<iota>
#include<numeric>
#include<vector>

using namespace std;

int main()
{
    vector<int> v(10);
    iota(v.begin(), v.end(), 1);

    cout << "Sum = "                              // init + ∑ᵢvᵢ
         << accumulate(v.begin(), v.end(), 0)     // 55
         << endl;

    cout << "Product = "
         << accumulate(v.begin(), v.end(), 1L,    // init · ∏ᵢvᵢ
                    multiplies<long>())            // 3 628 800
         << endl;
}
```

5.11.2 inner_product

This algorithm adds the inner product of two containers u and v, which will mostly be vectors, to the initial value `init`:

$$\text{Result} = \text{init} + \sum_i v_i \cdot u_i$$

Instead of addition and multiplication, other operations may be chosen as well. The prototypes are:

```cpp
template<class InputIterator1, class InputIterator2, class T>
T inner_product(InputIterator1 first1,
                InputIterator1 last1,
                InputIterator2 first2,
                T init);

template<class InputIterator1, class InputIterator2, class T,
         class binaryOperation1, class binaryOperation2>
T inner_product(InputIterator1 first1,
                InputIterator1 last1,
                InputIterator2 first2,
                T init,
                binaryOperation1 binOp1,
                binaryOperation2 binOp2);
```

In a Euclidean n-dimensional space R^n, the length of a vector is defined as the root of the inner product of the vector with itself. The example calculates the length of a vector in R^4. The value of `init` must again be 0.

```cpp
//  k5/innerpro.cpp
#include<numeric>
#include<vector>
#include<cmath>
#include<iota>

//  functor for calculating the square of a difference (see below)
template<class T>
struct difference_square
{
    T operator()(const T& x, const T& y)
    {
        T d = x - y;
        return d*d;
    }
};

using namespace std;

int main()
{
```

```
int Dimension = 4;
vector<int> v(Dimension,1);

cout << "Length of vector v = "
    << sqrt((double) inner_product(v.begin(), v.end(),
                                    v.begin(), 0))
    << endl;

/*
```

In order to show the application of other mathematical operators, the following part of the example calculates the distance between two points. Besides the functors of Section 1.6.3, user-defined functors are allowed as well, such as, in this case, the functor difference_square.

```
*/

//  2 points p1 and p2
vector<double> p1(Dimension,1.0),      // unit vector
               p2(Dimension);

iota(p2.begin(), p2.end(), 1.0);       // arbitrary vector

cout << "Distance between p1 and p2 = "
    << sqrt((double) inner_product(p1.begin(), p1.end(),
            p2.begin(), 0,
            plus<int>(), difference_square<int>()))
    << endl;
}
```

The first operator is the addition (summation), the second operator the quadrature of the differences:

$$\text{Distance} = \sqrt{\sum_i (v_i - u_i)^2}$$

5.11.3 *partial_sum*

Partial summation functions in the same way as accumulate(), but the result of each step is stored in a result container given by the result iterator. The prototypes are:

```
template<class InputIterator, class OutputIterator>
OutputIterator partial_sum(InputIterator first,
                           InputIterator last,
                           OutputIterator result);

template<class InputIterator, class OutputIterator,
         class binaryOperation>
OutputIterator partial_sum(InputIterator first,
                           InputIterator last,
                           OutputIterator result,
                           binaryOperation binOp);
```

The example shows both variations. The last number of each sequence corresponds to the result of `accumulate()` in the earlier example.

```cpp
//  k5/partials.cpp
#include<numeric>
#include<vector>
#include<showseq>
#include<iota>

using namespace std;

int main()
{
    vector<long> v(10), ps(10);
    iota(v.begin(), v.end(), 1); //  natural numbers

    cout << "vector          = ";
    showSequence(v);             //  1 2 3 4 5 6 7 8 9 10

    partial_sum(v.begin(), v.end(), ps.begin());
    cout << "Partial sums    = ";
    showSequence(ps);            //  1 3 6 10 15 21 28 36 45 55

    //  Sequence of factorials
    cout << "Partial products = ";
    partial_sum(v.begin(), v.end(), v.begin(),
                multiplies<long>());
            //  1 2 6 24 120 720 5040 40320 362880 3628800
    showSequence(v);
}
```

5.11.4 adjacent_difference

This algorithm calculates the difference between consecutive elements of a container v and writes the result into a result container e pointed to by the `result` iterator. Since there is exactly one difference value less than there are elements, the first element is retained. If the first element has the index 0, the following holds:

$$e_0 = v_0$$
$$e_i = v_i - v_{i-1}, i > 0$$

Besides calculation of differences, other operations are possible. The prototypes are:

```cpp
template<class InputIterator, class OutputIterator>
OutputIterator adjacent_difference(InputIterator first,
                                   InputIterator last,
                                   OutputIterator result);
```

```
template<class InputIterator, class OutputIterator,
         class binaryOperation>
OutputIterator adjacent_difference(InputIterator first,
                                   InputIterator last,
                                   OutputIterator result,
                                   binaryOperation binOp);
```

The example shows both variations. In the first one, the differences are calculated; in the second one, a sequence of Fibonacci numbers is calculated.

```
//  k5/adjdiff.cpp
#include<numeric>
#include<vector>
#include<iota>
#include<showseq>

using namespace std;

int main()
{
    vector<long> v(10), ad(10);
    iota(v.begin(), v.end(), 0);

    cout << "vector        = ";
    showSequence(v);                     // 0 1 2 3 4 5 6 7 8 9

    cout << "Differences   = ";
    adjacent_difference(v.begin(), v.end(), ad.begin());
    showSequence(ad);                    // 0 1 1 1 1 1 1 1 1 1

    //  Fibonacci numbers
    vector<int> fib(16);
    fib[0] = 1;                          //  initial value

    /*
```

One initial value is sufficient here because the first value is written to position 1 (see formula $e_i =...$ above and the result iterator which is shifted by one position). Therefore, after the first step of the algorithm, `fib[1]` equals 1.

```
    */
    cout << "Fibonacci numbers  = "; //  see below
    adjacent_difference(fib.begin(), fib.end(),
                (fib.begin()+1), plus<int>());

    showSequence(fib);
    //  1 1 2 3 5 8 13 21 34 55 89 144 233 377 610 987
}
```

If, instead of the difference, the sum of both predecessors is used, the result container is filled with a sequence of Fibonacci numbers. Fibonacci (an Italian mathematician, c. 1180–1240) asked himself, how many pairs of rabbits there would be after n years, if, beginning with the second year, each couple generates another couple. The fact that rabbits eventually die was ignored for the purpose of this problem. The answer to this question is that the number of rabbits in the year n is equal to the sum of the numbers of the years $n-1$ and $n-2$. Fibonacci numbers play an important role in information science (Wirth, 1979 and Cormen *et al.*, 1994). It should be noted that at the beginning of the construction of the sequence, the `result` iterator must be `fib.begin()+1`.

Part III

Beyond the STL: components and applications

Set operations on associative containers

6

Summary: This chapter presents global operations which are not included in the STL and which overcome the limitations described in Section 5.6.6. This has its price: these algorithms no longer work on simple C arrays and thus do not satisfy the requirements put on their algorithms by the authors of the STL. The price, however, is not too high, because algorithms and data structures should match. Thus, the data structures suitable for set operations are not necessarily sorted C arrays, but sets, represented, for example, by the set *class.*

The algorithms in this chapter have a further advantage: they work not only on the sorted set containers of the C++ Standard Template Library, but also on unsorted associative containers as described in Chapter 7. Then, they are not slower than the set operations of Section 5.6. The algorithms of this chapter are not designed for multisets, but they can be extended accordingly.

The names of the algorithms differ from those of the STL because they lack the set prefix and have an upper case initial letter. All algorithms and examples in Part III, which starts with this chapter, are also available via the Internet.

The set_type placeholder for the data type used in the following templates applies to all set containers that provide the following methods:

```
begin()
end()
find()
insert()
swap()
```

In addition, just one public type

```
set_type::iterator
```

must be available, by means of which elements of the set can be accessed. Obviously, the semantics of the methods and the iterator type must conform to the STL.

6.1 Subset relation

This algorithm determines whether a set s2 is contained in a set s1. Each element of s2 is checked to see whether it is included in s1:

```
//  include/setalgo
#ifndef setalgo
#define setalgo

template<class set_type>
bool Includes(const set_type& s1, const set_type& s2)
{
    //  Is s2 contained in s1?
    if(&s1 == &s2)          //  save time if the sets are identical
        return true;

    /*
    The check for identity must not be confused with the check for equality which would
    have to be formulated as if(s1 == s2)...! The identity check is very fast, because
    only addresses are compared. The equality check can take a long time, because the
    sets must be compared element by element.
    */
    set_type::iterator i2 = s2.begin(), i1;

    while(i2 != s2.end())
    {
        i1 = s1.find(*i2++);
        if(i1 == s1.end())      //  not found
            return false;
    }
    return true;
}
```

The complexity is $O(N_2 \log N_1)$ for the STL class set and $O(N_2)$ for the class HSet in Chapter 7. Here and in the following sections, N_1 and N_2 denote the number of elements in s1 and s2.

The check for identity of the arguments saves time because the loop is not executed. A further possible optimization is to run the loop on the smaller of the two sets (see Exercise 6.1). Then, the complexity is $O(\min(N_1, N_2)\log(\max(N_1, N_2))$ for the STL class set and $O(\min(N_1, N_2))$ for the class HSet of Chapter 7.

6.2 Union

This and the following algorithms have three sets as parameters, with the third parameter result containing the result after the end of the algorithm. When calling the function, result can be identical with s1 or s2, so a temporary set is used to store the intermediate results. In order to save an assignment `result` = `temp`, which is expensive when many elements are involved, the element function `swap()` of the container is employed. `Union()` initializes `temp` with `s2` and adds all the elements of `s1`.

```
template<class set_type>
void Union(const set_type& s1, const set_type& s2,
           set_type& result)
{
    set_type temp(s2);
    if(&s1 != &s2)
    {
        set_type::iterator i = s1.begin();
        while(i != s1.end())
            temp.insert(*i++);
    }

    temp.swap(result);
}
```

The `if` condition is used for speed optimization. If both sets are identical, there is no need for the loop. The complexity is $O(N_2 \log N_2 + N_1 \log N_1)$ for the STL class `set` and $O(N_2 + N_1)$ for the class `HSet` in Chapter 7. The first summand refers to the initialization of `temp`, the second to the loop.

6.3 **Intersection**

The `Intersection()` algorithm begins with an empty container and inserts all the elements that are contained both in `s1` and in `s2`.

```
template<class set_type>
void Intersection(const set_type& s1, const set_type& s2,
                  set_type& result)
{
    set_type temp;
    set_type::iterator i1 = s1.begin(), i2;

    //  An identity check makes no sense, because in case
    //  of identity, temp must be filled anyway.

    while(i1 != s1.end())
    {
        i2 = s2.find(*i1++);
        if(i2 != s2.end())
            temp.insert(*i2);
    }
    temp.swap(result);
}
```

The complexity is $O(N_1 \log N_2)$ for the STL class set and $O(N_1)$ for the class HSet (Chapter 7). The factor N_1 refers to the loop, the rest to the find() operation. The function insert() is only called a maximum of $(\min(N_1, N_2))$ times and is therefore not considered in the complexity analysis.

Here too, a gain in speed could be achieved by running the loop on the smaller of the two sets.

6.4 Difference

Here, all the elements are inserted into result which are contained in s1, but not in s2.

```
template<class set_type>
void Difference(const set_type& s1, const set_type& s2,
                set_type& result)
{
    set_type temp;
    set_type::iterator i1 = s1.begin(), i2;

    if(&s1 != &s2)
        while(i1 != s1.end())
        {
            i2 = s2.find(*i1);
            if(i2 == s2.end())   // not found
                temp.insert(*i1);
            ++i1;
        }
    temp.swap(result);
}
```

The complexity is $O(N_1 \log(\max(N_1, N_2)))$ for the STL class set and $O(N_1)$ for the class HSet (Chapter 7). Calculation of the maximum is necessary, because for a small set s2, very many elements of s1 must be inserted into temp, or for a large N_2, the number of insert() operations may also be small.

The check for non-identity (&s1 != &s2) saves the loop in case of identical arguments and immediately returns an empty set. Initializing of temp with s1 and deletion of all elements contained in s2 does not lead to a gain in time, because the possible savings in the loop are compensated by the cost of the initialization. Some time could, however, be saved by choosing the smaller set for the loop (see Exercise 6.1).

6.5 Symmetric difference

This algorithm finds all the elements that occur in s1 or in s2, but not in both. The symmetric difference is equivalent to $(s1 - s2) \cup (s2 - s1)$ (implemented here) or $(s1 \cup s2) - (s1 \cap s2)$.

```
template<class set_type>
void Symmetric_Difference(const set_type& s1,
                          const set_type& s2,
                          set_type& result)
{
    set_type temp;
    set_type::iterator i1 = s1.begin(), i2;

    if(&s1 != &s2)
    {
        while(i1 != s1.end())
        {
            i2 = s2.find(*i1);
            if(i2 == s2.end())   // not found
                temp.insert(*i1);
            ++i1;
        }

        i2 = s2.begin();
        while(i2 != s2.end())
        {
            i1 = s1.find(*i2);
            if(i1 == s1.end())   // not found
                temp.insert(*i2);
            ++i2;
        }
    }
    temp.swap(result);
}
#endif   // File setalgo
```

The complexity is $O((N_1 + N_2) \log(\max(N_1, N_2)))$ for the STL class set and $O(N_1 + N_2)$ for the class HSet (Chapter 7). The check for non-identity (&s1 != &s2) saves the loop in case of identical arguments and directly returns an empty set.

6.6 Example

This example contains a compiler switch STL_set which allows you to compile the program both with the set container of the STL and with the faster HSet container

(Chapter 7). This shows the compatibility of the algorithms with two different set implementations. The switch controls not only the type definitions, but also the inclusion of a class `HashFun` used for the creation of a function object for the address calculation. `HashFun` serves as standard hash-function object, provided that no different object is required, and is stored in the file *hashfun*:

```
//   Standard function object, see Chapter 7
#ifndef Hash_function
#define Hash_function

template<class T>
class HashFun
{
   public:
     HashFun(long prime=1009) : tabSize(prime) {}
     long operator()(T p) const
     {
         return long(p) % tabSize;
     }
     long tableSize() const { return tabSize;}
   private:
     long tabSize;
};
#endif
```

In order not to repeat the example in Chapter 7, it is recommended that you try it out again after reading the next chapter, commenting out the macro

```
//  #define STL_set
```

This does not change the behavior of the program, only the underlying implementation – and with this, the running time.

```
//   k6/mainset.cpp
//   Example for sets with set algorithms
//   alternatively for set (STL) or HSet(hash) implementation
#include<showseq>

//   compiler switch (see text)
#define STL_set

#include<setalgo>

#ifdef STL_set
#include<set>
#else
#include<hset>
```

EXAMPLE **173**

```
#include<hashfun>
#endif

using namespace std;

int main()
{
// type definition according to selected implementation
#ifdef STL_set
    // default setting for comparison: less<int>
    typedef set<int> SET;
#else
    typedef HSet<int, HashFun<int> > SET;
#endif
    SET   Set1, Set2, Result;
    int i;
    for(i = 0; i < 10; i++) Set1.insert(i);
    for(i = 7; i < 16; i++) Set2.insert(i);

    // display
    showSequence(Set1);
    showSequence(Set2);
    cout << "Subset:\n";
    cout << "Includes(Set1, Set2) = "
         << Includes(Set1, Set2) << endl;

    cout << "Includes(Set1, Set1) = "
         << Includes(Set1, Set1) << endl;

    cout << "Union:\n";
    Union(Set1, Set2, Result);
    showSequence(Result);

    cout << "Intersection:\n";
    Intersection(Set1, Set2, Result);
    showSequence(Result);

    cout << "Difference:\n";
    Difference(Set1, Set2, Result);
    showSequence(Result);

    cout << "Symmetric difference:\n";
    Symmetric_Difference(Set1, Set2, Result);
    showSequence(Result);

    cout << "Copy constructor:\n";
    SET newSet(Result);
    showSequence(newSet);
```

```
    cout << "Assignment:\n";
    Result = Set1;
    showSequence(Set1);
    showSequence(Result);
}
```

Exercise

6.1   Implement the optimization proposals made in this chapter.

Fast associative containers

7

Summary: *This chapter introduces associative containers which, because of hashing, allow significantly faster access times than the sorted associative containers of the STL. The chapter concludes with suitable overloaded operators for set operations on these containers.*

As already mentioned in Section 4.4, containers of this kind were not incorporated into the C++ standard draft for reasons of time, although the STL developers had made a corresponding proposal. An unofficial implementation of their proposal, together with a description, can be obtained via FTP (see page 286). Therefore, there is no standard for this kind of containers. On the other hand, under certain conditions which will be explained below, access to the elements of these containers is independent of the number of elements, making it particularly fast ($O(1)$), so that containers of this kind are frequently employed.

This is reason enough to discuss hashing more extensively and, in particular, to present a solution based on the elements of the STL. To make the underlying concepts as simply as possible, no reference is made to the above-mentioned implementation. By omitting less important functions, such as the one for automatic adaptation to container size, the description can be made even clearer. Most compiler producers offer hash-based containers in their libraries; however they are not (yet) compatible with the STL.

Applications, for example a sparse $1\,000\,000 \times 1\,000\,000$ matrix with fast access, will be shown in subsequent chapters. Matrices with large index ranges occur in simulations of networks (gas and electricity supplies, telecommunication, and so on). Compared with the sorted associative containers of the STL, the solutions presented are not only faster, but also more economical in their memory consumption.

7.1 Fundamentals

Sometimes, the sorting provided by the associative containers is not needed. The order of the elements of a set or map need not be defined. If we do not implement sorting we can calculate the address of a sought element directly from the key. For example, a compiler builds a symbol table whose elements must be able to be accessed very quickly. The complexity of the access is $O(1)$, independent of the number N of elements in the table.

> The preconditions are that the address can be calculated in constant time with a simple formula, that sufficient memory is available, and that the address calculation supplies an even distribution of elements in memory.

This kind of storage is called hashing. It is always suitable when the actual number of keys to be stored is small compared to the number of possible keys. A compiler can have a symbol table with 10 000 entries; the number of possible variable names with, for example, only 10 characters is much larger. If, for simplicity, we assume that only the 26 lower case letters are to be used, the result already shows 26^{10} = approx. $1.4 \cdot 10^{14}$ possibilities. The same problem arises with the storage of huge matrices in which only a small percentage of the elements is not equal to zero.

The function $h(k)$ for the transformation of the key k into the address is called the *hash function* because all N possibilities of keys must be mapped to M storage places by hashing and mixing up information. M is supposed to be very much smaller than N, which immediately creates a problem: two different keys may result in the same address. Such collisions must be taken into account. The function $h(k), 0 \leq k < N$ must yield only values between 0 and $M - 1$. A very simple hash function for numeric keys is the modulo function

$$h(k) = k \bmod M$$

Here, in order to achieve an even distribution, a prime number is chosen for the table size M. Nevertheless, the distribution strongly depends on the kind and occurrence of the keys, and it is sometimes difficult to find a function that leads to only a few collisions. A hash function for character strings should ensure that similar character strings do not lead to agglomerations in the hash table. The best way is to check the distribution by way of 'actual' data, in order to adapt the hash function appropriately before a software product is used.

7.1.1 Collision handling

What happens if two keys land on the same address? The second one comes off worse if the place is already occupied. One method is the so-called 'open addressing,' in which the attempt is made, by repeated application of the same (or another) hash function, to jump to a new, free address. This method assumes that there must be a tag for an address which shows whether it is free or not. When the table is filled, searching for and entering an element will take longer. Thus, the complexity $O(1)$ is an expectation value for a table which is not too full. Good addressing methods need approximately three or four calculations and associated jumps in order to find a free place with an occupation rate α of 90%. The occupation rate α is defined as the ratio of the number of entries and the size of the hash table.

MAP **177**

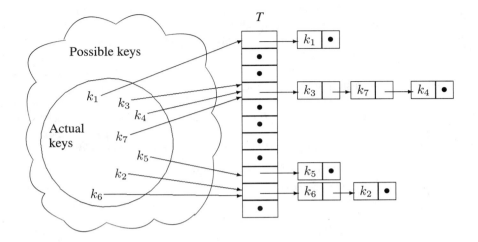

Figure 7.1 Hashing with collision resolution by chaining.

Open addressing is problematic when elements are to be deleted, because the corresponding table entry cannot simply be marked as 'free.' It might well be that the entry has been previously used as a jumping point for finding the next address during insertion of another element. After the deletion, this other element can no longer be found.

Here is another common method in which the keys are not stored directly. Instead, each entry in the table consists of a reference to a singly-linked list in which all keys with the same hash function value are stored. This method is called 'hashing with collision resolution by chaining' and is shown in Figure 7.1.

A table element $T[i]$ points to a list of all keys whose hash function value equals i. In Figure 7.1 it holds that $h(k_1) = 0, h(k_3) = h(k_4) = h(k_7) = 3, h(k_5) = 8$ and $h(k_2) = h(k_6) = 9$. Deletion of an element is simpler, and because of the nearly unlimited length of a list, more elements can be stored than the table has positions. Such an occupation rate > 1 obviously entails a loss of performance, because in the worst case, the search or insertion time is proportional to the length of the longest list.

7.2 Map

This section gives a complete description of the hash-based class HMap, whose name differs from that of the STL class map by its upper case initial and a prefixed H. Under the assumption made on page 176, search or insertion of an element in HMap is carried out in constant time, that is, independently of the number N of already existing elements, whereas in map, the same process is of complexity $O(\log N)$.

The internal data structure for the hash table is a vector v whose elements are pointers to singly-linked lists, as shown in Figure 7.1. The hash table T of the figure is implemented by means of the vector v. A list is realized by means of the slist class of page 9, assuming the solution of Exercise 1.1. The list class of the STL would function just as well, but it uses more memory because of the backward pointers. Since with a proper choice of the hash function and a not too full table, lists mostly consist of only one element, a singly-linked list is sufficient.

For reasons of simplicity and clearness, HMap implements only the most important type names and functions of the map class. However, the functions available in HMap have the same interface as map, so that all the following examples which do not assume sorting can work as well with map, only more slowly.

```
//  File include/hmap (= hash map)
#ifndef hashmap
#define hashmap

//  implicit data structures
#include<vector>
#include<slist>

//  hash map class
template<class Key, class T, class hashFun>
class HMap
{
public:
    typedef size_t size_type;
    typedef pair<const Key,T> value_type;

    //  define more readable denominations
    typedef slist<value_type> list_type;
    typedef vector<list_type*> vector_type;

    /*
```

The template parameter Key stands for the type of the key; T stands for the class of data associated to a key; and hashFun is the placeholder for the data type of the function objects used for address calculation. Below, a function object for address calculation is proposed, but any other one can be used as well. Analogous to map, value_type is the type of the elements that are stored in an HMap object. value_type is a pair consisting of a constant key and the associated data.

```
    */

    class iterator;
    //  maintain compatibility with the STL:
    typedef iterator const_iterator;
    friend class iterator;

    /*
```

The nested class iterator cooperates closely with HMap, so that both are mutually declared as friend. iterator is only supposed to allow forward traversal and therefore inherits forward_iterator from the standard class. An iterator object allows

MAP **179**

you to visit all the elements of an HMap object one after the other. Neither an order nor a sorting is defined for the elements. The visiting order of the iterator is given by the implicit data structure (see below, operator++()).
*/

```
class iterator : public
        forward_iterator<value_type, size_type>
{
  friend class HMap<Key, T, hashFun>;
  private:
  list_type::iterator current;
  size_type Address;
  const vector_type *pVec;
```

    /*
    Privately, the HMap iterator must remember three things:

  - current, an iterator for a list which begins at an element of the vector,

  - pVec, a pointer to the vector on which the HMap iterator walks, and

  - Address, the number of the vector element where the currently processed list begins.

    The constructors initialize the private data, with the standard constructor initializing the pointer to the vector with 0 and current with a list end iterator.
    */

```
  public:
  iterator()
  : current(list_type::iterator()),
    pVec(0)
  {}

  iterator(list_type::iterator LI,
           size_type A,   const vector_type *C)
  : current(LI), Address(A), pVec(C)
  {}
```

    /*
    The following operators allow you to check an HMap iterator in the condition part of if or while as to whether it is at all defined:
    */

```
  operator const void* () const
  {
      return pVec;
  }

  bool operator!() const
  {
```

```
        return pVec == 0;
}

/*
```

The operator for dereferencing occurs both in the const variation and in the non-const variation. Thus, dereferencing of an undefined iterator is punished with a program abort, which is a clear message to you to check the program that uses the iterator.

```
*/

const value_type& operator*() const
{
    assert(pVec);
    return *current;
}

value_type& operator*()
{
    assert(pVec);
    return *current;
}

/*
```

The non-const variation is required to modify data independently of the key. Modification of the key must be excluded because it requires a new address calculation. Constancy is guaranteed by the const declaration in the type definition of value_type.

```
*/
/*
```

How does the HMap iterator move from one element to the other with operator++()? First, current is incremented:

```
*/

iterator& operator++()
{
    ++current;

        /*
```

If after this, current points to a list element, a reference to the iterator is returned (see below: return *this). Otherwise, the end of the list is reached.

```
        */

        if(current == (*pVec)[Address]->end())
        {

            /*
```

At this point, one address after the other is checked in the vector, until either a list entry is found or the end of the vector is reached. In the latter case, the iterator becomes invalid, because it can only move forward. In

MAP **181**

order to exclude further use, pVec is set to 0:
```
        */

    while(++Address < pVec->size())
       if((*pVec)[Address])
       {
           current = (*pVec)[Address]->begin();
           break;
       }

    if(Address == pVec->size()) // end of vector reached
       pVec = 0;
  }
  return *this;
}
```

```
/*
```
The postfix variation does not show any peculiarities. It remembers the old state in the variable `temp`, calls the prefix form, and returns the old state.
```
*/

iterator operator++(int)
{
    iterator temp = *this;
    operator++();
    return temp;
}
```

```
/*
```
The last two methods compare two HMap iterators. Two undefined or invalidated iterators are always considered as equal:
```
*/

bool operator==(const iterator& x) const
{
    return current == x.current
         || !pVec && !x.pVec;
}

bool operator!=(const iterator& x) const
{
    return !operator==(x);
}
}; // iterator
```

```
/*
```
With this, the nested class `iterator` is concluded, so that now the data and methods of the `HMap` class can follow:
```
*/
```

```
private:
  vector_type v;
  hashFun hf;
  size_type Count;

  /*
  Count is the number of stored pairs of keys and data, v is the vector whose elements
  are pointers to singly linked lists, and hf is the function object used for calculation of
  the hash address.
  */

  void construct(const HMap& S)
  {
      hf = S.hf;
      v = vector_type(S.v.size(),0);
      Count = 0;

      // begin(), end(), insert(): see below
      iterator t = S.begin();
      while(t != S.end())
          insert(*t++);
  }


  /*
  The construct() function is an auxiliary function which is called both in the copy
  constructor and in the assignment operator. It constructs an HMap object out of an-
  other one and has been extracted in order to avoid code duplication in copy constructor
  and assignment operator.
  */

public:
  iterator begin() const
  {
      size_type adr = 0;
      while(adr < v.size())
      {
          if(!v[adr])      // found nothing?
            adr++;          // continue search
          else
            return iterator(v[adr]->begin(), adr, &v);
      }
      return iterator();
  }

  iterator end() const
  {
      return iterator();
  }
```

MAP **183**

```
/*
```

The method `begin()` supplies an iterator to the first element – provided it exists – in the HMap object. Otherwise, as with `end()`, an end iterator is returned. Iterators can become invalid if, after their generation, elements have been inserted or deleted in the HMap object.

The following HMap constructor needs a hash function object f as the parameter. If no function object is passed, a default object f is generated by means of the standard constructor of the `hashFun` class. The vector is created in the suitable size `f.tableSize()`, and all elements are initialized with 0. It is assumed that the hashFun class provides the method `tableSize()` (see Section 7.2.1).

```
*/

HMap(hashFun f = hashFun())
: v(f.tableSize(),0), hf(f), Count(0)
{}

/*
```

What is meant by 'suitable size'? The hash table has a capacity P, with a prime number generally being chosen for P. On the other hand, the hash function object is used for address calculation; thus, this object too must know P. It is important that both function and vector denote the same P; therefore, a separate specification in the initialization of HMap and hash function object would be prone to errors.

In order to avoid the hash function object having to procure the information on the capacity of the vector, the opposite method is followed: the vector is created in a size determined by the hash function object, assuming that the hash function object provides a method `tableSize()` for finding out the size of the table. This assumption is checked at compile time.

Copy constructor, destructor, and assignment operator are of a very simple construction. The `clear()` method deletes the contents of an HMap object.

```
*/

HMap(const HMap& S)
{
    construct(S);
}

~HMap()
{
    clear();                              //  see below
}

HMap& operator=(const HMap& S)
{
    if(this != &S)
    {
        clear();
        construct(S);
```

```
        }
        return *this;
}

/*
```

clear() uses delete to call the destructor of each list referred to by a vector element. Subsequently, the vector element is marked as unoccupied.
```
*/

void clear()
{
    for(size_t i = 0; i < v.size(); i++)
        if(v[i])                        //  does list exist?
        {
            delete v[i];
            v[i] = 0;
        }
    Count = 0;
}

/*
```

In the following find() and insert() functions, the sought address within the vector v is calculated directly by means of the hash function object. If the vector element contains a pointer to a list, the list is searched in find() by means of the list iterator temp until either an element with the correct key is found or the list has been completely processed:
```
*/

iterator find(const Key& k) const
{
    size_type address = hf(k);      //  calculate address

    if(!v[address])
        return iterator();          //  non-existent
    list_type::iterator temp =  v[address]->begin();

    //  find k in the list
    while(temp != v[address]->end())
        if((*temp).first == k)
            return iterator(temp,address,&v); //  found
        else ++temp;

    return iterator();
}

/*
```

A map stores pairs of keys and associated data, where the first element (first) is the key and the second element (second) contains the data. find() returns an iterator which can be interpreted as a pointer to a pair. In order to obtain the data belonging to

MAP **185**

a key, the index operator can be called with the key as argument:

```
*/

T& operator[](const Key& k)
{
    return (*find(k)).second;
}

/*
```

If the key does not exist, that is, if find() returns an end iterator, a run time error occurs while dereferencing! (See the dereferencing operator on page 180.)

The HMap class allows the insertion of an element only if an element with that key does not yet exist. If this is not desirable, it is easily possible to use HMap to build a MultiHMap class that allows multiple insertion of elements with identical keys. As in the STL, insert() returns a pair whose first part consists of the iterator that points to the found position. The second part indicates whether the insertion has taken place or not.

```
*/

pair<iterator, bool> insert(const value_type& P)
{
    iterator temp = find(P.first);
    bool inserted = false;

    if(!temp) // not present
    {
        size_type address = hf(P.first);
        if(!v[address])
            v[address] = new list_type;
        v[address]->push_front(P);
        temp = find(P.first); // redefine temp
        inserted = true;
        Count++;
    }
    return make_pair(temp, inserted);
}

/*
```

After the insertion, temp is redefined, because the iterator at first does not point to an existing element. The known auxiliary function make_pair() (page 20) generates a pair object to be returned.

```
*/

void erase(iterator q)
{

    /*
```

If the iterator is defined at all, the element function erase() of the associated list is called. Subsequently, the list is deleted, provided it is now empty, and the vector element to which the list is attached is set to 0.

```
*/
    if(q.pVec)                    //  defined?
    {
        v[q.Address]->erase(q.current);
        if(v[q.Address]->empty())
        {
            delete v[q.Address];
            v[q.Address] = 0;
        }
        Count--;
    }
}
```

```
/*
```

Sometimes, we would probably like to delete all the elements of a map that have a given key. In an HMap, this can at most be one element, but in an HMultimap, several elements might be affected.

```
*/
```

```
//   suitable for HMap and HMultimap
size_type erase(const Key& k)
{
    size_type deleted_elements = 0; //  Count

    //   calculate address
    size_type address = hf(k);
    if(!v[address])
        return 0;              //  not present

    list_type::iterator temp =  v[address]->begin();
```

```
    /*
```

In the following loop, the list is searched. A iterator called pos is used to remember the current position for the deletion itself.

```
    */
```

```
    while(temp != v[address]->end())
    {
        if((*temp).first == k)
        {
            list_type::iterator pos = temp++;

            v[address]->erase(pos);
            //  pos is now undefined

            Count--;
            deleted_elements++;
        }
```

MAP **187**

```
          else ++temp;
    }
```

```
    /*
```

The temporary iterator `temp` is advanced in *both* branches of the `if` instruction. The operation `++` cannot be extracted in order to save the `else`, because `temp` would then be identical with `pos` which is undefined after the deletion, and a defined `++` operation would no longer be possible.

```
    */
```

```
    //  delete hash table entry if needed
    if(v[address]->empty())
    {
        delete v[address];
        v[address] = 0;
    }
    return deleted_elements;
}
```

```
/*
```

Here are a couple of very simple methods. As opposed to other containers, `max_size()` does not indicate the maximum number of elements that can be stored in an HMap container, which is limited only by the capacity of the lists, but the number of available hash table entries. This information is more sensible, because the efficiency of an HMap depends on the occupation range α, assuming a good hash function. The occupation rate can easily be determined: $\alpha = $ `size()`/`max_size()`.

```
*/
```

```
size_type size()       const { return Count;}
```

```
size_type max_size() const { return v.size();}
```

```
bool empty()           const { return Count == 0;}
```

```
void swap(HMap& s)
    {
        v.swap(s.v);
        std::swap(Count, s.Count);
        std::swap(hf, s.hf);
    }
};
#endif    // File hmap
```

The `swap()` method swaps two HMap containers, using both a method of the vector container (see page 50) and an algorithm (see page 113) for swapping the remaining private data. Depending on the implementation, the latter is global or is located in the namespace `std`.

7.2.1 Example

The following example is taken from Section 4.4.3 and has been slightly modified. As in the example at the end of Chapter 6, the modification consists in the introduction of a compiler switch STL_map which allows you to compile the program both with the map container of the STL and with the HMap container just presented. The switch controls not only the type definitions, but also the inclusion of a class HashFun (file *hashfun*), used to create a function object for the address calculation.

```
//  function object for hash address calculation
#ifndef Hash_function
#define Hash_function

template<class IndexTyp>
class HashFun
{
   public:
     //  size of hash table: 1009 entries
     HashFun(long prime=1009) //  other prime numbers are possible
     : tabSize(prime)
     {}
     //  simple hash function
     long operator()(IndexTyp p) const
     {
        return long(p) % tabSize;
     }

     //  tableSize() is used by the constructor of an HMap
     //  or HSet container for determination of the size
     long tableSize() const
     {
        return tabSize;
     }

   private:
     long tabSize;
};
#endif

//  k7/maph.cpp
//  Example for a map with hash map
#include<string>
using namespace std;

//  compiler switch (see text)
// #define STL_map

#ifdef STL_map
#include<map>
```

```
typedef map<long, string, less<long> > MapType;
#else
#include<hmap>
#include<hashfun>

typedef HMap<long, string, HashFun<long> > MapType;
#endif

typedef MapType::value_type ValuePair;

int main()
{
    //  see page 88
}
```

The source code of the `main()` program remains unchanged with respect to page 88. However, the running program behaves differently when the compiler switch `STL_map` is not set and therefore an HMap container is used as underlying implementation: the output is *not* sorted.

7.3 Set

A set differs from a map in that the keys are also the data, that is, no separation exists. By changing the parts concerning pairs of keys and data, it is very easy to derive a corresponding HSet class from the HMap class of Section 7.2. Apart from pure name changes (`HMap` becomes `HSet`), these parts are so few that the HSet class is not listed here, especially since it is included in the examples available via the Internet.

Further modifications concern only the following points:

- Overloaded operators for set operations are added which will be discussed in the following sections.
- `HSet` has no index operator, because keys and data are the same.
- In the `HSet` class, the dereferencing operator for an iterator is present only in the `const` variation, since direct modification of an element must not be allowed because of the necessary address recalculation. In contrast, in the `HMap` class, the non-`const` variation is desirable for modifying data independently from their keys. As can be seen from the definition of `HMap::value_type`, constancy of the key is guaranteed.

7.4 Overloaded operators for sets

Once you design a class for sets, it is only reasonable to provide the usual set operations as overloaded operators. In the STL, these operators do not exist for set containers, so an extension is presented here which is based on three design criteria:

- The choice of operator symbols partly orients with the symbols known from the Pascal programming language:

  + for the union of two sets

  – for the difference of two sets

  * for the intersection of two sets

  For the symmetric difference, which corresponds to the exclusive or, the corresponding C++ operator ^ is chosen. The Pascal keyword in does not exist in C++ and it does not seem reasonable to choose another C++ symbol instead, so no operator for the subset relation is defined.

- The operators are implemented by means of the global set operations shown in Chapter 6.

- The binary operators +, –, *, and ^ are implemented as member functions using the short form operators +=, and so on. With permanently defined types, an implementation as a global function is usual, but here we are dealing with templates. This design decision avoids conflicts with other global template operators of the same names. An alternative is namespaces; however, these will not be discussed.

The following description is based on the fact that all methods are defined inline in the class definition of HSet (file *hset*).

7.4.1 Union

Exceptionally, no use is made of the global function Union() of Chapter 6 to prevent creation of a copy of *this:

```
HSet& operator+=(const HSet& S)              // Union
{
    HSet::iterator i = S.begin();
    while(i != S.end()) insert(*i++);
    return *this;
}

// binary operator
HSet operator+(const HSet& S)                // Union
{
    HSet result = *this;
    return result += S;
}
```

7.4.2 Intersection

```
HSet& operator*=(const HSet& S)              // intersection
{
    Intersection(*this, S, *this);
```

```
      return *this;
   }

   //  binary operator
   HSet operator*(const HSet& S)              //  intersection
   {
      HSet result = *this;
      return result *= S;
   }
```

7.4.3 Difference

```
   HSet& operator-=(const HSet& S)            //  difference
   {
      Difference(*this, S, *this);
      return *this;
   }

   //  binary operator
   HSet operator-(const HSet& S)              //  difference
   {
      HSet result = *this;
      return result -= S;
   }
```

7.4.4 Symmetric difference

```
   HSet& operator^=(const HSet& S)            //  symmetric difference
   {
      Symmetric_Difference(*this, S, *this);
      return *this;
   }

   //  binary operator
   HSet operator^(const HSet& S)              //  symmetric difference
   {
      HSet result = *this;
      return result ^= S;
   }
```

7.4.5 Example

This shows the application of the overloaded operators for set operations without giving a choice between the set implementation of the STL and an HSet container, because the former does not provide these operators.

```cpp
#include<showseq>
#include<hset>
#include<hashfun>

int main()
{
    int i;
    typedef HSet<int, HashFun<int> > SET;
    SET   Set1, Set2, Result;
    for(i = 0; i < 10; i++) Set1.insert(i);
    for(i = 7; i < 16; i++) Set2.insert(i);

    showSequence(Set1);      // 0 1 2 3 4 5 6 7 8 9
    showSequence(Set2);      // 7 8 9 10 11 12 13 14 15

    cout << "Union:\n";
    Result = Set1;
    Result += Set2;

    showSequence(Result);   // 0 1 2 3 4 5 6 7 8 9 10 11 12 13 14 15

    cout << "Intersection:\n";
    Result = Set1;
    Result *= Set2;

    showSequence(Result);   // 7 8 9

    cout << "Union:\n";
    Result = Set1 + Set2;

    showSequence(Result);   // 0 1 2 3 4 5 6 7 8 9 10 11 12 13 14 15

    cout << "Intersection:\n";
    Result = Set1 * Set2;
    showSequence(Result);   // 7 8 9

    cout << "Difference:\n";
    Result = Set1 - Set2;

    showSequence(Result);   // 0 1 2 3 4 5 6

    cout << "Symmetric difference:\n";
    Result = Set1 ^ Set2;

    showSequence(Result);   // 0 1 2 3 4 5 6 10 11 12 13 14 15
}
```

Various applications $\boxed{8}$

Summary: *While the following chapters deal with complex data structures and algorithms, this chapter looks at smaller applications that show how, thanks to the power of the C++ Standard Template Library, much can be achieved with relatively short programs. The applications are: output of a cross-reference list of identifiers in a text, generation of a permuted index, and search for related concepts of a given term (thesaurus).*

8.1 Cross-reference

The first example is a program for printing a cross-reference list, that is, a list which contains the words or identifiers occurring in the text in alphabetical order, together with the position of their occurrence, in this case, their line numbers.

This is the beginning of the cross-reference list that belongs to the following program:

```
    _              : 50 59
    a              : 11 19 22 22 22 24 73 74 78
    all            : 11
    and            : 10
    are            : 74 75
    avoid          : 10
    b              : 19 23 23 23 24
    back           : 64
    be             : 11 73
    because        : 73
    begin          : 82
    beginning      : 47 75
    bool           : 19
    buf            : 37 48 50 50 52 53 59 59 61 64 65 67 68 74
    ⋮
```

In the simple variation described here, words occurring in comments are output as well. The appropriate data structure is a map container. The value pairs consist of the identifier of type `string` as key and a list of line numbers. Because of the sorted storage, no special sorting process is needed.

```
//  k8/crossref.cpp : program for printing cross-references
#include<fstream>
#include<string>
#include<list>
#include<cctype>
#include<showseq>
#include<map>

/*
```

To avoid different sorting of upper case and lower case letters, the class `Compare` is used which converts all strings to be compared into lower case, since a corresponding function is not provided in the `string` class:

```
*/

using namespace std;

struct Compare
{
    bool operator()(string a, string b) const
    {
      int i;
      for(i = 0; i < a.length(); i++) a[i] = tolower(a[i]);
      for(i = 0; i < b.length(); i++) b[i] = tolower(b[i]);
      return a < b;
    }
};

int main( )
{
    //  This program generates its own cross-reference list.
    ifstream Source("crossref.cpp");

    typedef map<string, list<int>, Compare > MAP;
    MAP CrossRef;

    const unsigned int maxi = 100;
    char buf[maxi];                     //  buffer
    int LineNo = 1;

    /*
```

The next section largely corresponds to the `operator>>()` on page 43. The difference lies in the counting of lines.

```
    */
```

```
while(Source)
{
    //  find beginning of identifier
    buf[0] = 0;

    while(Source && !(isalpha(buf[0]) || '_' == buf[0]))
    {
        Source.get(buf[0]);
        if(buf[0] == '\n') LineNo++;
    }

    //  collect rest of identifier
    int i = 0;
    while(Source &&  i < maxi
        && (isalnum(buf[i]) || '_' == buf[i]))
    {
        Source.get(buf[++i]);
    }

    Source.putback(buf[i]);     //  back to input stream
    buf[i] = char(0);           //  end mark

    if(buf[0])
        CrossRef[string(buf)].push_back(LineNo);   //  entry
}

/*
```

Putting the line number in the list utilizes the fact that the `MAP::operator[]()` returns a reference to the entry, even if this has still to be created because the key does not yet exist. The key entry `string(buf)` is a list. Since the line numbers are inserted with `push_back()`, they are in the correct order from the very beginning.

The output of the cross-reference list profits by the sorted storage. The `first` element of a value pair is the identifier (key), the `second` element is the list which is output by means of the known template.

```
*/

MAP::iterator iter = CrossRef.begin();

while(iter != CrossRef.end())
{
    cout << (*iter).first;                      //  identifier
    cout.width(20 - (*iter).first.length());
    cout << ": ";
    showSequence((*iter++).second);   //  line numbers
}

}
```

8.2 Permuted index

A permuted index is printed by some journals at the beginning of a new year to facilitate retrieving articles from the previous year using the terms contained in the titles. The permuted index is alphabetically sorted by words in the title and thus facilitates the search for articles on a given subject. Table 8.1 shows an example with three titles.

	Search term	Page
	Electronic Mail and POP	174
Electronic	Mail and POP	174
	Objects in the World Wide Web	162
Electronic Mail and	POP	174
	Unix or WindowsNT?	12
Objects in the World Wide	Web	162
Objects in the World	Wide Web	162
Unix or	WindowsNT?	12
Objects in the	World Wide Web	162

Table 8.1   Example of a permuted index.

The alphabetical order of the terms in the second column allows quick orientation. Table 8.1 was generated by the following sample program which exploits a map container and its property of sorted storage. A pointer to each relevant word – here, all words beginning with an upper case letter are included – is stored in the map container together with the current title number. Subsequently, the contents may be output only in a formatted way.

```
//  k8/permidx.cpp
//  Program for generation of a permuted index
#include<iostream>
#include<vector>
#include<string>
#include<map>
#include<cctype>

using namespace std;

struct StringCompare
{
   bool operator()(const char* a, const char* b) const
   {
       return string(a) < string(b);
   }
};
```

```
/*
```
The class `StringCompare` is needed for the creation of a function object for the map container. No use is made of the well-known function `strcmp()`, since in the coming C++ standard, application of the functions from *string.h* is regarded as a 'C hangover' and is no longer recommended.

Normally, titles and page numbers would be read from a file, but for simplicity, in this example both are wired in:
```
*/
int main()
{
    vector<string> Title(3);
    vector<int> Page(Title.size());

    // read titles here. Only for the example:
    Title[0] = "Electronic Mail and POP";        Page[0] = 174;
    Title[1] = "Objects in the World Wide Web" ;  Page[1] = 162;
    Title[2] = "Unix or WindowsNT?";              Page[2] =  12;

    typedef map<const char*, int, StringCompare> MAP;
    MAP aMap;

    /*
```
All pointers to words that begin with an upper case letter are stored in the map container together with the page numbers of the titles. It is assumed that words are separated by spaces. An alternative could be to store not the pointers, but the words themselves as string objects.

On average, however, this would require more memory, and a multimap container would have to be used, because the same words can occur in different titles. The pointers, in contrast, are unique. The same words in different titles have different addresses.
```
    */

    for(int i = 0; i < Title.size(); i++)
    {
        int j = 0;

        do
        {
            const char *Word = Title[i].c_str() + j;
            if(isalpha(*Word) && isupper(*Word))
                aMap[Word] = i;                   // entry

            // find next space
            while(j < Title[i].length()
                && Title[i][j] != ' ') j++;

            // find beginning of word
            while(j < Title[i].length()
```

```
                    && !isalpha(Title[i][j])) j++;
        } while(j < Title[i].length());
}

/*
```
The map container is filled, now we need the output. As usual in such cases, the
formatting requires more program lines than the rest.
```
*/

MAP::iterator I = aMap.begin();
const int leftColumnWidth = 25,
          rightColumnWidth = 30;

while(I != aMap.end())
{
    // determine left column text
    // = 1st character of title no. (*I).second
    // up to the beginning of the search term
    // which begins at (*I).first.
    const char *begin = Title[(*I).second].c_str();
    const char *End = (*I).first;

    // and output with leading spaces
    cout.width(leftColumnWidth-(End-begin));
    cout << ' ';
    while(begin != End)
        cout << *begin++;

    // output right column text
    cout << ' ';      // highlight separation left/right
    cout.width(rightColumnWidth);
    cout.setf(ios::left, ios::adjustfield); // ranged left
    cout << (*I).first;

    cout.width(4);
    cout.setf(ios::right, ios::adjustfield); // ranged right
    cout << Page[(*I).second]        // page number
        << endl;
    ++I;                    // go to next entry
}
}
```

8.3 Thesaurus

A thesaurus is a systematic collection of words and terms that allows you to find
terms related to a given concept. The terms can be similar, but they can also represent
opposites or antonyms. In this respect, a thesaurus is a counterpart to a dictionary.

The dictionary explains the concept belonging to a given term; the thesaurus presents words related by subject and meaning to a given concept.

The thesaurus used in this example was published in its original form by Peter Mark Roget in 1852. It is contained in the file *roget.dat*, which is used in Knuth (1994) for the generation of a directed graph of 1022 nodes and 5075 edges (= references). The file can be obtained via FTP (see page 287).

Instead of building a graph, this section shows how very fast access to related terms is possible with the lower-bound algorithm. A possible application could be in a text processing system, to provide an author with a formulation aid. The lines of the file look as follows:

```
1existence:2 69 125 149 156 166 193 455 506 527
2inexistence:1 4 167 192 194 368 458 526 527 771
3substantiality:4 323 325
4unsubstantiality:3 34 194 360 432 452 458 527 and so on.
```

The numbers after the concept substantiality mean that corresponding entries can be found in lines 4, 323, and 325. There are several possibilities to allow fast access. Here, the lower_bound() algorithm is employed, which assumes a sorted container and works with the principle of binary search. It finds the first position that can be used for insertion into the container without violating the sorting order. Thus, the algorithm is also suitable for finding an entry in a container.

Three different containers are needed:

- a vector to contain all terms,
- a vector of lists containing the references, and
- a vector that contains the sorting order and is used as an index vector for fast access.

The alternative of not using an index vector and sorting the first two vectors is not chosen, because it is a rather long-winded process to update all references in the lists.

```cpp
//   k8/thesaur.cpp : program for the output of terms
//   related to a given concept
#include<fstream>
#include<vector>
#include<string>
#include<slist>
#include<cctype>
#include<algorithm>

using namespace std;

struct indirectCompare
{
    indirectCompare(const vector<string>& v) : V(v) {}

    bool operator()( int x,  int y) const
```

```
        {
            return V[x] < V[y];
        }
        bool operator()( int x, const string& a) const
        {
            return V[x] < a;
        }

        const vector<string>& V;
};
```

```
/*
```
The class `indirectCompare` compares the corresponding values in the vector V for passed indices, and the reference is initialized during construction of the object. The second overloaded function operator directly compares a value with a vector element whose index is given.
```
*/
```

```
void readRoget(vector<string>& Words,
               vector<slist<int> >& lists)
{
    //  see Appendix
}
```

```
/*
```
The procedure `readRoget()` reads the file *roget.dat* and has nothing much to do with the STL. It mainly concentrates on analysis and conversion of the data format and has therefore been relegated to the Appendix.
```
*/
```

```
int main( )
{
    const int Maxi = 1022;   // number of entries in roget.dat

    vector<string> Words(Maxi);
    vector<slist<int> > relatedWords(Maxi);
    vector<int> Index(Maxi);

    //  read thesaurus file
    readRoget(Words,relatedWords);

    //  build index vector
    int i;
    for(i = 0; i < Index.size(); i++)
        Index[i] = i;

    indirectCompare aComparison(Words);      // functor

    sort(Index.begin(), Index.end(), aComparison);
```

```
/*
```
The index vector now indicates the ordering, so that Words[Index[0]] is the first term according to the alphabetical sorting order. This creates the precondition for a binary search.
```
*/

cout << "Search term? ";
char buf[50];
cin.getline(buf, sizeof(buf));
string SearchTerm = buf;

//  binary search
vector<int>::iterator TableEnd,
            where = lower_bound(Index.begin(), Index.end(),
                                SearchTerm, aComparison);
/*
```
If the iterator where points to the end of the table, the term was not found. Otherwise, a check must be made as to whether the found term matches the search term in its first characters. This does not have to be the case, because lower_bound() only returns a position which is suitable for sorted insertion.
```
*/

bool found = true;            //  hypothesis to be checked
if(where == TableEnd)
    found = false;
else

        //  next possible entry is ≥ search term
        //  do they match?
{
    int i = 0;
    while(i < Words[*where].length()
        && i < SearchTerm.length()
        && found)
      if(Words[*where][i] != SearchTerm[i])
          found = false;
      else ++i;
}

/*
```
If the term is found, the list of references, provided that references exist, is 'scoured' with the iterator here, and the corresponding terms are displayed on screen.
```
*/

if(found)
{
    cout << "found   : "
        << Words[*where] << endl
        << "related words:\n";
```

```
        slist<int>::iterator atEnd,
            here = relatedWords[*where].begin();

    if(here == atEnd)
        cout << "not found\n";
    else
        while(here != atEnd)
            cout << '\t' << Words[*here++] << endl;
    }
    else  cout << "not found\n";
}
```

To conclude, the output of the program for the search term 'free' is shown:

Search term? free
found : freedom
related words:
    cheapness
    permission
    liberation
    subjection
    hindrance
    facility
    will

Vectors and matrices $\boxed{9}$

Summary: The elements of the STL can easily be used for constructing arrays or vectors in which the access to elements is checked at run time to determine an index overflow. Construction of matrices for different memory models is quite possible, as is shown for C matrices (row-wise storage), FORTRAN matrices (column-wise storage), and symmetric matrices. A class for sparse matrices is implemented by means of an associative container.

9.1 Checked vectors

The vector templates of the STL do not carry out an index check. The example

```
vector<string> stringVec(4);
//  ...
stringVec[0] = stringVec[34];  // Error!
```

shows a nonsensical assignment. If a program goes on working with values generated by erroneous indices, the error is often detected only through consequential errors and is therefore difficult to identify. It is, however, possible to construct a new vector class named, for example, checkedVector, that carries out an index check. This class is not part of the STL, but it builds on it.

The principle is straightforward: checkedVector *is a* vector which carries out additional checks. In C++, the relation 'is a' is expressed through public inheritance. The derived class must only provide the constructors of the base class and overwrite the index operator:

```
//  include/checkvec : vector class with checked limits
#ifndef checkvec
#define checkvec
#include<cassert>
#include<vector>

using namespace std;

template<class T>
```

```
class checkedVector : public vector<T>    // inherit from std::vector<T>
{
  public:
      // type names like iterator are also inherited
      checkedVector()
      {}

      checkedVector(size_type n, const T& value = T())
      : vector<T>(n, value)
      {}

      checkedVector(iterator i, iterator j)
      : vector<T>(i, j)
      {}

      reference operator[](difference_type index)
      {
          assert(index >=0 && index < size());
          return vector<T>::operator[](index);
      }

      const_reference operator[](difference_type index) const
      {
          assert(index >=0 && index < size());
          return vector<T>::operator[](index);
      }
};
#endif
```

> *Note:* The STL allows inheritance, but does *not* support polymorphism!
> In this sense, methods of derived classes may be called, but not via
> pointers or references of the base class type. In the case of vectors, this
> is certainly no problem, but be aware of it.

difference_type is deliberately chosen as the argument type, so that negative erroneous index values are recognized as well. The type size_type would lead to an int → unsigned conversion, and a negative index would be recognized only because it is converted into a significantly large number. Applying this template generates error messages at run time, when the permitted index range is exceeded in either direction. The index check can be switched off with the preprocessor instruction #define NDEBUG, if it is inserted before #include<assert>. The following program provokes a run time error by accessing a non-existent vector element:

```
//  k9/a1/strvec.cpp
//  string vector container with index check
```

```
#include"checkvec"     //  contains checkedVector
#include<iostream>
#include<string>

int main()
{
    //  a string vector of 4 elements
    checkedVector<string> stringVec(4);
    stringVec[0] = "first";
    stringVec[1] = "second";
    stringVec[2] = "third";
    stringVec[3] = "fourth";
    cout << "provoked program abort:" << endl;
    stringVec[4] = "index error";
}
```

Thus, the `checkedVector` class puts a so-called safety wrapper around the vector class. One interface, namely the access to elements of the vector, is adapted to the safety requirements, which is why the `checkedVector` class can be called a kind of 'vector adaptor.'

9.2 Matrices as nested containers

Besides one-dimensional arrays, two- and three-dimensional matrices are widely used in mathematical applications. This section is based on Breymann and Hughes (1995). The implementation by means of containers from the STL is, however, new. Mathematical matrices are special cases of arrays of elements which are of the data types `int`, `float`, `complex`, `rational`, or similar. The `checkedVector` class (Section 9.1) is a one-dimensional matrix in this sense, with the difference that, unlike a normal C array, the class allows safe access via the index operator, as we would also expect for two- and more-dimensional matrix classes. Access to the elements of a one- or more-dimensional matrix object should

- be safe by checking all indices, and
- be carried out via the index operator `[]` (or `[][]`, `[][][]`, ...), so that the usual notation can be maintained.

A possible alternative would be to overload the bracket operator for round parentheses (), which is shown in Section 9.3. It may be argued that it is more pleasing to the eye to write `M(1,17)` instead of `M[1][17]`. When writing new programs, this is really not important. But what if you are responsible for maintaining and servicing existing large programs which use the `[]` syntax? A further argument is that a matrix class should behave as similarly as possible to a conventional C array.

The first requirement is often dismissed, the decrease in efficiency being the justification. This argument is not a hard and fast rule, for more than one reason:

- A correct program is more important than a fast one. As industry practice shows, index errors occur quite frequently. Finding the source of the error is difficult when calculation is continued with erroneous data and the error itself becomes evident only through consequential errors.

- The increased run time caused by checked access is often comparable to further operations relative to the array element, and is sometimes negligible. In the fields of science and engineering, there are programs in which the index check is significantly disadvantageous; however, it depends on the specific case. Only if a program is too slow *because of* the index check, might one consider, after thorough testing, taking the index check out.

9.2.1 Two-dimensional matrices

What is a two-dimensional matrix whose elements are of type int? An int matrix *is a* vector consisting of int vectors! This view allows a significantly more elegant formulation of a matrix class in comparison to the assertion: 'The matrix *has* or consists of mathematical int vectors.' The formulation of the *is a* relation as inheritance shows the class Matrix. Again, it is not the standard vector container which is employed, but the checkedVector class of page 203 derived from it, so that automatic index checking is achieved. Only if no index check is required at all should the checkedVector be replaced with the vector:

```
//  File matrix
#ifndef matrix_t
#define matrix_t

#include<checkvec>      //  checked vector of Section 9.1
#include<iostream>      //  for operator<<(), see below

/*  matrix as vector of vectors*/
template<class T>
class Matrix : public checkedVector<checkedVector<T> >
{
    protected:
      size_type rows,
                columns;

    public:
      Matrix(size_type x = 0, size_type y = 0)
      : checkedVector<checkedVector<T> >(x,
              checkedVector<T>(y)), rows(x), columns(y)

      {}

      /*
```

Thus, the Matrix class inherits from the checkedVector class, with the data type of the vector elements now being described by a checkedVector<T> template. With this, the matrix is a nested container that exploits the combination of templates with inheritance.

The constructor initializes the implicit subobject of the base class type (checked-Vector< checkedVector<T> >) with the correct size x.

Exactly as with the standard vector container, the second parameter of the constructor specifies with which value each vector element is to be initialized. Here, the value is no more than a vector of type checkedVector<T> and length y.

Some simple methods follow for returning the number of rows and columns, initializing all matrix elements with a given value (init()), and generation of the identity matrix (I()), in which all diagonal elements = 1 and all other elements = 0. For comparison: init() does not return anything and I() returns a reference to the matrix object, so that the latter method allows chaining of operations:
*/

```
size_type Rows() const {return rows; }

size_type Columns() const {return columns; }

void init(const T& Value)
{
    for (size_type i = 0; i < rows; i++)
        for (size_type j = 0; j < columns ; j++)
            operator[](i)[j] = Value; // that is, (*this)[i][j]
}

/*
```

The index operator operator[]() is inherited from checkedVector. Applied to i, it supplies a reference to the ith element of the (base class subobject) vector. This element is itself a vector of type checkedVector<T>. It is again applied to the index operator, this time with the value j, which returns a reference to an object of type T, which is then assigned the value.
*/

```
    // create identity matrix
    Matrix<T>& I()
    {
        for (size_type i = 0; i < rows; i++)
            for (size_type j = 0; j < columns ; j++)
                operator[](i)[j] = (i==j) ? T(1) : T(0);
        return *this;
    }

    // here, mathematical operators could follow ...
}; // class Matrix
#endif
```

Further mathematical operations are omitted, because the point is not to describe a voluminous matrix class, but to show the flexible and varied way in which elements of the STL can be used for the construction of new data structures. In light of this, it is not easy to understand why the C++ standardization committee has chosen a numeric library which is not based on the STL, but is no easier to handle. `Matrix` has no dynamic data outside the base class subobject. Therefore, no special destructor, copy constructor, or an own assignment operator is needed. The corresponding operations of the base class subobject are carried out by the `checkedVector` class or its superclass `vector`.

To facilitate the output of a matrix, we can quickly formulate an output operator which displays a matrix together with its row numbers:

```
template<class T>
ostream& operator<<(ostream& s, const Matrix<T>& m )
{
    typedef Matrix<T>::size_type size_type;

    for (size_type i = 0; i < m.Rows(); i++)
    {
        s << endl << i <<" :   ";
        for (size_type j = 0; j < m.Columns(); j++)
            s << m[i][j] <<" ";
    }

    s <<endl;
    return s;
}
#endif     // file matrix
```

Further operations and functions can be built following this scheme. A sample application shows that applying the matrix class is extremely simple:

```
//  Excerpt from k9/a2/matmain.cpp
//  Examples for matrix as nested container
#include"matrix"

int main()
{
    Matrix<float> a(3,4);
    a.init(1.0);                    //  set all elements = 1
    cout << " Matrix a:\n" << a;

    /*
    The output of this simple program part is

    Matrix a:
    0 : 1 1 1 1
    1 : 1 1 1 1
    2 : 1 1 1 1


    Chaining of operations by returning the reference to the object is shown in the line
    */

    cout << "\n Identity matrix:\n" << a.I();
```

```
/*
```
As with a simple C array, the index operator can be chained, but with the advantage that the index is checked for limits:
```
*/
```

```
Matrix<float> b(4,5);
```

```
int i;
for (i=0; i< b.Rows(); i++)
    for (int j=0; j< b.Columns(); j++)
        b[i][j] = 1+i+(j+1)/10.;        //  index operator
```

```
cout << "\n Matrix b:\n" << b;
```

Output:

Matrix b:
0 : 1.1 1.2 1.3 1.4 1.5
1 : 2.1 2.2 2.3 2.4 2.5
2 : 3.1 3.2 3.3 3.4 3.5
3 : 4.1 4.2 4.3 4.4 4.5

Owing to the check in `operator[]()`, an assignment of the kind `b[100][99] = 1.0` leads to the erroneous program being aborted. Now, how do element access and index check work? Let us consider the following example:

```
b[3][2] = 1.0;
```

Access is very simple; both indices are checked. Explaining how it works, however, is not that easy. In order to see what happens, we now rewrite `b[3][2]` and resolve the function calls:

```
(b.checkedVector<checkedVector<float>>::operator[](3)).operator[](2)
```

The anonymous base class subobject is a `checkedVector` whose `[]` operator is called with the argument '3.' The elements of the vector are of type `checkedVector<float>`; that is, a reference to the third `checkedVector<float>` of the base class subobject is returned. If, for simplicity, we call the return value `X`, then

```
X.operator[](2)
```

is executed, which means no more than executing the index operation `operator[]()` for a `checkedVector<float>` with the result `float&`, that is, a reference to the sought element. In each of these index operator calls, the limits are checked in a uniform way. Apart from the equivalent definition for constant objects, there exists *only one* definition of the index operator!

9.2.2 **Three-dimensional matrix**

The scheme used for two-dimensional matrices can now easily be extended for matrices of arbitrary dimensions. Here, as a conclusion, an example for dimensions is given. What is a three-dimensional matrix whose elements are of type `int`? The question can easily be answered in analogy to the previous section. A three-dimensional `int` matrix *is a* `vector` of two-dimensional `int` matrices! The formulation of the *is a* relation as inheritance is shown by the `Matrix3D` class:

```
//  k9/a2/matrix3d
#ifndef matrix3d_t
#define matrix3d_t

#include"matrix"

/*  3D matrix as vector of 2D matrices*/
template<class T>
class Matrix3D : public checkedVector<Matrix<T> >
{
  protected:
    size_type rows,
              columns,
              zDim;         //  3rd dimension

  public:
    Matrix3D(size_type x = 0, size_type y = 0,
             size_type z = 0)
     : checkedVector<Matrix<T> >(x, Matrix<T>(y,z)),
       rows(x), columns(y), zDim(z)
    {}
    /*
```

The constructor initializes the base class subobject, a `checkedVector` of length `c`, whose elements are matrices. Each element of this vector is initialized with a (y,z) matrix.
```
    */

    size_type Rows() const { return rows;}

    size_type Columns() const { return columns;}

    size_type zDIM() const { return zDim;}

    /*
```
The other methods resemble those of the `Matrix` class. The `init()` method needs only one loop over the outermost dimension of the three-dimensional matrix, because `operator[](i)` is of type `&Matrix<T>` and therefore `Matrix::init()` is called for each two-dimensional submatrix:
```
    */

    void init(const T& Value)
    {
        for (size_type i = 0; i < rows; i++)
```

```
                    operator[](i).init(Value);
    }
    //  here, mathematical operators could follow ...
};
#endif
```

Since, like `Matrix`, `Matrix3D` has no dynamic data outside the base class subobject, no special destructor, copy constructor, or own assignment operator is needed. The corresponding operations for the base class subobject are carried out by the `checkedVector` class itself. The index operator is inherited. Three-dimensional matrices can be defined and used in a simple way, for example:

```
//  Excerpt from k9/a2/matmain.cpp
#include"matrix3d"

int main()
{
    Matrix3D<float> M3(2,4,5);

    for (i=0; i< M3.Rows(); i++)
        for (int j=0; j< M3.Columns(); j++)
            for (int k=0; k< M3.zDIM(); k++)
            //  chained index operator
                M3[i][j][k] = 10*(i+1)+(j+1)+(k+1)/10.;
    cout << "\n 3D matrix:\n";
    for (i=0; i< M3.Rows(); i++)
        cout << "Submatrix " << i
            << ":\n"
            << M3[i];
    //  ... and so on
```

Since for `M3[i]`, as with a two-dimensional matrix, the output operator is already defined, the output only needs one loop level. The result is:

3D matrix:
Submatrix 0:
0 : 11.1 11.2 11.3 11.4 11.5
1 : 12.1 12.2 12.3 12.4 12.5
2 : 13.1 13.2 13.3 13.4 13.5
3 : 14.1 14.2 14.3 14.4 14.5

Submatrix 1:
0 : 21.1 21.2 21.3 21.4 21.5
1 : 22.1 22.2 22.3 22.4 22.5
2 : 23.1 23.2 23.3 23.4 23.5
3 : 24.1 24.2 24.3 24.4 24.5

An index error can easily be provoked and is 'rewarded' with program abortion, no matter in which of the three dimensions the error occurs. The functioning of the index operator can be described analogous to the `Matrix` class, but there is one more chained operator call. Let us, for example, reformulate an access `M[1][2][3]`:

```
M.checkedVector<Matrix<float> >::
        operator[](1).operator[](2).operator[](3)}
```

The first operator returns something of type `Matrix<float>&` or, more precisely, a reference to the first element of the `checkedVector` subobject of `M`. For readability, we now abbreviate the returned 'something' with `Z` and obtain

```
Z.operator[](2).operator[](3)
```

We know that a reference is only another name (an alias), so that, in the end, `Z` represents a matrix of type `Matrix<float>`. We have already seen that a `Matrix<float>` is a vector of type `checkedVector<checkedVector<float> >`, from which `operator[]()` was inherited. This operator is now called with the argument '2' and returns a result of type `checkedVector<float>&` which, for brevity, will be called '`X`':

```
X.operator[](3)
```

The rest is easy when we think back to the end of Section 9.2.1. Here too, as with the `Matrix` class, access to an element is simpler than the underlying structure.

9.2.3 Generalization

The method for construction of classes for multi-dimensional matrices can easily be generalized: an n-dimensional matrix can always be considered as a vector of $(n-1)$-dimensional matrices, the existence of a class for $(n-1)$-dimensional matrices is assumed. In practice, however, four- and higher-dimensional matrices are seldom employed. The index operator, assignment operator, copy constructor, and destructor do not have to be written, they are provided by the `vector` class; whereas the constructor, the initialization methods, and the required mathematical operators still have to be written.

9.3 Matrices for different memory models

This section will show how matrices for different memory layouts can easily be implemented by means of the STL programming methodology. Here, for a change, the index operator is realized with round parentheses, that is, by overlaying the function operator `operator()()`, because otherwise, an auxiliary class would be needed.

Different memory models can play a role when matrices from or in FORTRAN programs are to be processed, for example when FORTRAN matrix subroutines are called from within a C++ program. The matrices of the previous section are vectors which, depending on the allocator, are not necessarily stored in memory one after the other. Each matrix of this section is, however, mapped to a linear address space, the reason for which a vector container is chosen as a basis. This address space shall be of fixed, unchangeable size, which is expressed by the name `fixMatrix` for the matrix class.

The position of a matrix element `X[i][j]` inside the vector container depends, however, on the kind of storage. Three cases will be discussed:

- C memory layout
  Storage occurs *row-wise*, that is, row 0 lies at the beginning of the container. It is followed by row 1, and so on. The linear order of the six elements M_{ij} of a matrix M with two rows and three columns is as follows:

  $$M_{00}, M_{01}, M_{02}, M_{10}, M_{11}, M_{12}, M_{20}, M_{21}, M_{22}$$

- FORTRAN memory layout
  In the FORTRAN programming language, storage occurs *column-wise*. Column 0 lies at the beginning of the container, followed by column 1, and so on. The linear order of the six elements of a matrix with two rows and three columns is therefore:

  $$M_{00}, M_{10}, M_{20}, M_{01}, M_{11}, M_{21}, M_{02}, M_{12}, M_{22}$$

- Memory layout for symmetric matrices
  A symmetric matrix M satisfies the condition $M = M^{\mathrm{T}}$. The raised T stands for 'transposed matrix' and means that $M_{ij} = M_{ji}$ holds for all elements. It follows that a symmetric matrix is quadratic, that is, it has as many rows as columns. Furthermore, it follows that by exploiting the symmetry, one needs only slightly more than half the memory, compared with an arbitrary square matrix. For example, for a symmetric matrix with three rows and three columns, it is sufficient to store the following six instead of nine elements:

  $$M_{00}, M_{01}, M_{02}, M_{11}, M_{12}, M_{22}$$

An element M_{10} must be searched for at position 1 of the container, where the associated element M_{01} is located.

To implement all three possibilities in a flexible way using the STL, a class `fixMatrix` is defined which provides the most important methods of a matrix, namely the constructor and methods for determining number of rows and columns, together with an operator for accessing individual elements, implemented here by means of the overloaded function operator:

```
template<class MatrixType>
class fixMatrix
{
  public:
    typedef MatrixType::ValueType ValueType;
    typedef MatrixType::IndexType IndexType;
    typedef MatrixType::ContainerType ContainerType;
```

```
fixMatrix(IndexType z, IndexType s)
: MType(z,s,C), C(MType.howmany())
{}

IndexType Rows() const { return MType.Rows(); }

IndexType Columns() const { return MType.Columns(); }

ValueType& operator()(IndexType z, IndexType s)
{
    return MType.where(z,s);
}
// ... further methods and operators

private:
    MatrixType MType;            // determines memory layout
    ContainerType C;             // container C
};
```

The kind of data storage is undefined; it is determined by the placeholder MatrixType which is supposed to supply the required properties. The requirements for MatrixType result from fixMatrix:

- Data types must be provided for the container, the elements to be stored, and the data type of the index.
- The method howmany() is used to determine the size of the container.
- The method where(), when applied to the object which determines the matrix type, returns a reference to the sought element.
- Rows() and Columns() methods return the corresponding number.

What is still needed is a proper formulation of the matrix types for the above-mentioned possibilities of element order. Properties common to all three types are formulated as a superclass which is parametrized with the value and index types. In this superclass, the container type is defined as vector.

```
#include<cassert>                // used in subclasses
#include<vector>

template<class ValueType, class IndexType>
class MatrixSuperClass
{
  public:
    // public type definitions
    typedef ValueType ValueType;
    typedef IndexType IndexType;
    // define vector as container type:
    typedef vector<ValueType> ContainerType;

    IndexType Rows()  const { return rows; }
```

```
     IndexType Columns() const { return columns;}

protected:
     MatrixSuperClass(IndexType z, IndexType s, ContainerType &Cont)
     : rows(z), columns(s), C(Cont)
     {}

     ContainerType &C;

private:
     IndexType rows, columns;
};
```

Because of the `protected` constructor, `MatrixSuperClass` is an abstract class. Outside the derived class, no single object of type `MatrixSuperClass` can be instantiated. With the same result, one could have declared the functions `howmany()` and `where()` common to all as purely virtual methods. The resulting advantage of a compulsory definition of an interface for all derived classes would, however, be overcome by the cost of an internal management table for virtual functions. This is the reason why this alternative is not implemented. Furthermore, it is neither usual nor necessary to access matrices via superclass pointers or references. See also the hint on page 204.

The reference to the container which is physically located in the `fixMatrix` class allows derived classes to access it. The following sections present the outstanding peculiarities.

9.3.1 C memory layout

In the following, r stands for 'row' and c for 'column.' `CMatrix` inherits, as described, from `MatrixSuperClass`.

```
template<class ValueType, class IndexType>
class CMatrix : public MatrixSuperClass<ValueType, IndexType>
{
  public:
    CMatrix(IndexType r, IndexType c, ContainerType& C)
    : MatrixSuperClass<ValueType,IndexType>(r,c,C)
    {}

    //  The size of the vector can easily be calculated:
    IndexType howmany() const
    {
        return Rows()*Columns();
    }

    /*
```

The position of an element with the indices r and c is calculated in the `where()` method. Checking of index limits in the vector container is only possible to a limited

extent, because the check could only be carried out against the entire length (Rows × Columns). Therefore, a checkedVector is not sufficient, and the index check is carried out directly inside the where() method.
```
  */
ValueType& where(IndexType r, IndexType c) const
{
   assert(r < Rows() && c < Columns());
   return C[r * Columns() + c];
}
}; // CMatrix

   /*
```

A simple program shows the application in which the fixMatrix class is parametrized with a CMatrix that, for example, assumes values of type float and an index type int.
```
   */
// Excerpt from k9/a3/divmat.cpp
int main()
{
   int i;
   fixMatrix<CMatrix<float,int> > MC(5,7);
   cout << " CMatrix " << endl;

   // fill rectangle
   for(i = 0; i < MC.Rows(); i++)
     for(int j = 0; j < MC.Columns(); j++)
         // application of operator()():
         MC(i,j) = i + float(j/100.);

   // display rectangle
   for(i = 0; i < MC.Rows(); i++)
   {
     for(int j = 0; j < MC.Columns(); j++)
        cout << MC(i,j) << ' ';
     cout << endl;
   }
```

9.3.2 FORTRAN memory layout

The class for FORTRAN memory layout differs only by the kind of address calculation:

```
template<class ValueType, class IndexType>
class FORTRANMatrix : public MatrixSuperClass<ValueType, IndexType>
{
  public:
    FORTRANMatrix(IndexType r, IndexType c, ContainerType& C)
```

```
            : MatrixSuperClass<ValueType, IndexType>(r,c,C)
            {}

            IndexType howmany() const
            {
                return Rows()*Columns();
            }

            /*
```
In the address calculation, rows and columns are exchanged in contrast to the `CMatrix` class:
```
            */

            ValueType& where(IndexType r, IndexType c) const
            {
                assert(r < Rows() && c < Columns());
                return C[c * Rows() + r];
            }
    };
```

A simple example shows the application:

```
fixMatrix<FortranMatrix<float, int> > MF(5,7);
//  and so on, as above in the C matrix layout
```

9.3.3 Memory layout for symmetric matrices

There are several differences between this and the two previous classes: the constructor checks equality of numbers of rows and columns; the address and memory requirement calculations also differ.

```
template<class ValueType, class IndexType>
class symmMatrix : public MatrixSuperClass<ValueType, IndexType>
{
  public:
    symmMatrix(IndexType r, IndexType c, ContainerType& C)
    : MatrixSuperClass<ValueType, IndexType>(r,c,C)
    {
        assert(r == c);     // matrix must be quadratic
    }

    // reduced memory consumption thanks to symmetry
    IndexType howmany() const
    {
        return Rows()*(Rows()+1)/2;
    }

    // the symmetry is exploited
    ValueType& where(IndexType r, IndexType c) const
```

```
     {
        assert(r < Rows() && c < Columns());
        if (r <= c) return C[r + c*(c+1)/2];
        else        return C[c + r*(r+1)/2];
     }
  };
```

In the example, only one half-triangle of the matrix, including the diagonal, is equipped with values; nothing further is provided by the available memory. The subsequent display shows the complete matrix as a square where, obviously, the elements mirrored at the diagonal are equal.

```
//  Example of a symmetric matrix
    int i;
    fixMatrix<symmMatrix<float, int> > MD(5,5);
    cout << "\n symmMatrix " << endl;

//  fill triangle
    for(i = 0; i < MD.Rows(); i++)
      for(int j = i; j < MD.Columns(); j++)
          MD(i,j) = i + float(j/100.);

//  output square
    for(i = 0; i < MD.Rows(); i++)
    {
       for(int j = 0; j < MD.Columns(); j++)
          cout << MD(i,j) << ' ';
       cout << endl;
    }
```

9.4 Sparse matrices

A sparse matrix is one whose elements are nearly all zero. Sparse matrices find their application in simulation calculations of large networks in which mainly neighboring nodes are connected to each other. Examples include road networks, local and world-wide computer networks, telephone networks, compound systems for supplying the population with electricity, gas, and water, and many more. A characteristic feature of all these networks is their large number of nodes.

A matrix M may, for example, represent a road network in which the element M_{ij} contains the distance in kilometers between town i and town j. By convention, a value $M_{ij} = 0, (i \neq j)$ shall mean that no direct connection between towns i and j exists. A direct connection in this sense is a connection that connects exactly two towns. A road that touches several towns is therefore not considered as a direct connection between starting point and end point, but as a compound connection composed of direct connections. When one-way roads or direction-dependent routes play a role, $M_{ij} \neq M_{ji}$ may hold, so that M is not necessarily symmetric.

Network nodes	Matrix elements	of which $\neq 0$	Occupation rate in %
100	10 000	500	5
1 000	1 000 000	5 000	0.5
10 000	100 000 000	50 000	0.05

Table 9.1 Typical occupation rate in sparse matrices.

The fact that towns are directly connected with neighboring towns, but that there are barely any *direct* connections between distant towns, leads to the effect that the elements near the matrix diagonal are mostly not equal to 0. The ratio of the number of elements not equal to 0 and the total number of elements in the matrix is called the occupation rate. The occupation rate of a high-voltage network for energy supply, for example, is approximately $\frac{5\pm2}{N}$, where N is the number of network nodes and N^2 the number of matrix elements.

With 100 nodes, the matrix would have 10 000 elements, of which only about 500 would be not equal 0 (= 5%). Table 9.1 gives an idea of the dependency of the occupation rate on the number of nodes. It is obvious that it would be a waste of main and mass storage to store all the zeros. Therefore, typically only the non-zero elements are stored, together with an index pair (i, j) for identification.

Which abstract data type is best suited for storage of a sparse matrix? Imagine a column as a map which via a `long` index returns a `double` value. A matrix could then be a map which via a `long` index returns a row. Thus, a sparse matrix of double elements could be described quite simply as:

```
//  k9/a4/sparse1.cpp
#include<map>
#include<iostream>

//  matrix declaration
typedef map<long, double> doubleRow;
typedef map<long, doubleRow> SparseMatrix;

    /*
```
The first index operator applied to a `SparseMatrix` returns a row on which the second index operator is applied, as shown in the program:
```
    */
int main()
{
    SparseMatrix M;              //  see declaration above
    M[1][1] = 1.0;
    M[1000000][1000000] = 123456.7890;
    cout.setf(ios::fixed);
    cout.precision(6);

    cout << M[1][1] << endl;                          //  1.000 000
```

```
cout << M[1000000][1000000] << endl;        //  123 456.789 000
cout << "M.size() :" << M.size() << endl;    //  2

/*
```

Unfortunately, this very simple form of a sparse matrix has a couple of 'minor blemishes.' Access to a not yet defined element creates a new one:

```
*/

cout << M[0][0] << endl;
cout << "M.size() :" << M.size() << endl;    //  3

/*
```

This is not desirable, since the point is *saving* storage space. The next flaw is the uncontrolled access to unwanted positions, once again with the effect of generating additional elements:

```
*/

cout << M[-1][0] << endl;                    //  index error
cout << "M.size() :" << M.size() << endl;    //  4
}
```

The maximum index cannot be defined anyway, because it is given by the number range of long. It would, however, be desirable to have a matrix which did not have these properties and which ensured that elements of value 0 did not contribute to memory consumption. Therefore, a different approach is presented which, however, requires more effort.

Here, access to the elements is carried out in a matrix via a pair of indices – row and column. Thus, an index pair constitutes the key for which the value of the matrix element is sought. This is a typical application of an associative container; thus, the classes map of the STL and HMap of Chapter 7 would be suitable, but in a different way than described above.

The following solution works with both kinds of map container, controlled by a compiler switch, but the second container is faster. Obviously, accessing an element of an associative container is slower when compared to a simple C array. This is the price that has to be paid for being able, for example, to represent a 1 000 000 000 × 1 000 000 000 matrix on a small PC and calculate with it, provided that the occupation rate is very, very small.

An example of the usage of a sparse matrix is shown in the following program segment in which a matrix with ten million rows and columns, that is, 10^{14} (fictitious) elements is defined. Control of whether the underlying container is to be taken from the STL is exercised by the switch STL_map which takes effect in the file sparmat. If the line is commented out using //, the HMap container of Chapter 7 is used.

```
//  k9/a4/main.cpp
#include<iostream>
//  #define STL_map
#include"sparmat"   //  class sparseMatrix, see below

//  example of a very big sparse matrix
```

```
int main()
{
    //  ValueType double, IndexType long
    sparseMatrix<double, long> M(10000000,10000000);

    //  Documentation
    cout << "matrix with "
         << M.Rows()                        //  10000000
         << " rows and "
         << M.Columns()                     //  10000000
         << " columns" << endl;

    //  occupy some elements
    M[999998][777777]    = 999998.7777770;
    M[1][8035354]        = 123456789.33970;
    M[1002336][0]        = 444444444.1111;
    M[5000000][4900123]  = 0.00000027251;

    //  display of two elements
    cout.setf(ios::fixed|ios::showpoint);
    cout.precision(8);
    cout << "M[1002336][0]         = "
         << M[1002336][0]        << endl;

    cout << "M[5000000][4900123] = "
         << M[5000000][4900123]  << endl;
```

The output is

M[1002336][0]   = 444444444.11110002
M[5000000][4900123]   = 0.00000027

The small deviations with respect to the above assignments result from formatting with `precision(8)`. Besides row and column number, it is also possible to output the number of non-zero elements:

```
cout << "Number of non-zero elements = "
     << M.size() << endl;

cout << "max. number of non-zero elements = "
     << M.max_size() << endl;
```

To satisfy the need to output all non-zero elements of the sparse matrix for display or storage, the `sparseMatrix` class should provide forward iterators:

```
cout << "Output all non-zero elements via iterators\n";
sparseMatrix<double, long>::iterator
        temp = M.begin();

while(temp != M.end())
{
    cout << "M["   << M.Index1(temp)    // i
```

```
                    << "][" << M.Index2(temp)    // j
                    << "] = " << M.Value(temp)    // value
                    << endl;
             ++temp;
        }
        // ...
```

The above lines lead to the following display

Output all non-zero elements via iterators
M[1][8035354] = 123456789.33970000
M[5000000][4900123] = 0.00000027
M[1002336][0] = 444444444.11110002
  ⋮

The output is only ordered when the map container of the STL is chosen. In the above example, this is obviously not the case.

9.4.1 Index operator and assignment

Because of the selective storage of matrix elements, some peculiarities must be considered during the design, particularly of the index and assignment operators. A matrix element can stand both on the left-hand and on the right-hand side of an assignment. In both cases, it must be taken into account that the element might not yet exist in the container, that is, if it has not yet been assigned a value not equal to zero. Three cases must be distinguished (the matrix elements are to be of type double):

1. Matrix element as lvalue: M[i][j] = 1.23;
   In order to analyze it, the instruction must be broken down into its function parts:

   ```
   sparseMatrix::operator[](i).operator[](j).operator=(1.23);
   ```

   The first index operator checks the line index i for maintaining the limits, the second operator checks the column index j. Furthermore, the second index operator must supply an object that possesses an assignment operator to enter a double value into the associative container together with the indices. This object must have available all necessary information. When the double value is zero, however, *no* entry is to be made, but the element M[i][j] is to be deleted, provided it already exists.

   As usual in C++, some auxiliary classes are invented for the solution of this problem. The first class, named Aux, is the return type of the first index operator. The second index operator, which checks the column number, is the index operator of the Aux class. It returns an object of type MatrixElement, the second auxiliary class. The assignment operator of this object caters for the rest, as illustrated by the following lines:

$$\underbrace{\text{sparseMatrix::operator[](i)}}.\text{operator[](j).operator=(1.23);}$$

$$\underbrace{\text{Aux::operator[](j)}}.\text{operator=(1.23);}$$

$$\underbrace{\text{MatrixElement::operator=(1.23);}}$$

On the surface, this highly flexible method of proceeding may seem costly. However, this cost must be compared with the insertion and search processes of the underlying container; then, the balance looks significantly better. Substituting the usual index operator `operator[]()` with the function operator `operator()()` brings no advantage.

2. Matrix element as rvalue: `double x = M[i][j];`
   In addition, the `MatrixElement` class needs an operator which converts an object of type `MatrixElement` into the appropriate value type, in this case `double`.

3. Matrix element on both sides: `M1[n][m] = M2[i][j];`, where `M1` and `M2` may be identical.
   The `MatrixElement` class needs a second assignment operator with the argument `const MatrixElement&`.

9.4.2 Hash function for index pairs

In this section, the file *sparmat* is presented which contains the classes and auxiliary classes discussed above. It is included via `#include` into a program which is designed to work with sparse matrices (see example on page 220). The file begins with some preprocessor directives for determining the underlying implementation.

```
//  File sparmat, templates for sparse matrices
#ifndef sparsematrix
#define sparsematrix

//  selection of implementation
#ifdef STL_map              //  defined in main()
#include<map>
#include<assert>
#else
#include<hmap>

/*
```

If at this point the HMap container of Chapter 7 is chosen, a function for calculating the hash table addresses is needed. As opposed to the hash functions described up to now, not just one value, but two are used for the calculation. Therefore, the function operator of the `PairHashFun` class takes a pair as argument. The address calculation itself is simple, but sufficient for the examples in this book.

```
*/

template<class IndexType>  //  int, long or unsigned
class PairHashFun
{
  public:
```

```
      PairHashFun(long prime=65537) //  another prime number is possible
      //  for example, 2111 for smaller matrices

  : tabSize(prime)
  {}

  //  Address calculation with two values
  long operator()(const pair<IndexType, IndexType>& p) const
  {
      return (p.first + p.second) % tabSize;
  }

  long tableSize() const
  {
      return tabSize;
  }

private:
  long tabSize;
};
#endif
```

9.4.3 Class MatrixElement

An element stored in a container has a determined type denoted in the STL by
value_type. In this case, the value_type is a pair consisting of the key and the
associated value, where the key itself is a pair of two indices. In the class described
below, a pair of indices is defined as type IndexPair.

```
template<class ValueType, class IndexType, class ContainerType>
class MatrixElement
{
  private:
    ContainerType& C;
    ContainerType::iterator I;
    IndexType row, column;

  public:
    typedef pair<IndexType, IndexType> IndexPair;
    typedef MatrixElement<ValueType, IndexType,
                          ContainerType>&  Reference;

    MatrixElement(ContainerType& Cont, IndexType r, IndexType c)
    : C(Cont), I(C.find(IndexPair(r,c))),
      row(r), column(c)
    {}

    /*
```

The constructor initializes the private variables with all information that is needed.

(Normally, the private objects are placed at the end of a class definition. For reasons of contextual consistency, this rule is sometimes not observed.) The container itself is located in the `sparseMatrix` class; here, the reference to it is entered. If the passed indices for row and column belong to an element not yet stored in the container, the iterator has the value `C.end()`.
`*/`

```
ValueType asValue() const
{
    if(I == C.end())
        return ValueType(0);
    else
        return (*I).second;
}

operator ValueType () const    // type conversion operator
{
    return asValue();
}

/*
```

According to the definition of the sparse matrix, 0 is returned if the element is not present in the container. Otherwise, the result is the second part of the object of type `value_type` stored in the container. The type conversion operator fulfils the requirements of point 2 on page 223. The assignment operator (see point 1 on page 222) is structured in a slightly more complicated way.
`*/`

```
Reference operator=(const ValueType& x)
{
    if(x != ValueType(0))          //  not equal to 0?
    {
        /*
        If the element does not yet exist, it is put, together with the indices, into an
        object of type value_type and inserted with insert():
        */
        if(I == C.end())
        {
            assert(C.size() < C.max_size());
            I = (C.insert(ContainerType::value_type(
                    IndexPair(row,column), x))
                ).first;
        }
        else (*I).second = x;
    }
    /*
    insert() returns a pair whose first part is an iterator pointing to the inserted
```

object. The second part is of type `bool` and indicates whether the insertion took place because no element with this key existed. This is, however, not evaluated here because, due to the precondition (`I == C.end()`), the second part must always have the value `true`. If, instead, the element already exists, the value is entered into the second part of the `value_type` object.

If the value is equal to 0, then to save space the element is deleted if it existed.
```
        */

        else                    //  x = 0
           if(I != C.end())
           {
               C.erase(I);
               I = C.end();
           }
        return *this;
    }

    /*
```
Point 3 on page 223 requires an assignment operator which in turn requires a reference to an object of type `MatrixElement`. When both the left- and right-hand sides are identical, nothing has to happen. Otherwise, as above, it has to be checked whether the value of the right-hand element is 0 or not. The resulting behavior is described together with the above assignment operator, so that here it is simply called:
```
    */

    Reference operator=(const Reference rhs)
    {
        if(this != &rhs)        //  not identical?
        {
            return operator=(rhs.asValue());   //  see above
        }
        return *this;

    }
};   //  class MatrixElement
```

9.4.4 Class sparseMatrix

Depending on the selected implementation, the data types for the container and other aspects are set:

```
template<class ValueType, class IndexType>
class sparseMatrix
{
    public:
        typedef pair<IndexType, IndexType> IndexPair;

    /*
```

The switch STL_map controls the compilation:
```
*/

#ifdef STL_map
      typedef map<IndexPair, ValueType,
                  less<IndexPair> >          ContainerType;
#else
      typedef HMap<IndexPair, ValueType,
                   PairHashFun<IndexType> > ContainerType;
#endif

      typedef MatrixElement<ValueType, IndexType,
                            ContainerType> MatrixElement;
   public:
      typedef IndexType size_type;

      /*
```
The constructor initializes only the row and column information. The container is created by its standard constructor, where in the case of hash implementation, the size of the container is given by the hash function object of type PairHashFun (see typedef above).
```
      */

   private:
      size_type rows, columns;
      ContainerType C;
   public:
      sparseMatrix(size_type r, size_type c)
      : rows(r), columns(c)
      {}

      /*
```
The following list of methods, besides determining the number of rows and columns, provides the common container methods, which are not discussed in detail.
```
      */

   size_type Rows()   const { return rows;}
   size_type Columns() const { return columns;}

   //  usual container type definitions
   typedef ContainerType::iterator iterator;
   typedef ContainerType::const_iterator const_iterator;

   //  usual container functions
   size_type size()        const { return C.size();}
   size_type max_size()    const { return C.max_size();}

   iterator begin()             { return C.begin();}
   iterator end()               { return C.end();}
```

```
const_iterator begin() const { return C.begin();}
const_iterator end()   const { return C.end();}

void clear() { C.clear();}

  /*
  The index operator of the sparseMatrix class returns the auxiliary object described
  on page 222, whose class is defined as nested inside sparseMatrix.
  */

Aux operator[](size_type r)
{
   assert(r >= 0 && r < rows);
   return Aux(r, columns, C);
}

class Aux
{
  public:
    Aux(size_type r, size_type maxs, ContainerType& Cont)
    : Row(r), maxColumns(maxs), C(Cont)
    {}

    /*
    After checking the number of columns, the index operator of Aux returns a ma-
    trix element which is equipped with all the necessary information to carry out a
    successful assignment.
    */

    MatrixElement operator[](size_type c)
    {
        assert(c >= 0 && c < maxColumns);
        return MatrixElement(C, Row, c);
    }

  private:
    size_type Row, maxColumns;
    ContainerType& C;
};
```

/*
Up to this point, from a functionality point of view, the sparseMatrix class is suffi-
ciently equipped. However, to avoid writing such horrible things as '(*I).first.first'
for accessing the elements, some of the following auxiliary functions determine the
indices and associated values of an iterator in a more readable way. Their application
can be seen in the example on page 221.
*/

```
size_type Index1(iterator& I) const
{
    return (*I).first.first;
}

size_type Index2(iterator& I) const
{
    return (*I).first.second;
}

ValueType Value(iterator& I) const
{
    return (*I).second;
}
};          //  class sparseMatrix
#endif    //  file sparmat
```

From the point of view of the information needed in the auxiliary functions, it is not necessary to formulate these functions as element functions. It would also be possible to create global template definitions. These, however, would need an extra parameter to determine the type of the index or the values, thus the first way is followed.

Access time/μs

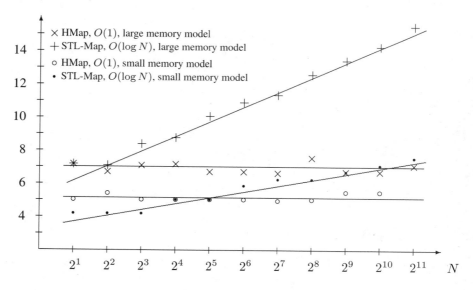

Figure 9.1 Access times for elements of a sparse matrix (measured on Pentium 90 and with the Borland C++ compiler 4.5 under MS-DOS).

9.4.5 **Run time measurements**

Owing to its more complicated storage, access to an element of a sparse matrix takes significantly longer than access to elements of the matrices discussed in the previous sections.

Figure 9.1 shows how the access time to a matrix element depends on the number N of elements already in the container. The access time depends on the kind of computer, the operating system, and the compiler and its settings.

The continuous lines show the trend. The horizontal lines of nearly constant access time apply to the implementation of the `sparseMatrix` class with an HMap container; the ascending lines show the linear dependency of the access time from the logarithm of the number N of already stored elements of the sorted map container of the STL.

The choice of memory is not insignificant, as can be seen from the figure. The reason for the different measured values is that because of the 'longer' pointers, the CPU has more work to do. In the small memory model, a `ptrdiff_t` object occupies 2 bytes; in the large or huge models, 4 bytes. UNIX users are lucky enough not to have to worry about memory models.

External sorting

10

Summary: External sorting is needed if a file cannot be sorted in memory because available memory is too small or the file is too large, and so mass storage must be used as a medium for sorting. The elements of the STL are used to construct an iterator for sorted subsequences which is used for external sorting. A priority queue can accelerate the sorting process.

To start with, the following questions should be answered to establish whether external sorting can be avoided:

- Is the entire available RAM used as virtual memory without having to swap memory pages?

- Can keys and an index file be used? For example, an address file could be sorted by using only the names for sorting. Then, the index file contains only the sorted names and, for each name, a pointer to the location of the complete address file, where all other information, such as street and town, can be found.

Copy processes in mass storage are very expensive compared to copy processes in RAM. When memory access takes 50 nanoseconds, and hard disk access 10 milliseconds, then the mass storage is slower by a factor of 200 000, if no buffer is used. When all else fails, it could be helpful to divide the problem into smaller subproblems:

1. The large file of N elements is split into n small files of approximately equal size, where n is chosen in such a way that the small file fits into memory.
2. All small files are sorted separately.
3. The sorted files are merged back into one large file. Section 5.5.4 describes how two sorted subsequences are merged into one single sorted sequence.

10.1 External sorting by merging

Step 3 above hardly consumes any memory because only n elements are read and compared. However, the operating system creates a buffer for each open file, which can amount to a considerable quantity of memory. Frequently, the maximum number of open files allowed is also insufficient for this purpose.

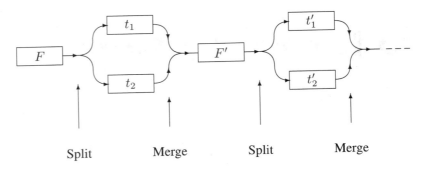

Figure 10.1   External sorting with two runs shown.

Therefore, the process is modified: the large file F is only split into two temporary auxiliary files t_1 and t_2 which are again put together in a large file with a higher degree of sorting. The files F, F', and so on are the same; they are reused. The same applies to t_1 and t_2. Therefore, someone with a little foresight creates a backup copy of F.

This process is repeated with the new file until sorting is achieved (see Figure 10.1). Thus, you only need a total of three files. You could, however, take more than two files for splitting. The only important point is that the temporary files contain sorted subsequences which are merged into each other. A sorted subsequence is also called *run*.

As an example, an unsorted sequence of 17 numbers is to be sorted in ascending order into a file. The numbers are:

F :   13 44 7 3 3 9 99 37 61 71 2 6 8 11 14 15 1

This sequence is split into the auxiliary files in such a way that sorted subsequences are maintained. These are shown by way of square brackets:

F :   [13 44] [7] [3 3 9 99] [37 61 71] [2 6 8 11 14 15] [1]

Splitting yields:

t_1 :   [13 44] [3 3 9 99] [2 6 8 11 14 15]
t_2 :   [7] [37 61 71] [1]

The first two subsequences of t_2 can be considered as *one* sorted subsequence:

F :   [13 44] [7] [3 3 9 99] [37 61 71] [2 6 8 11 14 15] [1]
t_1 :   [13 44] [3 3 9 99] [2 6 8 11 14 15]
t_2 :   [7 37 61 71] [1]

Now, the subsequences of the auxiliary files are merged, resulting in the new file F. Merging is carried out in the sense of Section 5.5.4: when one subsequence is exhausted, the remainder of the other subsequence is copied.

merge:
F :   [7 13 37 44 61 71] [1 3 3 9 99] [2 6 8 11 14 15]

Further split and merge operations yield:

<pre>
    split:
t₁ :   [7 13 37 44 61 71] [2 6 8 11 14 15]
t₂ :   [1 3 3 9 99]
    merge:
F :   [1 3 3 7 9 13 37 44 61 71 99] [2 6 8 11 14 15]
    split:
t₁ :   [1 3 3 7 9 13 37 44 61 71 99]
t₂ :   [2 6 8 11 14 15]
    merge:
F :   [1 2 3 3 6 7 8 9 11 13 14 15 37 44 61 71 99]
</pre>

Thus, only three runs with one split and one merge process each are needed. A closer analysis shows that for a file of N elements, a total of about $\log_2 N - 1$ runs is needed. Each run means N copy processes (read + write), so that the total cost is $O(N \log N)$. Later, we will see how we can accelerate this process. Those who find the description too brief should refer to the 'essential' Wirth (1979).

Thus, we have three files, which can also be magnetic tapes, and two passes, namely splitting and merging. Therefore, the method is called 3-way 2-pass sort-merge. When we talk about merging and tapes, it is understood that only sequential access to individual elements is possible. An algorithm for external sorting must take this into account.

The following `main()` program calls a function for external sorting. The file is arbitrarily called *random.dat* and contains numbers of type `long`.

```
//  k10/extsort.cpp    Sorting of a large file
#include"extsort.t"           //  see below

int main()
{
//  less<long> Comparison;         // descending
    greater<long> Comparison;                  //  ascending
    istream_iterator<long, ptrdiff_t> suitable_iterator;

    cout << externalSorting(
                suitable_iterator,    //  type of file
                "random.dat",         //  file name
                "\n",                 //  separator
                Comparison)           //  sorting criterion
            << " sorting runs" << endl;
}
```

The function returns the number of necessary runs. Since no information on the type of elements can be derived from the file name, a suitable iterator is passed whose type contains the necessary information. The separator string is inserted between two elements which are written to a temporary file, because this example uses the >> operator for input and the << operator for output. The comparison object determines the sorting criterion. The components needed for this algorithm are described individually.

One important component is an iterator that works on a stream and recognizes subsequences. This iterator will be called `SubsequenceIterator`. It inherits from the class `istream_iterator` and uses its `protected` variables, which were described on page 40. The subsequence iterator behaves in the same way as an `istream_iterator`, but in addition determines whether the elements of the stream are sorted according to the sorting criterion `comp`. This requires a comparison between a read object and the previous one which here is a private variable named `previousValue`.

```
//  Template classes and functions for sorting of large files
//  k10/extsort.t
#ifndef extsort_t
#define extsort_t

#include<fstream>
#include<algorithm>
#include<iterator>
using namespace std;

template<class T, class Distance, class Compare>
class SubsequenceIterator : public istream_iterator<T, Distance>
{
  public:
    SubsequenceIterator()
    : comp(Compare())
    {}


    SubsequenceIterator(istream& is, Compare& c)
    : istream_iterator<T, Distance>(is),
      comp(c), previousValue(value), sorted_(true)
    {}

    /*
```

`previousValue` can be initialized with `value`, because the initialization of the base class subobject has already read a value. The following `++` operators now ensure that the end of a sorted subsequence is recognized by setting the private variable `sorted_`. A subsequence is in any case also closed when the stream is terminated; therefore, `end_marker` is checked. The `end_marker` attribute is inherited from the `istream_iterator` class (see page 41).

It is important to write `!comp(previousValue, value)` and not `comp(value, previousValue)`. The second notation would erroneously already signal the end of a subsequence when two *equal* elements follow each other. You can easily imagine this by assuming, for example, `Compare = less<int>`.

```
    */
```

```
        SubsequenceIterator& operator++()
        {
            istream_iterator<T, Distance>::operator++();
            sorted_ = !comp(previousValue, value) && end_marker;
            previousValue = value;
            return *this;
        }

        SubsequenceIterator operator++(int)
        {
            SubsequenceIterator tmp = *this;
            operator++();
            return tmp;
        }

        bool sorted() const { return sorted_;}
        /*
```
When the end of a subsequence is recognized, the internal flag for this can be reset with nextSubsequence() to process the next subsequence:
```
        */

        void nextSubsequence()
        {
            sorted_ = end_marker;
        }

        Compare Compareobject() const { return comp;}
        /*
```
Compareobject() supplies a copy of the internal comp object. In addition to the inherited variables, the following ones are needed:
```
        */
    private:
        Compare comp;
        T previousValue;
        bool sorted_;
};
```

Next, the function externalSorting() is described, which constitutes the user interface in main(). This function calls an overloaded function of the same name which differs by two pointers in the parameter list. These pointers are exclusively used to determine the type of the values contained in the file and the suitable distance type, following the method described in Section 3.4.1. This detour need not be followed, but it does allow the user of the function to define a narrower interface.

```
template<class IstreamIterator,    // template for type determination
         class Compare>
int externalSorting(IstreamIterator& Input,
```

```
                              char *Filename,
                              char *Sep,
                              Compare& comp)
{
    return externalSorting(Filename, Sep, comp,
             value_type(Input), distance_type(Input));
}

template<class Compare, class T, class Distance>
int externalSorting(char *SortFile,
                              char *Separator,
                              Compare& comp,
                              T*, Distance*)
{
    bool sorted = false;

    // arbitrary names for auxiliary files
    char *TempFile1 = "esort001.tmp",
         *TempFile2 = "esort002.tmp";

    int Run = 0;            // number of sort-merge cycles
    do
    {
        ifstream Input(SortFile);
        SubsequenceIterator<T, Distance, Compare>
                    FileIterator(Input, comp);
```

/*
The file to be sorted must exist. A suitable subsequence iterator for reading is passed to the function split() which writes sorted subsequences of the main file F, as it was called earlier, into the two auxiliary files t_1 and t_2.
*/

```
        split(FileIterator, TempFile1, TempFile2, sorted);
        Input.close();
```

/*
During this process, split() determines whether F is already sorted. Only if this is not the case are further steps necessary. These steps consist in generating subsequence iterators for the function mergeSubsequences() and opening the output file F'. Then, the subsequences are merged.
*/

```
        if(!sorted)
        {
            // prepare for merging
            ifstream Source1(TempFile1);
            ifstream Source2(TempFile2);
```

```
SubsequenceIterator<T, Distance, Compare>
                                I1(Source1, comp);
SubsequenceIterator<T, Distance, Compare>
                                I2(Source2, comp);
SubsequenceIterator<T, Distance, Compare> End;

//  open SortFile for writing
ofstream Output(SortFile);
ostream_iterator<T> Result(Output, Separator);

mergeSubsequences(I1, End, I2, End, Result, comp);
++Run;
        }
    } while(!sorted);
    return Run;
}
```

The function `mergeSubsequences()` has the same interface as the standard function `merge()` (see Section 5.5.4). `merge()` cannot be used because `merge()` extracts one element at a time via the input iterators according to `comp`, but ignores the subsequence structure.

The `split()` function is also called indirectly via the type derivation template, because the iterators of the output streams that are written to must know the type of the elements.

```
//  type derivation template.
//  TF_iterator is a placeholder for the data type of a subsequence iterator.
template<class TF_iterator>
void split(TF_iterator& Input,
            const char *Filename1,
            const char *Filename2,
            bool& sorted)
{
    split(Input, Filename1, Filename2, sorted,
          value_type(Input));
}

template<class TF_iterator, class T>
void split(TF_iterator& Input,
            const char *Filename1,
            const char *Filename2,
            bool& sorted,
            T*)
{
    ofstream Target1(Filename1);
    ofstream Target2(Filename2);

    ostream_iterator<T> Output1(Target1, "\n");
```

```
   ostream_iterator<T> Output2(Target2, "\n");
   TF_iterator End;

   /*
```

The functioning is quite simple: as long as the input stream supplies a sorted subsequence, all data is written to an output stream. Once the end of a sorted subsequence is reached, `flipflop` is used to switch to the other output stream. In order to save the caller unnecessary work, the variable `sorted` remembers whether there has been any violation of the sorting order in the input stream.

```
   */

   sorted = true;
   bool flipflop = true;

   while(Input != End)
   {
      while(Input.sorted())
         if(flipflop) *Output1++ =  *Input++;
         else         *Output2++ =  *Input++;

      if(Input != End)
      {
         sorted = false;
         flipflop = !flipflop;
         Input.nextSubsequence();
      }
   }
}

/*
```

After splitting a file into two temporary auxiliary files, the file is rebuilt on a 'higher sorting level' by merging the auxiliary files.

```
*/

template <class SubsequenceIterator, class OutputIterator,
          class Compare>
void mergeSubsequences(SubsequenceIterator first1,
                       SubsequenceIterator last1,
                       SubsequenceIterator first2,
                       SubsequenceIterator last2,
                       OutputIterator result,
                       Compare& comp)

{
   // as long as both the auxiliary files are not exhausted
   while (first1 != last1 && first2 != last2)
   {
      // merge sorted subsequences
      while(first1.sorted() && first2.sorted())
```

```
if (comp(*first1, *first2))
    *result++ = *first2++;
else
    *result++ = *first1++;
```

```
//  At this point, (at least) one of the subsequences is terminated.
//  Now copy the rest of the other subsequence:
while(first1.sorted()) *result++ = *first1++;
while(first2.sorted()) *result++ = *first2++;
```

```
//  Process the next subsequence in both auxiliary files,
//  provided there is one:
first1.nextSubsequence();
first2.nextSubsequence();
}
```

```
//  At least one of the temporary files is exhausted.
//  Copy the rest of the other one:
copy(first1, last1, result);
copy(first2, last2, result);
}
```

10.2 External sorting with accelerator

External sorting is designed only for sorting processes where the internal memory of the computer is not sufficient. However, (almost) no memory was used in the above program. The best solution for external sorting is to employ as much internal memory as possible.

An ideal tool for this purpose is the priority queue presented in Section 4.3. It has the property of putting all incoming elements into the correct position, so that when one element is removed, the one with the highest priority according to the sorting criterion is immediately available, for example, the greatest element.

If the priority queue can take N_p elements, then for all input files F with N_p or less elements, only one sorting run is needed. For larger input files, the priority queue allows longer sorted subsequences, so that fewer runs are needed. It is evident that the effect of a priority queue diminishes when the subsequences to be processed are longer than the size of the priority queue. For this reason, the effect of a priority queue is that in the first run, subsequences of a length $\geq N_p$ are already generated, thus saving $(\log_2 N_p - 1)$ runs. At least one run is needed.

The complexity of external sorting does not change when a priority queue is employed. Since, however, copy operations to mass storage are time-consuming, the saving of constant $(\log_2 N_p - 1)$ runs is very desirable.

When placing and using the priority queue in the data flow, care must be taken not to use it directly as a sorting filter. The reason for this is that the initial fast generation of long subsequences would become impossible.

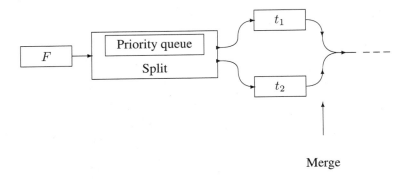

Figure 10.2   External sorting with priority queue.

Let us assume that the number of elements in a file substantially exceeds N_p and that the sorting criterion is to generate a descending sequence, that is, the greatest element is removed from the priority queue. This removal frees a place, and the next element is inserted into the priority queue. This element, however, can be greater than the element just removed, so that the subsequence of removed elements is immediately terminated.

Figure 10.2 shows that to achieve the longest possible subsequences, the priority queue is used inside the splitting process.

The decisive factor is that the read elements are not simply passed sorted. Instead, reading of an element greater than the one that stands at the top of the priority queue must lead to the whole priority queue being emptied. Only then can the new element be inserted. As can be seen from the figure, this involves the `split()` function whose modified variation is shown as a conclusion. `#include<algorithm>` can now be omitted, since `copy()` is no longer used. Instead,

```
#include<vector>
// #include<stack>   contains priority_queue after ISO96
#include<queue>   //  ISO97
```

are required if the priority queue is to be implemented with a vector. Since the priority queue must know not only the data type of the elements, but also the sorting criterion, the function is called with the known template for type derivation with a `Compare` parameter. The parameter is the `comp` object of the passed subsequence iterator.

```
template<class TF_iterator>    //  type derivation template
void split(TF_iterator& Input,
             const char *Filename1,
             const char *Filename2,
             bool& sorted)
{
    split(Input, Filename1, Filename2, sorted,
          value_type(Input),
```

```
                    Input.Compareobject());
}
```

In the example, the size of the priority queue is specified as 30 000: depending on the computer type, memory size, and operating system, it should, on the one hand, be set as large as possible; on the other hand, it should still be small enough not to need memory swapping to hard disk.

Unfortunately, there is no element function `capacity()` for the priority queue of the STL, which would return the capacity of the underlying container. It would be sensible to check `capacity()`, instead of using `maxSize`. Since the container in the priority queue is `protected`, one could write one's own priority queue class which inherits from the standard priority queue and provides this function (which has not happened here). Unfortunately, such a function is not easy to write, because it strongly depends on the operating system.

How much space can be allocated to the program depends on the current usage of the computer by other users and programs, and can therefore only be determined at a given time. Information on the amount of available memory can be given only by the operating system. Therefore, it is best to allocate the program a guaranteed amount of memory at the call.

```
template<class TF_iterator, class T, class Compare>
void split(TF_iterator& Input,
           const char *Filename1,
           const char *Filename2,
           bool& sorted,
           T*, Compare comp)
{
    const size_t maxSize = 30000; // maximize, see text

    // The size of the priority queue is dynamically increased
    // up to the given limit (see below)
    priority_queue<T, vector<T>, Compare > PQ(comp);

    ofstream Target1(Filename1);
    ofstream Target2(Filename2);
    ostream_iterator<T> Output1(Target1, "\n");
    ostream_iterator<T> Output2(Target2, "\n");
    TF_iterator End;

    sorted = true;
    bool flipflop;              // for switching the output

    while(Input != End)
    {
        // fill priority queue
        while(Input != End && PQ.size() < maxSize)
        {
            if(!Input.sorted())
                sorted = false;
```

```
        PQ.push(*Input++);
    }

    while(!PQ.empty())
    {
        //  Write to output files. Selection of file
        //  by way of the variable flipflop
        if(flipflop) *Output1++ =  PQ.top();
        else         *Output2++ =  PQ.top();

        //  create space and fill if needed
        PQ.pop();
        if(Input != End)
        {
          if(!Input.sorted())
              sorted = false;

          //  The next element is inserted only if it does not
          //  violate the subsequence ordering.
          if(!comp(PQ.top(), *Input))
              PQ.push(*Input++);
        }
    }

    //  The priority queue is now empty; the sorted sequence
    //  output is terminated. For outputting the next sorted
    //  sequence we switch to the next channel.
    flipflop = !flipflop;
  }
}
```

A final hint: the last run generates a completely sorted file. This is, however, determined only by the following split, where one of the temporary files is empty and the other one is identical to the result file. The above algorithm could be optimized, so that the last split is no longer needed. For this, it would be necessary to determine during merging whether the result is sorted. One method of achieving this is to construct a more 'intelligent' output iterator `result` which determines this information.

Graphs

11

Summary: *Graphs and their associated algorithms are widely used for the process-*
ing of problems in information science. A common problem for which graphs are
suited is finding the shortest path between two given points. Another problem is cal-
culating a minimal path that passes a number of points. This is an interesting problem
for a carrier who has to deliver goods to a series of customers in different towns. An-
other typical application is the maximization of message or material throughput in
a network. The components of the STL allow the construction of graphs for a multi-
tude of applications and of a library of suitable fast algorithms. This chapter deals
with the structure of a graph class on the basis of STL components and a selection of
algorithms (shortest paths, topological sorting).

A graph consists of a set of vertices and edges that connect two vertices. If an edge
is assigned a direction, the graph is called *directed*, otherwise it is undirected. Figure 11.1 shows one directed and one undirected graph with five vertices and five
edges each.

If an edge leads from a vertex A to a vertex B, A is called the *predecessor* of
B and B is called the *successor* of A. A sequence of vertices e_1, e_2, ..., e_k is called a
path if each vertex e_j with $j = 2$, ..., k is successor of vertex e_{j-1}.

There are different ways to represent a graph. The most frequently used repre-
sentations are *adjacency matrices* (Latin *adiacere* = lie next to, border) and *adjacency
lists*. In the adjacency matrix, a '1' at position (i, j) means that there is an edge from
vertex i to vertex j. Each edge can be equipped with numbers which represent costs
or distances. In this case, instead of the '1,' the corresponding numbers are entered.
Furthermore, there must be one special number (normally 0) which means that no
connection exists between the two vertices.

The adjacency matrix of an undirected graph is symmetric with regard to
the main diagonal. Table 11.1 shows the adjacency matrices corresponding to
Figure 11.1.

The second common representation using adjacency lists consists of a vector
or a list of all vertices, where for each vertex a sublist with all successive vertices
exists (Figure 11.2).

This kind of representation has the advantage that only memory which is actually required is used and that, notwithstanding, the successors of each vertex can

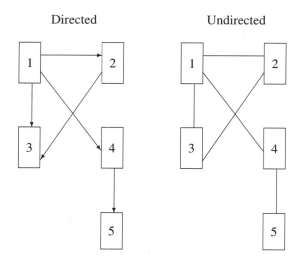

Figure 11.1 Directed and undirected graphs.

Vertex	1 2 3 4 5
1	0 1 1 1 0
2	0 0 1 0 0
3	0 0 0 0 0
4	0 0 0 0 1
5	0 0 0 0 0

Vertex	1 2 3 4 5
1	0 1 1 1 0
2	1 0 1 0 0
3	1 1 0 0 0
4	1 0 0 0 1
5	0 0 0 1 0

Table 11.1 Adjacency matrices for directed and undirected graphs.

be found very quickly. For this reason, we will use the list representation, albeit in a slightly modified form.

Instead of taking lists for the references, as shown in Figure 11.2, the information about successors and edge values is stored in a map `map`. The key to an edge value is the number of a successive vertex. The advantage this gives over a list is that during the construction or reading of the graph, we can be certain that no multiple edges will exist. Thus, a vector element consists of a pair: the vertex and the set of its successors.

There is an alternative to this construction: imagine a graph as a map in which the set of successors and the edge values are accessed via a vertex, in analogy to the simple model of the sparse matrix on page 219. If the vertices are of type `string` and the edge values of type `double`, a graph type could be defined as follows:

```
typedef map<string, double> Successor;
typedef map<string, Successor> GraphType;
```

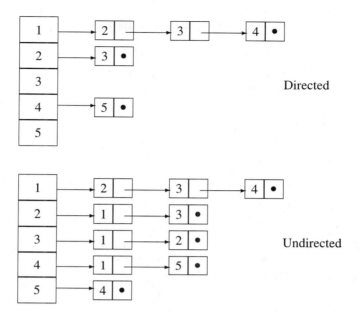

Figure 11.2   Adjacency lists.

Now, the definition of vertices and edge values is very simple:

```
string vertex1("firstVertex");
string vertex2("secondVertex");
GraphType theGraph;
theGraph[vertex1][vertex2] = 4.568;
```

This solution is not favored for various reasons:

- In many instances, the information about whether a graph is directed plays a role and should therefore be included.
- Inadvertent access to an undefined vertex with the `[]` operator leads to a new vertex being created without an error message (see page 88).
- At each access to a vertex, a search process is carried out. The process is fast ($O(\log N)$), but a direct access is even faster.
- Sometimes an order is needed, for example, the order of vertices in a shortest path. A vector of vertex numbers is a suitable and, above all, very simple tool for this purpose. Solutions based on the `GraphType` of the above listing are more expensive from a programming point of view.

The complexity of programs involving graphs is generally expressed in relation to the number of vertices and edges.

Edges without weighting?

Edges can be equipped with parameters to express distances or costs. In case *no* parameters are needed, an empty class with a minimum set of operations is defined as a placeholder:

```
struct Empty
{
  public:
    Empty(int=0) {}
    bool operator<(const Empty&) const { return true;}
};
ostream& operator<<(ostream& os, const Empty&) { return os;}
istream& operator>>(istream& is, Empty& ) { return is;}
```

With this class, it is possible to formulate a uniform class for graphs, together with auxiliary routines for input and output, valid for graphs with and without weighted edges.

11.1 Class Graph

According to Figure 11.2, the class Graph consists of a vector V of all vertices. As the advanced private part shows, the additional information about whether the graph is directed or not is present. An undirected graph is represented by the fact that for each edge, a second edge exists in the opposite direction. This takes up memory for what, in the final analysis, is redundant information, but has the advantage that each successor of an arbitrary vertex can be reached quickly.

The class is equipped with various checking methods whose diagnostic messages are output on the channel pointed to by the ostream pointer pOut.

```
template<class VertexType, class EdgeType>
class Graph
{
  public:
    // public type interface
    typedef map<int, EdgeType, less<int> > Successor;
    typedef pair<VertexType, Successor> vertex;
    typedef checkedVector<vertex> GraphType;
    typedef GraphType::iterator iterator;
    typedef GraphType::const_iterator const_iterator;

  private:
    bool directed;
    GraphType C;                // container
    ostream* pOut;
  public:
```

```
/*
```
The following constructor initializes the output channel with cerr. A parameter must be specified as to whether the graph is directed or undirected, because this is an essential property of a graph.
```
*/

Graph(bool g, ostream& os = cerr)
: directed(g), pOut(&os) { }

bool isDirected() const { return directed;}

/*
```
A graph is a special kind of container to which something can be added and whose elements can be accessed. Therefore, in the following typical container methods, their extents are limited to those needed for the examples. Thus, there is no method for explicit removal of a vertex or an edge from the graph.
```
*/

size_t size() const   { return C.size();}

iterator begin()      { return C.begin();}
iterator end()        { return C.end();}

// access to vertex i
vertex& operator[](int i)
{
    // the access is safe, because C is a checkedVector
    return C[i];
}

// addition of a vertex
int  insert(const VertexType& e);

// addition of an edge between e1 and e2
void insert(const VertexType& e1, const VertexType& e2,
            const EdgeType& Value);

// addition of an edge between vertices no. i and j
void connectVertices(int i, int j, const EdgeType& Value);

/*
```
The following methods are useful tools for displaying information on a graph and checking its structure. These methods are described in detail in the next sections.
```
*/

// checking of a read data model
// output on the channel passed to check()
void check(ostream& = cout);

// determine the number of edges
size_t CountEdges();
```

```
//  determine whether the graph contains cycles
//  and in which way it is connected
void CycleAndConnect(ostream& = cout);
};      // Graph
```

The last method combines two tasks, because they can be carried out in a single run. The terms are explained in the description of the methods.

11.1.1 Insertion of vertices and edges

To avoid ambiguities, a vertex is entered only if it did not previously exist. The sequential search is not particularly fast; however, this process is needed only once during the construction of the graph.

```
template<class VertexType, class EdgeType>
int Graph<VertexType,EdgeType>::insert(const VertexType& e)
{
    for(int i = 0; i < size(); ++i)
       if(e == C[i].first)
          return i;

    //  if not found, insert:
    C.push_back(vertex(e, Successor()));
    return size()-1;
}
```

An edge is inserted by first inserting the vertices, if needed, and by determining their positions. The edge construction itself is carried out by the function connectVertices(). It is passed the vertex numbers and, because there is no search procedure, it is very fast.

```
template<class VertexType, class EdgeType>
void Graph<VertexType,EdgeType>::insert(const VertexType& e1,
                                        const VertexType& e2,
                                        const EdgeType& Value)
{
    int pos1 = insert(e1);
    int pos2 = insert(e2);
    connectVertices(pos1, pos2, Value);
}

template<class VertexType, class EdgeType>
void Graph<VertexType,EdgeType>::connectVertices(
             int pos1, int pos2, const EdgeType& Value)
{
    (C[pos1].second)[pos2] = Value;

    if(!directed)   // automatically insert opposite direction too
       (C[pos2].second)[pos1] = Value;
}
```

11.1.2 Analysis of a graph

The method check() sets the output channel and calls all other checking methods.

```
template<class VertexType, class EdgeType>
void Graph<VertexType,EdgeType>::check(ostream& os)
{
    os << "The graph is ";
    if(!isDirected())
        os << "un";

    os << "directed and has "
        << size() << " vertices and "
        << CountEdges()
        << " edges\n";
    CycleAndConnect(os);
}
```

Determining the number of edges

Determining the number of edges of a given graph is simple: all that is required is to add the lengths of all adjacency lists. Undirected graphs are represented by two opposed edges for each connected pair of vertices; thus, in this case, the sum is halved.

```
template<class VertexType, class EdgeType>
size_t Graph<VertexType,EdgeType>::CountEdges()
{
    size_t edges = 0;
    iterator temp = begin();

    while(temp != end())
        edges += (*temp++).second.size();

    if(!directed)
        edges /= 2;
    return edges;
}
```

Cycles, connection, and number of components

A graph has a *cycle* if there is a path with at least one edge whose first node is identical with the last node.

An undirected graph is *connected* if each vertex can be reached from each of the other vertices. For directed graphs, a distinction is made between a strong and a weak connection. A directed graph has a strong connection if a path exists from each vertex to each of the other vertices, that is, all vertices are mutually reachable.

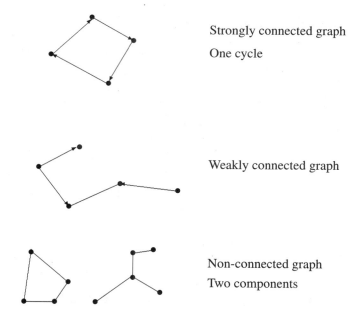

Strongly connected graph

One cycle

Weakly connected graph

Non-connected graph

Two components

Figure 11.3   Different types of graph.

The connection is weak if an arbitrary vertex A is reachable from a vertex B, but not vice versa.

A graph is not connected if it is composed of two or more non-connected components. Figure 11.3 shows some examples.

CycleAndConnect() works with a *depth-first search*. Starting with an initial vertex, a successor is visited, then the successor of this successor, and so on, until no further successor is found. Then the next successor of the initial vertex is visited, applying the same process again. A breadth-first search, in contrast, processes all successors of the initial vertex in the first step, without considering their successors. Only then is the second level of successors tackled.

Unlike Cormen *et al.* (1994), no recursion is employed because, depending on the system, even smaller graphs can cause a stack overflow. For undirected graphs, the stack depth corresponds to the number of edges + 1. In a user-defined stack, only the necessary information is stored, not all sorts of data used for function call management, such as local variables, return addresses, and so on.

```
template<class VertexType, class EdgeType>
void Graph<VertexType, EdgeType>::CycleAndConnect(ostream& os)
{
    int Cycles = 0;
    int ComponentNumber = 0;
    stack<int> verticesStack;          //  vertices to be visited
```

```
/*
```
To prevent multiple visits to vertices in possible cycles, which entails the risk of in-
finite loops, the vertices are earmarked as having been visited or as finished being
processed. This is executed by the vector `VertexState`.
```
*/
```

```
// assign all vertices the state 'not visited'
enum VertStatus {notVisited, visited, processed};
vector<VertStatus> VertexState(size(), notVisited);
```

```
/*
```
If, starting from one vertex, an attempt is made to reach all other vertices, success is
not guaranteed in weakly or non-connected graphs. Therefore, each vertex is visited.
If it is found that a vertex has already been visited, it does not need to be processed
any further.
```
*/
```

```
// visit all vertices
for(int i = 0; i < size(); ++i)
{
  if(VertexState[i] == notVisited)
  {
     ComponentNumber++;
     // store on stack for further processing
     verticesStack.push(i);

     // process stack
     while(!verticesStack.empty())
     {
        int theVertex = verticesStack.top();
        verticesStack.pop();
        if(VertexState[theVertex] == visited)
           VertexState[theVertex] = processed;
        else

           if(VertexState[theVertex] == notVisited)
           {
              VertexState[theVertex] = visited;
              // new vertex, earmark for processed mark
              verticesStack.push(theVertex);
```

```
              /*
```
If one of the successors of a newly found vertex bears the `visited`
mark, the algorithm has already passed this point once, and there is
a cycle.
```
              */
```

```
              // earmark successor:
              Graph<VertexType,EdgeType>::Successor::iterator
```

```
                  start  = operator[](theVertex).second.begin(),
                  end    = operator[](theVertex).second.end();

              while(start != end)
              {
                  int Succ = (*start).first;

                  if(VertexState[Succ] == visited)
                  {
                      ++Cycles;     //  someone's been here already!
                      (*pOut) << "at least vertex "
                      << operator[](Succ).first
                      << " lies in a cycle\n";
                  }

                  /*
```

Otherwise, the vertex has already been processed and therefore should not be considered again, or it has not yet been visited and is earmarked on the stack.

```
                  */
                    if(VertexState[Succ] == notVisited)
                        verticesStack.push(Succ);
                  ++start;
              }
          }
      }   //  stack empty?
  }       //  if(VertexState...
}         //  for() ...
```

```
/*
```
Now we only need the output. In case of directed, weakly connected graphs, the algorithm counts several components. To make the output conform to the above definitions, although with a lesser information content, a distinction is made as to whether the graph is directed or not.
```
*/
```

```
if(directed)
{   if(ComponentNumber == 1)
        os << "The graph is strongly connected.\n";
    else
        os << "The graph is not or weakly "
              "connected.\n";
}

else
    os << "The graph has "
        << ComponentNumber
        << " component(s)." << endl;
```

```
        os << "The graph has ";
        if(Cycles == 0)
          os << "no ";
        os << "cycles." << endl;
    }
```

Display of vertices and edges

The output operator is used to display the vertices and edges of a graph. The output format corresponds to the format assumed by the routines of the next section.

```
template<class VertexType, class EdgeType>
ostream& operator<<(ostream& os, Graph<VertexType,EdgeType>& G)
{
    //  display of vertices with successors
    for(int i = 0; i < G.size(); ++i)
    {
        os << G[i].first << " <";

        Graph<VertexType,EdgeType>::Successor::iterator
                startN = G[i].second.begin(),
                endN   = G[i].second.end();

        while(startN != endN)
        {
            os << G[(*startN).first].first << ' ' // vertex
               << (*startN).second << ' ';         // edge value
            ++startN;
        }
        os << ">\n";
    }
    return os;
}
```

11.1.3 Input and output tools

This section presents some tools that facilitate experimenting with algorithms involving graphs. All auxiliary programs and sample data files are also available via the Internet.

Reading data

Besides information on the connection of vertices, many graphs need only the labelling of vertices and in some cases the length of edges. A simple way of representing this information in a file is the following format:

vertex < successor1 cost1 successor2 cost2 ...>

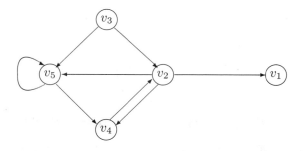

Figure 11.4   Directed graph. (Example taken from Maas (1994), by kind permission of Wißner publishers.)

If they are not needed, the costs can be omitted. A # character at the beginning of a line starts a comment. Figure 11.4 corresponds to the simple file *gra1.dat*.

```
# gra1.dat
v1
v2 <v1 v4 v5 >
v3 <v2 v5 >
v4 <v2 >
# cycle, loop to itself:
v5 <v5 v4 >
```

For the vertices, the graph needs only an identifier of type `string`. The edge parameters can be of a numeric type or, as in this example, of type `Empty` (see page 246).

A program for reading and documenting a graph may then look as follows:

```
int main()
{
    //  no edge weighting, therefore type Empty:
    Graph<string,Empty> V(true);          // directed

    //  file gra1.dat see above
    ReadGraph(V, "gra1.dat");

    V.check();                    // display properties

    //  display of vertices with successors
    cout << V;
}
```

The result of method `check()` is:

The graph is directed and has 5 vertices and 8 edges.
The graph is not connected or is weakly connected.
The graph has cycles.

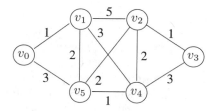

Figure 11.5   Undirected graph with weighted edges. (Example from Maas (1994).)

The display of the vertices with successors corresponds to the format of the input file. The function `ReadGraph()` is less interesting from an algorithmic point of view; it can therefore be found in Section A.1.2.

A second example is an undirected graph with integer edge weights:

```
Graph<string,int> G(false);        // undirected
```

This graph is described by the following file, in which slight errors have been inserted for demonstration purposes:

```
# gra2.dat
v0 <v1 1 v5 3 >
#double edge v2
v1 <v2 5 v2 9 v4 3 v5 2 v0 1 >
v2 <v1 5 v5 2 v4 2 v3 1 >
v3 <v2 1 v4 3>
v4 <v5 1 v1 3 v2 2 v3 3 >
v5 < v1 2 v2 2 v4 1 >
```

The result of the above program, including output of the corrected graph with vertices and successors shown in Figure 11.5 is as follows:

The graph is undirected and has 6 vertices and 10 edges.
The graph has 1 component(s).
The graph has cycles.

v0 <v1 1 v5 3 >
v1 <v0 1 v2 5 v4 3 v5 2 >
v2 <v1 5 v3 1 v4 2 v5 2 >
v3 <v2 1 v4 3 >
v4 <v1 3 v2 2 v3 3 v5 1 >
v5 <v1 2 v2 2 v4 1 v0 3 >

11.2 Dynamic priority queue

The STL provides the priority queue described in Section 4.3. For some purposes, the functions provided are not sufficient. For example, it is not possible specifically to change the priority of an element stored in a priority queue. Nor is removing and reinserting it with changed priority possible.

Exactly this property, however, is required in the algorithm for the topological sorting of a graph (see Section 11.3.2) and, furthermore, this property is advantageous in an algorithm for finding the shortest path from one node to another. This algorithm is described in Section 11.3.1. It could also be solved with a conventional STL priority queue, but only with a relatively higher number of push calls.

Since the required priority queue allows modification of stored elements without losing the priority queue property, this type will be called a 'dynamic priority queue.' It is intended as a special extension, so that it is not necessary to reproduce all the methods of an STL priority queue, but only those needed in this application.

At first sight, it seems a good idea to exploit the existing STL implementation. Two mechanisms are available:

- Inheritance
  The container used in the STL priority queue is `protected`, so that it can be accessed from within a derived class. However, the declaration would be very complex: the elements would be of type `pair<key, Index>`, with the priority being defined by the key `key` and the index representing a reference to the corresponding node of the graph. At the declaration, not only the underlying container, but also a comparison object `Greater` or something similar must be specified, since smaller keys are to signify a higher priority.
  Furthermore, the size of the additional code to be written is of the order of a whole new class, as experiments which are not documented here have shown.

- Delegation
  It is conceivable to invent a class that *uses* an STL priority queue by making it an attribute of this class and forwarding method calls to it. This possibility is ruled out because, owing to its `protected` property, the container cannot be accessed, but an access would be impossible to prevent.

Thus, it is more appropriate to write a special class. Even from the point of view of total cost, it is more advantageous than copying and complementing an existing implementation of a priority queue.

11.2.1 Data structure

The dynamic priority queue should allow an algorithm of more or less the following kind:

1. Initialize the dynamic priority queue DPQ with a vector V which consists of the elements $0 \ldots n - 1$, and $n = V.size()$ holds.

2. As long as the DPQ is not empty:

   (a) determine from DPQ the element k of V that has the smallest value,

   (b) read the corresponding position k from DPQ,

(c) modify one or more of the not yet read elements of V,

(d) update DPQ accordingly.

Elements of V should be modified only via a dynamic priority queue method, because the information on the element to be modified must be kept. All this should also be *fast*, which excludes linear search processes or a reinitialization of the dynamic priority queue at each modification. To satisfy these requirements, the data structure shown in Figure 11.6 is chosen.

In Figure 11.6, c is a vector of pointers to the elements of the external vector V. After initialization, c is converted into a heap with the property that c[0] now points to the smallest element inside V. After the heap conversion, the order of elements in c no longer corresponds to the order in V. To guarantee fast access in spite of this fact, an auxiliary array Indices is created with the necessary information, that is, element i of the array contains the address of array c, where the pointer to element i of vector V can be found (inverted addressing). This allows fast changes without search processes:

```
//  modify element V[i] from within the dynamic priority queue:
*c[Indices[i]] = newValue;
```

At each modification of the heap c, the auxiliary array must be updated, which takes place in constant time.

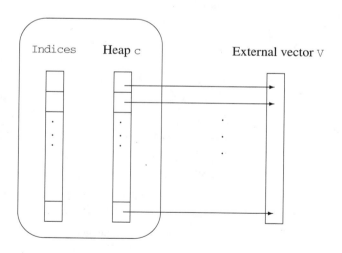

dynamic_priority_queue

Figure 11.6   Internal data structure of the dynamic priority queue.

11.2.2 Class dynamic_priority_queue

The heap inside the dynamic priority queue is indirect because it consists of pointers whose ordering obviously does not correspond to the pointers themselves, but to the values pointed to by these pointers. The class `PtrGreater` allows the creation of suitable function objects:

```
//  compares the associated values of passed pointers
template<class T>
struct PtrGreater
{
    bool operator()( T x,  T y) const { return *y < *x;}
};
```

It should be noted that only the < operator is needed for the template data type *T and that the required relation is created by swapping the arguments.

The class template `dynamic_priority_queue` needs only the type `key_type` of the elements of the external vector, which represent the priorities.

```
#ifndef dyn_pq
#define dyn_pq
#include<checkvec>
#include<algorithm>
#include<showseq>

template <class key_type>
class  dynamic_priority_queue
{
  public:
      //  public type definitions
      typedef vector<key_type>::size_type size_type;
      typedef vector<key_type>::difference_type index_type;

      //  constructor
      dynamic_priority_queue( vector<key_type>& v);

      //  change a value at position at
      void changeKeyAt(index_type at, key_type k);

      //  index of the smallest element (= highest priority)
      index_type topIndex() const { return (c.front() - first); }

      //  value of the smallest element (= highest priority)
      const key_type& topKey() const { return *c.front(); }

      void pop();        // remove smallest element from the heap

      bool empty() const { return csize == 0;}
      size_type size() const { return csize;}

  private:
      checkedVector<index_type> Indices;   //  auxiliary vector
```

```
checkedVector<key_type*> c;          //  heap of pointers
key_type* first;                     //  beginning of the external vector
PtrGreater<key_type*> comp;          //  comparison object
size_type csize;                     //  current heap size

    //  heap update (see below)
    void goUp(index_type);
    void goDown(index_type);
};
```

The class definition is followed by the implementation together with explanations about the way of functioning. In the initialization list, the vectors Indices and c are created, among others. Subsequently, the addresses of all the elements of the external vector are entered and a heap is generated. An entry of the auxiliary array Indices is simply the difference between the address stored in c and the starting address of the vector V.

```
template <class key_type>
dynamic_priority_queue<key_type>::
                    dynamic_priority_queue(vector<key_type>& v)
 : Indices(v.size()), c(v.size()), first(v.begin()),
   csize(v.size())
{
    index_type i;

    //  store pointers and generate heap
    for(i = 0; i< csize; i++)
       c[i] = &v[i];
    make_heap(c.begin(), c.end(), comp);          //  STL

    //  construct index array
    for(i = 0; i< csize; i++)
       Indices[c[i] - first] = i;
}
```

The method changeKeyAt() allows a value of the external vector at position at to be changed without violating the heap property. This process is of complexity $O(\log N)$ and therefore very fast. N is the number of elements still present in the heap. The main cost lies in the procedures for the reorganization of the heap which, however, never require more steps than $\log N$, the height of the heap.

The theory is that, if a modified element has become greater (= 'heavier'), then this element is allowed to sink down in the heap until it has reached its proper position. Vice versa, a 'lighter' element should rise by a corresponding amount towards the top.

```
template <class key_type>
void dynamic_priority_queue<key_type>::
                    changeKeyAt(index_type at, key_type k)
{
```

```
index_type idx = Indices[at];
assert(idx < csize);      // value still present in the queue?

if(*c[idx] != k)          // in case of equality, do nothing
   if(comp(&k, c[idx]))
   {
        *c[idx] = k;      // enter heavier value
        goDown(idx);      // reorganize heap
   }
   else
   {
        *c[idx] = k;      // enter lighter value
        goUp(idx);        // reorganize heap
   }
}
```

The method goUp(idx) causes an element to rise at position idx. Figure 11.7 shows, from top to bottom, the effect of changeKeyAt() and goUp(), starting with an arbitrary external vector whose ninth element is set to 0. The lighter element at idx rises through gradual sinking of the heavier predecessors and entry at the freed position.

```
template <class key_type>
void dynamic_priority_queue<key_type>::goUp(index_type idx)
{
    index_type Predecessor = (idx-1)/2;
    key_type* temp = c[idx];

    /*
```

In the figure, the process is exemplified by swapping the values of predecessor and successor. In the following program segment, however, in order to save unnecessary assignments, entry of the element temp (0 in the figure) is postponed until all the necessary exchange operations have been carried out.

```
    */       while(Predecessor != idx && comp(c[Predecessor], temp))
         {
             c[idx] = c[Predecessor];
             Indices[c[idx]-first] = idx;
             idx = Predecessor;
             Predecessor = (idx-1)/2;
         }

    c[idx] = temp;
    Indices[c[idx]-first] = idx;
}
```

The method goDown() functions correspondingly. The heavy element at idx sinks down through gradual rising of the lighter successor and entry at the freed position.

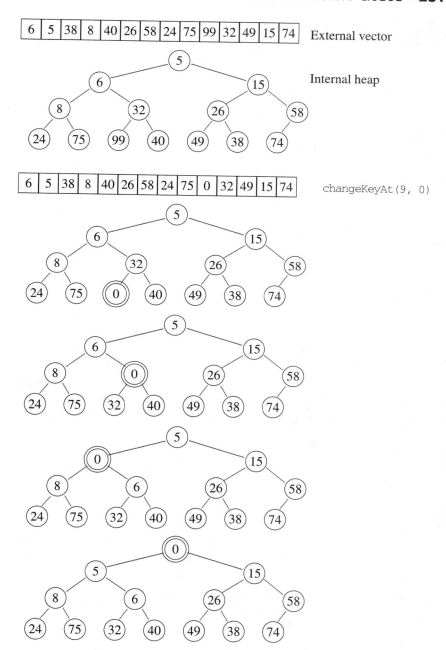

Figure 11.7   Effect of `changeKeyAt()` and `goUp()`.

```
template <class key_type>
void dynamic_priority_queue<key_type>::goDown(index_type idx)
{
    index_type Successor = (idx+1)*2-1;

    if(Successor < csize-1
       && comp(c[Successor], c[Successor+1]))
          ++Successor;
    key_type* temp = c[idx];

    while(Successor < csize && comp(temp, c[Successor]))
    {
       c[idx] = c[Successor];
       Indices[c[idx]-first] = idx;
       idx = Successor;
       Successor = (idx+1)*2-1;

       if(Successor < csize-1
          && comp(c[Successor], c[Successor+1]))
             ++Successor;
    }
    c[idx] = temp;
    Indices[c[idx]-first] = idx;
}
```

The method `pop()` removes the topmost element from the heap. This is done by moving the last element to the top and blocking the freed position with `--csize`. Subsequently, the element sinks down to its proper position.

```
template <class key_type>
void dynamic_priority_queue<key_type>::pop()
{
    // overwrite pointer at the top with the
    // address of the last element
    c[0] = c[--csize];

    // enter the new address 0 at the position belonging
    // to this element in the auxiliary array
    Indices[c[0]-first] = 0;

    // let the element at the top sink to the correct
    // position corresponding to its weight
    goDown(0);
}
#endif
```

Example

A program fragment shows the application:

```
checkedVector<double> V(8);

// ... assign values to the elements V[i]

dynamic_priority_queue<double> DPQ(V);

//  change value V[3]; correct insertion
//  into DPQ is carried out automatically
DPQ.changeKeyAt(3, 1.162);

//  outputting and emptying by order of priority
while(!DPQ.empty())
{
    cout << "Index: " << DPQ.topIndex();
    cout << " Value: " << DPQ.topKey() << endl;
    DPQ.pop();
}
```

11.3 Graph algorithms

There are vast numbers of algorithms for graphs. Here, only some of these are presented to show how such algorithms can be implemented using the STL and its techniques with the extensions of the previous sections.

Many problems involving graphs, such as finding the shortest path between two points or determining an optimal travelling route, involve specifying locations. For such problems, a vertex type suggests itself which contains the location's coordinates and a denomination. A suitable class for this is Place:

```
//  include/place.h
#ifndef place_h
#define place_h
#include<cmath>
#include<string>

class Place
{
  public:
    Place() {};

    Place(long int ax, long int ay, string& N = string(""))
    : x(ax), y(ay), Name(N)
    {}

    string readName()     const { return Name;}
    unsigned long int X() const { return x;}
    unsigned long int Y() const { return y;}

    bool operator==(const Place& O) const
    {
```

```
            return x == O.x && y == O.y;
    }

    //  for alphabetical ordering
    bool operator<(const Place& O) const
    {
            return Name < O.Name;
    }

  private:
      long int x, y;                    //  coordinates
      string Name;                      //  identifier
};
```

Sometimes additional information, such as the number of inhabitants of a place, is required and can easily be added. The distance between two places can easily be calculated. The corresponding function `DistSquare()` is formulated as a separate function, because often only the result of a comparison of distances is of interest. To carry out the comparison, the squares of the distances are sufficient, and calculation of the square root `sqrt()` can be omitted.

```
unsigned long int DistSquare(const Place& p, const Place& q)
{
    long int dx = p.X()-q.X();
    long int dy = p.Y()-q.Y();
    //  (arithmetic overflow with large numbers is not checked)
    return dx*dx + dy*dy;
}

double Distance(const Place& p, const Place& q)
{
    return sqrt(double(DistSquare(p,q)));
}
```

The output operator displays the name of the place and allows a simpler notation than the detour via `readName()`.

```
ostream& operator<<(ostream& os, const Place& S)
{
    os << S.readName();
    return os;
}
#endif
```

11.3.1 Shortest paths

Here, the problem is to find the shortest path between two points of a graph. Probably the best known algorithm for this purpose is Dijkstra's algorithm. It uses the

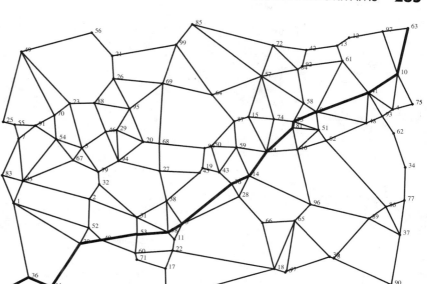

Figure 11.8   Graph with shortest path between two points.

dynamic priority queue of Section 11.2. Figure 11.8 shows an undirected graph with 100 places, in which the shortest path between point 0 and point 63 is highlighted.

The graph in Figure 11.8 was created with a number of small auxiliary programs. The function `create_vertex_set()` (Section A.1.3) generates a number of vertices with random coordinates within a given frame. The function `connectNeigh-bors()` (Section A.1.4) connects neighboring vertices of an undirected graph, and `createTeXfile()` (Section A.1.5) takes the graph and generates a file to be read into the LATEX typesetting program used to typeset this book.

How should the `Dijkstra()` algorithm be used? In the following example, a graph `G` with random coordinates is constructed, but any other graph would do as well:

```
#include<gra_algo>          // contains Dijkstra()
#include<gra_util>          // auxiliary functions from Appendix A

int main()
{
    unsigned int Count = 100;
    Graph<Place,float> G(false);                  // undirected
    create_vertex_set(G, Count, 12800, 9000); // range

    connectNeighbors(G);

    /*
```

The `Dijkstra()` function must be passed the graph, a vector of distances, and a

vector of the predecessors, which are modified by the algorithm. The distance type must match the edge parameter type of the graph.
*/

```
vector<float> Dist;
vector<int> Pred;

int start = 0;                          // starting point 0

Dijkstra(G, Dist, Pred, start);
```

/*
The last argument is the starting point which can be any vertex between no. 0 and no.
(G.size()-1). After the call, the distance vector contains the length of the shortest paths from each point to the starting point. Dist[k] is the length of the shortest possible path from vertex no. k to vertex no. 0. Dist[StartingPoint] is 0 by definition.
*/

```
// output
cout << "shortest path to "
     << G[start].first << ":\n";

cout << "predecessor of:  is:   "
         "distance to [indices in ()]:\n";

for(int i = 0; i < Pred.size(); ++i)
{
    cout.width(7);
    cout <<  G[i].first
         << '(' << i << ')';
    cout.width(12);

    if(Pred[i] < 0)
       cout << "-"              // no predecessor of starting point
            << '(' << Pred[i] << ')';

    else
       cout << G[Pred[i]].first
            << '(' << Pred[i] << ')';

    cout.width(9);
    cout << Dist[i] << endl;
}
}
```

The predecessor vector contains the indices of the predecessors on the path towards the starting point. Pred[StartingPoint] is undefined. If the starting vertex is 0, the predecessor and distance vectors of the graph in Figure 11.9 have the values shown in Table 11.2. It corresponds to the output of the above program, except that the table shows only the *vertex numbers* and not the *vertex names*.

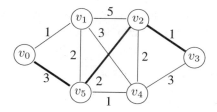

Figure 11.9   A shortest path.

i	Pred[i]	Dist[i]
0	undefined	0
1	0	1
2	0	3
3	2	5
4	1	4
5	3	6

Table 11.2   Example of predecessor and distance vectors.

The shortest path from vertex v_3 to vertex v_0 is 6 units long and leads through the vertices v_2 (=Pred[3]) and v_5 (=Pred[2]). The predecessor of 5 is 0. With this, the target is reached. There can be several equally short paths. The corresponding output of the program is:

shortest path to v0:

Predecessor of:	is:	Distance to	[indices in ()]:
v0(0)	*−(−1)*	*0*	
v1(1)	*v0(0)*	*1*	
v5(2)	*v0(0)*	*3*	
v2(3)	*v5(2)*	*5*	
v4(4)	*v1(1)*	*4*	
v3(5)	*v2(3)*	*6*	

How does the algorithm find the shortest path between two points? This algorithm is extensively described in Cormen *et al.* (1994), Maas (1994) and Owsnicki-Klewe (1995). Therefore only a brief outline is given. A preliminary hint: below, the distance vector is to be initialized with the value ∞, which is 'approached' by the maximum value possible for the data type in question:

```
numeric_limits<aScalarType>::max() // maximum value
```

aScalarType is one of the basic data types int, long, double, and so on. The class numeric_limits is declared in the header <limits>.

The inclusion of the include files is followed by the definition of the Dijkstra()

function which is passed the graph `Gr`, the two vectors of distances and predecessors, and the starting point of the search.

```
// include/gra_algo
#ifndef graph_algorithms
#define graph_algorithms
#include<dynpq>
#include<Graph>
#include<limits>

template<class graphType, class EdgeType>
void Dijkstra(
        graphType& Gr,
        vector<EdgeType>& Dist,
        vector<int>& Pred,
        int Start)
{
```

```
    /*
```
The algorithm proceeds in such a way that the distances are estimated and the estimates gradually improved. The distance to the starting point is known (0). For all other vertices, the worst possible estimate is entered.
```
    */
```

```
Dist = vector<EdgeType>(Gr.size(),
        numeric_limits<EdgeType>::max()); // as good as ∞
Dist[Start] = (EdgeType)0;
```

```
    /*
```
The predecessor vector too is initialized with 'impossible' values. Subsequently, a dynamic priority queue is defined and initialized with the distance vector:
```
    */
```

```
Pred = vector<int>(Gr.size(), -1);
dynamic_priority_queue<EdgeType> Q(Dist);
```

```
    /*
```
In the next step, all vertices are extracted one by one from the priority queue, and precisely in the order of the estimated distance towards the starting vertex. Obviously, the starting vertex is dealt with first. No vertex is looked at twice.
```
    */
```

```
int u;
while(!Q.empty())
{
    u = Q.topIndex();     // extract vertex with minimum
    Q.pop();

    /*
```
Now, the distance estimates for all neighboring vertices of `u` are updated. If the

previous estimate of the distance between the current neighbor of u and the starting vertex (Dist[Neighbor]) is worse than the distance between vertex u and the starting vertex (Dist[u]) plus the distance between u and the neighboring vertex (dist), the estimate is improved: this process is called relaxation. In this case, the path from the starting vertex to the neighbor cannot be longer than (Dist[u] + dist). In this case, u would have to be regarded as the predecessor of the neighbor.
```
*/

// improve estimates for all neighbors of u
graphType::Successor::iterator
            I = Gr[u].second.begin();

while(I != Gr[u].second.end())
{
    int Neighbor = (*I).first;
    EdgeType dist = (*I).second;

    // relaxation
    if(Dist[Neighbor] > Dist[u] + dist)
    {
        // improve estimate
        Q.changeKeyAt(Neighbor, Dist[u] + dist);
        // u is the predecessor of the neighbor
        Pred[Neighbor] = u;
    }
    ++I;
    }
}
}
// ... further graph algorithms (see later)
#endif
```

The loop cycles through all vertices. If the number of vertices is denoted by N_V and the number of edges by N_E, the complexity of the algorithm can be estimated as follows on the basis of the individual procedures:

1. N_V removals from the queue.
2. The removal (pop()) is of complexity $O(\log N_V)$.
3. Relaxation is carried out corresponding to the number of edges of a vertex. Since each vertex is looked at only once, its edges too are looked at only once. Therefore, a total of max. N_E edges are relaxed.
4. The relaxation of an edge is of complexity $O(\log N_V)$. The cost derives from reorganization of the heap in the method changeKeyAt().

The removals 'cost' a total of $O(N_V \log N_V)$, and the cost of all relaxations totals $O(N_E \log N_V)$. Thus, the complexity of the whole algorithm is $O((N_V +$

$N_E) \log N_V$). In Cormen *et al.* (1994) it is demonstrated that the path found really is the shortest one. Obviously, there can be several equally short paths in a graph. Which of these is chosen depends on the arrangement of vertices and edges.

11.3.2 Topological sorting of a graph

Topological sorting is a linear ordering of all vertices of a graph in such a way that in the ordering each successive vertex appears *after* its predecessor.

One example is the references in an encyclopedia, in which a term is explained with the aid of other terms. A topological order of the terms would be an order in which references are made only to already defined terms.

A Gantt chart, in which it is determined which activity must be terminated before another one can be started, also contains topological sorting. Thus, when building a house, painters and decorators can start only when electricians and joiners have finished. These, in turn, can start only after the builders have erected the walls. A graph that describes such dependencies must not contain cycles. In other words, it cannot be that the builders can only erect the walls after painters and electricians have finished their work and that these, in turn, wait for the builders.

Some things can be done in arbitrary order, for example wall painting and installing the central heating boiler. Thus, different topological sortings of a graph are possible. A directed acyclic graph is often abbreviated to *dag* or *DAG*. Figure 11.10 shows a DAG which is not yet sorted topologically.

The graph is defined by the following file with the structure known from page 253:

```
# topo.dat
a < l e f >
b < c e i >
c < f g j >
d < c g n >
e < h >
f < i m >
g < f >
h
i < h >
j < l k >
k < n >
l
m < j >
n
```

In the figure, activity a must be carried out before activity e. Activities h, l, and n are final activities; they have no successors and therefore stand at the end of the topological sorting shown in Figure 11.11. The essential difference is that all direction arrows point *to the right*. Vertices of the graph that have no topological

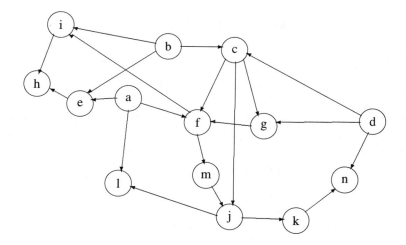

Figure 11.10 Directed acyclic graph.

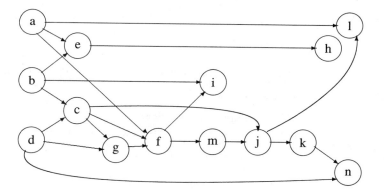

Figure 11.11 Topologically sorted DAG.

precedence over each other are drawn more or less above each other. All vertices that have no predecessor are on the extreme left.

The algorithms in the quoted literature mostly proceed by way of a depth first search (Cormen *et al.*, 1994) or by complicated list structures which are constructed for the analysis. Therefore, in contrast, a method will be described which successively reads those vertices from a dynamic priority queue that have no predecessors, and then removes these vertices by updating the predecessor numbers of the other vertices. This method has the advantage of being very compact and very fast.

Firstly, let us look at the program that calls the topological sorting:

```
//  topological sorting
#include<gr_input>
```

```
#include<gra_algo> //  contains topoSort(), see below

int main()
{
    Graph<string,Empty> G(true);                    //  directed

    ReadGraph(G, "topo.dat");

    /*
    After sorting, the vector Ordering passed as argument contains the indices of the
    graph's vertices.
    */

    vector<int> Ordering;

    if(topoSort(G, Ordering))               //  sort
    {
        for(int i = 0; i < G.size(); i++)
            cout << G[Ordering[i]].first << ' ';
        cout << endl;
    }
    else cout << "Error in the graph!\n";
}
```

The output of the program corresponds to the representation in Figure 11.11:

d b a c e g f i m j k h n l

The algorithm proper follows. The function returns `false` if the graph contains one or more cycles. In such a case, the result is meaningless.

```
//  File gra_algo (continued from page 269)
template<class graphType>
bool topoSort(
        graphType& G,
        vector<int>& Result)
{
    assert(G.isDirected());                 //  let's play it safe!
    int ResCounter = 0;
    Result = vector<int>(G.size(), -1);

    /*
    The vector Result takes the indices of the correspondingly distributed vertices. The
    counter ResCounter is the position in Result where the next entry belongs.
    */

    checkedVector<int> PredecessorCount(G.size(), 0);
    int VerticesWithoutSuccessor = 0;

    /*
    For each vertex, the vector PredecessorCount counts how many predecessors it
```

has. There are vertices without successors, whose number is kept in `VerticesWith-outSuccessor`. Furthermore, the algorithm remains stable if the precondition that a graph must not have cycles is violated. The variable `VerticesWithoutSuccessor` is used to recognize this situation (see below).
```
*/

for(int iv = 0; iv < G.size(); iv++)
{

    if(G[iv].second.size() > 0)         // is predecessor
    {
        graphType::Successor::iterator I =
            G[iv].second.begin();
        while(I != G[iv].second.end())

            //  update number of predecessors
            ++PredecessorCount[(*I++).first];
    }
    else     //  Vertex is no predecessor, that is, without successor
    {

        //  an excessively high number of predecessors is used
        //  for later recognition
        PredecessorCount[iv] =   G.size(); //  too many!
        VerticesWithoutSuccessor++;
    }
}

/*
```
The dynamic priority queue is initialized with the vector of numbers of predecessors. At the beginning of the queue we find those vertices that have no predecessors and therefore are to be processed next. Only the vertices which are predecessors themselves, that is, that have successors, are processed. The subsequent loop is terminated when the queue contains only successor vertices which themselves are not predecessors. Their number of predecessors can never be 0 because earlier they were initialized with too high a value.
```
*/

dynamic_priority_queue<int> Q(PredecessorCount);

// process all predecessors
while(Q.topKey() == 0)
{
    // determine vertex with predecessor number 0
    int oV = Q.topIndex();
    Q.pop();

    Result[ResCounter++] = oV;

    /*
```
To ensure that this vertex without predecessors oV is no longer considered in the

next cycle, the number of predecessors of all its successors is decreased by 1.
```
*/

graphType::Successor::iterator
        I = G[oV].second.begin();
while(I != G[oV].second.end())
{
        // decrease number of predecessors with
        // changeKeyAt(). Do not change directly!
        int V = (*I).first;
        Q.changeKeyAt(V, PredecessorCount[V] -1);
        ++I;
    }
}
```

```
/*
```
Now, all vertices without successors are entered. As a countercheck, the variable
`VerticesWithoutSuccessor` is decreased. If the queue contains too many vertices,
an error message is displayed.
```
*/

while(!Q.empty())
{
        Result[ResCounter++] = Q.topIndex();
        Q.pop();
        --VerticesWithoutSuccessor;
}

if(VerticesWithoutSuccessor < 0)
    cerr << "Error: graph contains a cycle!\n";
return VerticesWithoutSuccessor == 0;
}
```

The error occurs when the graph contains at least one cycle, since in the cycle
itself there can never be a vertex without a predecessor. In that case, more vertices
are caught in the queue than there should be according to the number `VerticesWith-
outSuccessor` counted at the beginning.

Complexity

For an estimate of the complexity, the following activities are relevant, where N_V
is the number of vertices and N_E the number of edges. An auxiliary measure $n = N_E/N_V$ is the average number of successors and predecessors per vertex:

1. Initialization of the vector with numbers of predecessors: $N_V + N_E$.
2. Initialization of the dynamic priority queue: N_V.
3. `while` loops: in all loops, each vertex is treated exactly once (N_V) and each
    edge (successor vertex) depending on the number of predecessors and suc-

cessors (nN_E). Each 'treatment' means removal from the queue ($\log N_V$) or modification of the queue with `changeKeyAt()` (again $\log N_V$).

The dominating part is $N_V \log N_V + nN_E \log N_V$. If the number of vertices and edges is approximately the same, the cost to be expected is $O(N_V \log N_V)$. The upper limit for the number of edges, however, is $N_V(N_V - 1)/2$ (every vertex is connected with every other vertex), so that the complexity is $O(N_V^2 \log N_V)$.

Exercise

11.1   What happens if you run the program on page 271 with a file *topo.dat* in which the line `j < 1 k >` is substituted with `j < f 1 k >`?

Appendix

A.1 Auxiliary programs

A.1.1 Reading the thesaurus file roget.dat

The function `readRoget()` reads the file *roget.dat* according to the given format, in order to build a data structure for a thesaurus (see Section 8.3).

```
void readRoget(checkedVector<string>& Words,
            checkedVector<slist<int> >& lists)
{
    ifstream Source("roget.dat");
    assert(Source);                     // let's play it safe!

    //  read thesaurus
    const int maxbuf = 200;
    char buf[maxbuf];
    char c;
    int i;

    while(Source.get(c))
    {
       if(c == '*')                     // skip line
          Source.ignore(1000,'\n');
       else
         if(isdigit(c))
         {
            Source.putback(c);
            Source >> i;                             // current no.
            Source.getline(buf, maxbuf, ':');   // word
            Words[--i] = buf;

            //  read line numbers if present,
            //  ignoring backslash:

            while(Source.peek() != '\n')
            {
```

```
                    int j;
                    Source >> j;

                    lists[i].push_front(--j);

                    if(Source.peek() == '\\')
                        Source.ignore(1000,'\n');
                }
            }
        }
    }
```

A.1.2 Reading a graph file

The ReadGraph() function is used to read a file for constructing a graph according to the format described in Section 11.1.3. The graph has only an identifier of type string for the vertices. The edge parameters can be of any numeric type or of type Empty (see page 246).

```
#ifndef gr_input_t
#define gr_input_t
#include<string>
#include<cctype>
#include<graph>
#include<fstream>

template<class EdgeParamType>
void ReadGraph(
                 Graph<string,EdgeParamType>& G,
                 char *Filename)
{
    ifstream Source;
    Source.open(Filename);
    if (!Source)        // error check
    {
        cerr << "Cannot open "
             << Filename
             << "!\n";
        exit(-1);
    }
    while(Source)
    {
        char c;
        string vertex, VertexSuccessor;
        Source.get(c);
        if(isalnum(c))
        {
```

```
            Source.putback(c);
            Source >> vertex;
            G.insert(vertex);
            //  collect successor now, if present
            bool SuccessorExists = false;

            Source >> c;
            if(c == '<') SuccessorExists = true;
            else Source.putback(c);

            while(SuccessorExists)
            {
                Source >> VertexSuccessor;
                if(!isalnum(VertexSuccessor[0]))
                    break;  //  illegal character

                EdgeParamType Par;
                Source >> Par;                  //  read parameters
                G.insert(vertex, VertexSuccessor, Par);
            }
        }
        else //  skip line
            while(Source && c != '\n') Source.get(c);
    }
}
#endif
```

A.1.3 Creation of vertices with random coordinates

The functions of the following sections can be found in the file *gra_util*. The prelims are:

```
#ifndef GraphUtilities
#define GraphUtilities

#include<place.h>
#include<graph>
#include<fstream>
#include<myrandom>
```

During automatic creation of an undirected graph, a name must be generated for each vertex. The following auxiliary function converts the current number into a string object which is entered as identifier.

```
//  auxiliary function for generating strings out of numbers
string i2string(unsigned int i)
{
```

```
if(!i) return string("0");
char buf[] = "0000000000000000";
char *pos = buf;
while(*++pos);  // search for end

do
  *--pos = i % 10 + '0';
while(i /=10);
return string(pos);
}
```

The function `create_vertex_set()` creates a number of vertices with random coordinates between 0 and `maxX` or `maxY` in a graph `G` according to its size (`G.size()`).

```
template<class EdgeType>
void create_vertex_set(Graph<Place, EdgeType>& G,
                       int count, int maxX, int maxY)
{
    Random xRandom(maxX),
           yRandom(maxY);

    // create vertices with random coordinates
    int i = -1;
    while(++i < count)
      G.insert(Place(xRandom(), yRandom(),i2string(i)));
}
```

A.1.4 Connecting neighboring vertices

This function connects neighboring vertices. Two places i and j are considered neighbors if there is no place located nearer to the mid-point between these two places than the two places themselves.

This definition of neighborhood is certainly arbitrary. It has the advantage that no place remains unconnected. Predefining a maximum distance between two places as a neighborhood criterion has the disadvantage that a point located slightly out of the way might not be connected.

The above definition resembles the definition of neighborhood used in graph theory for triangulation of a graph (Delaunay triangulation, see Knuth (1994)). The Delaunay triangulation postulates that there exists an interval on the mid-perpendicular between two places starting from which any point is nearer to these two places than to any other place. Usually, the mid-point of the two places lies inside this interval, but this is not mandatory.

We will not discuss the Delaunay triangulation algorithm because it is considerably more complicated than the algorithm presented here. Furthermore, we need only to connect neighboring places, not to subdivide the graph into triangles.

```
template<class EdgeType>
void connectNeighbors(Graph<Place, EdgeType>& G)
```

```
{
    int i;
    for(i = 0; i < G.size(); i++)
    {
        Place iPlace = G[i].first;

        for(int j = i+1; j < G.size(); j++)
        {
            Place jPlace = G[j].first;

            Place MidPoint((iPlace.X()+jPlace.X())/2,
                           (iPlace.Y()+jPlace.Y())/2);
            /*
```
The following loop is not run time optimized. A possible optimization could be to sort the places by their x-coordinates so that only a small relevant range must be searched. The relevant range results from the fact that the places to be compared must lie inside a circle around the mid-point whose diameter is equal to the distance between the places i and j.
```
            */

            int k = 0;
            long int e2 = DistSquare(iPlace, MidPoint);

            while(k < G.size())            //  not run time optimized
            {
                if(k != j && k != i &&
                    DistSquare(G[k].first, MidPoint) < e2)
                        break;
                ++k;
            }

            if(k == G.size()) //  no nearer place found
            {
                EdgeType dist = Distance(iPlace, jPlace);
                G.connectVertices(i, j, entf);
            }
        }
    }
}
```

A.1.5 Creating a LATEX file

Creation of a figure of a directed graph as a LATEX file is carried out by the following function. The image size is defined by xMax and yMax. The scaling factor increases or decreses the scaling of the image.

```
//  Only for undirected graphs!
template<class EdgeType>
```

```
void createTeXfile(char * Filename,
                   Graph<Place, EdgeType>& G,
                   double ScalingFactor,
                   int xMax, int yMax) .
{
    assert(!G.isDirected());
    ofstream Output(Filename);

    if(!Output)
    {
        cerr << Filename
             << " cannot be opened!\n";
        exit(1);
    }
    Output << "\\typeout{include emlines2.sty!}\n"
           << "\\unitlength 1.00mm\n"
           << "\\begin{picture}("
           << xMax << ','
           << yMax << ")\n";

    for(int iv = 0; iv < G.size(); iv++)
    {
        // Point
        Output << "\\put("
               << G[iv].first.X()*ScalingFactor
               << ','
               << G[iv].first.Y()*ScalingFactor
               << "){\\circle*{1.0}}\n";

        // node name
        Output << "\\put("
               << 1.0 + G[iv].first.X()*ScalingFactor
               << ','
               << G[iv].first.Y()*ScalingFactor
               << "){\\makebox(0,0)[lb]{{\\tiny "
               << G[iv].first            // name
               << "}}}\n";

        /*
```

All edges are drawn. To prevent them from appearing twice in the undirected graph, they are drawn only in the direction of the greater index.

```
        */

        Graph<Place,EdgeType>::Successor::iterator I =
                            G[iv].second.begin();

        while(I != G[iv].second.end())
        {
```

```
            int n = (*I).first;
            if(n > iv)                   //  otherwise, ignore
                Output  << "\\emline{"
                        << G[iv].first.X()*ScalingFactor
                        << "}{"
                        << G[iv].first.Y()*ScalingFactor
                        << "}{0}{"
                        << G[n].first.X()*ScalingFactor
                        << "}{"
                        << G[n].first.Y()*ScalingFactor
                        << "}{0}\n";
            ++I;
        }
    }
    Output << "\\end{picture}\n";
}
#endif   //  graphUtilities
```

A.2 Allocators

The allocator class provides the services needed for the procurement of memory space. Depending on the memory model, a suitable allocator is provided by the system, so that it normally does not have to be worried about, unless the user wants to implement special memory functions, for example the procurement of a large memory area for the user's own memory management, to minimize the time needed for the new operation.

Most important are the public types and methods provided by the allocator class, because they can be used in user-defined classes. The following definition of a standard allocator class is taken from the C++ standard draft. Member templates are currently not yet supported by the customary compilers.

```
namespace std
{
    class allocator          //  from C++ standard draft
    {
    public:
        typedef size_t size_type;
        typedef ptrdiff_t difference_type;

        template<class T>
        struct types
        {
            typedef T*         pointer;
            typedef const T*   const_pointer;
            typedef T&         reference;
```

```
    typedef const T& const_reference;
    typedef T          value_type;
};

allocator();
~allocator();
```

// return reference to x:
```
template<class T> typename types<T>::pointer
  address(types<T>::reference x) const;

template<class T> typename types<T>::const_pointer
  address(types<T>::const_reference x) const;
```

```
/*
```
Memory procurement with `allocate()` uses a second parameter U for special-izations of user-defined allocators. `hint` is a (non-mandatory) hint for the desired position in memory. The return value is a pointer to the beginning of the memory area of size `n*sizeof(T)`. The standard implementations use the global `new` operator for memory procurement.
```
*/
```

```
template<class T, class U> typename types<T>::pointer
  allocate(size_type n,
           types<U>::const_pointer hint = 0);
```

```
/*
```
Release of memory is achieved by means of `deallocate(p)`. It is assumed that p points to a range previously created with `allocate()`. As a standard, the global `delete` operator is used for releasing memory.
```
*/
```

```
template<class T> void deallocate(types<T>::pointer p);
```

// maximum possible number of memory locations
// for objects of type T
```
template<class T> size_type max_size() const;
```

```
/*
```
The `construct()` method creates space at position p for an object of type T1 whose constructor is called with `val` as the argument. `destroy()` calls the destructor for the object at position p without, however, freeing the space.
```
*/
```

```
template<class T1, class T2>
  void construct(T1* p, const T2& val);

template<class T> void destroy(T* p);
};

class allocator::types<void>   // specialization
{
```

```
public:
    typedef void* pointer;
    typedef const void* const_pointer;
    typedef void value_type;
};
```

```
// The global operator returns a.allocate<char,void>(N),
// that is, a pointer to a range of N bytes size created with
// the allocator a.
void* operator new(size_t N, allocator& a);
} // namespace std
```

A.2.1 Example

In the context of this book, all the allocator problems cannot be discussed, because the emphasis is on algorithms and data structures that can be implemented by means of the STL. Therefore, only a short example of a user-defined allocator for protocoling of memory allocation and deallocation, derived from a standard allocator, is shown.

```
#ifndef Allocator
#define Allocator myAllocator
#include<iostream>
#include <memory>

template<class T>
class myAllocator : public allocator<T>
{
  public:
    typedef allocator<T>::types::pointer pointer;

    pointer allocate(size_type n, const_pointer hint = 0)
    {
        pointer p = allocator<T>::allocate(n, hint);
        cerr << n*sizeof(T)
            << " bytes allocated at position "
            << p << endl;
        return p;
    }

    void deallocate(pointer p)
    {
        cerr << "Memory deallocation at position " << (p) << endl;
        allocator<T>::deallocate(p);
    }
};
#endif
```

A main() program can use this protocoling allocator as follows:

```
#include"myalloc.h"
#include<vector>

int main()
{
    using namespace std;
    vector<int, myAllocator<int> > v1(100);

    v1[0] = 1;
    cout << "v1[0]= " << v1[0] << endl; // display something
    vector<int, myAllocator<int> > v2 = v1;
    cout << "End of main\n";
}
```

The result of this program could be, for example (depending on the system):

200 bytes allocated at position 0x31730004
v1[0]= 1
200 bytes allocated at position 0x31800004
End of main
Memory deallocation at position 0x31800004
Memory deallocation at position 0x31730004

A.3 Sources and comments

The public domain HP implementation of the STL, which was the basis for the draft C++ Standard, can be obtained via

```
http://www.informatik.hs-bremen.de/~brey/stlbe.html
```

Commercial variations are supplied by several vendors, such as Modena, Rogue Wave, and others. Besides the source code, the above Internet address also contains the corresponding documentation (Stepanov and Lee, 1995) in PostScript format. The documentation can be freely used, provided that the following copyright notice is included:

Copyright(c) 1994 Hewlett-Packard Company

Permission to use, copy, modify, distribute and sell this document for any purpose is hereby granted without fee, provided that the above copyright notice appears in all copies and that both the copyright notice and this permission notice appear in supporting documentation.

The examples from this book can be found under the same Internet address, or they can be obtained via FTP from `ftp.informatik.hs-bremen.de/pub/brey/stl`.

The producers of C++ compilers are in the process of integrating their products with the STL as a part of the C++ standard library. Borland, for example, distributes Version 5 of their C++ compiler with the Rogue Wave implementation of the STL, and the public domain compiler GNU g++ has contained an adapted STL implementation since Version 2.7.

Articles on aspects of the STL can from time to time be found in the German journals *iX Magazin* and *OBJECTspektrum* and in the American journals *C++ REPORT* and *Dr. Dobbs Journal*.

`www.cs.rpi.edu/~musser/stl.html` is mentioned by the authors of Musser and Saini (1996).

The 'SafeSTL' is an STL implementation developed by Cay Horstmann, which makes usage of the STL safer by way of a large number of error checks. It can be obtained via the Internet (see instructions in `www.mathcs.sjsu.edu/faculty/horstman/cay.html`).

The new Silicon Graphics STL including a description is available under `www.sgi.com/Technology/STL`.

The thesaurus file *roget.dat* and other interesting files and programs dealt with in Knuth (1994) are contained in the *Stanford graphBase*, whose files can be obtained via FTP from `ftp.labrea.stanford.edu`, directory `sgb`.

A.4 Solutions to selected exercises

This section contains a selection of solutions which should be considered as suggestions. Often, several solutions exist, even though only one (or none) may be indicated.

Chapter 1

1.1 For clearness, `slist` is shown in its entirety.

```
//   list template for a singly-linked list
//   T = placeholder for the data type of a list element

//   supplements to slist:

    /*

        erase()

        clear()      for destructor and assignment operator

        empty()

        size()

        iterator::operator==()

        copy constructor, destructor, and assignment operator

    */

#ifndef slist
#define slist
#include<cassert>
```

```
template<class T>
class slist
{
    public:
      slist() : theBegin(0), Count(0) {}

      ~slist()
      {
         clear();      // see below
      }

      slist(const slist& S)
      {
          construct(S);  // see below
      }

      slist& operator=(const slist& S)
      {
         if(this != &S)
         {
            clear();         // see below
            construct(S); // see below
         }
         return *this;
      }

      void push_front(const T& Datum) // insert at the beginning
      {
          Listelement *temp =
                         new Listelement(Datum, theBegin);
          theBegin = temp;
          Count++;
      }

      size_t size() const { return Count;}
      bool empty() const { return Count == 0;}

    private:
      struct Listelement
      {
          T Data;
          Listelement *Next;
          Listelement(const T& Datum, Listelement* p)
          : Data(Datum), Next(p)   {}
      };
```

```
    Listelement *theBegin;
    size_t Count;

public:
  class iterator
  {
      friend class slist<T>;
      public:
        iterator(Listelement* Init = 0)
        : current(Init)
        {}

        const T& operator*() const    // dereferencing
        {
            return current->Data;
        }

        T& operator*()                // dereferencing
        {
            return current->Data;
        }

        iterator& operator++()        // prefix
        {
           if(current)
               current = current->Next;
           return *this;
        }

        iterator operator++(int)    // postfix
        {
           iterator temp = *this;
           ++*this;
           return temp;
        }

        bool operator==(const iterator& x) const
        {
           return current == x.current;
        }

        int operator-(iterator fromWhere)
        {
           int Dist = 0;
           while(fromWhere.current != current
                 && fromWhere != iterator())
           {
```

```
                ++Dist;
                ++fromWhere;
            }
        assert(current == fromWhere.current);
        // in case of inequality, this object cannot be
        // reached from fromWhere with ++
        return Dist;
    }

  private:
    // pointer to current element
    Listelement* current;
}; // iterator

// methods using the iterator class:
iterator begin() const
{
    return iterator(theBegin);
}

iterator end() const
{
    return iterator(); // 0-iterator
}

iterator erase(iterator position)
{
    if(!theBegin) return end(); // empty list
    iterator next_element = position;
    ++next_element;

    // search for predecessor
    Listelement *delem = position.current,
                *predecessor = theBegin;

    if(delem != theBegin)
    {
        while(predecessor->Next != delem)
            predecessor = predecessor->Next;
        predecessor->Next = delem->Next;
    }
    else // delete element at the beginning
        theBegin = delem->Next;
    delete delem;
    Count--;
    return next_element;
}
```

```
    void clear()
    {
       while(begin() != end())
           erase(begin());
    }

    void construct(const slist& S)
    {
       Count = 0;
       theBegin = 0;
       if(S.size())
       {
          //  in order to guarantee the correct order,
          //  a vector buf is used for intermediate storage
          Listelement **buf =
                    new Listelement*[S.size()];
          size_t index = S.size();
          Listelement* temp = S.theBegin;

          while(index)
          {
             //  storage in reverse order
             buf[--index] = temp;
             temp = temp->Next;
          }

          for(; index < S.size(); index++)
             push_front(buf[index]->Data);
          delete [] buf;
       }
    }
};
#endif
```

Chapter 4

4.1 The best way is to break down the expression step by step, giving temporary objects auxiliary names. The key k shall be of type Key. First, a pair P is created:

```
P = make_pair(k, T());
```

The expression

```
(*((m.insert(make_pair(k, T()))).first)).second
```

thus becomes

```
(*((m.insert(P)).first)).second
```

Insertion of this pair is carried out only if it does not yet exist. In any case, insert() returns a pair PIB of type pair<iterator, bool>, so that the expression is further simplified to:

```
(*((PIB).first)).second
```

The first element (first) is an iterator pointing to the existing, maybe just inserted, element of type value_type, that is, pair<Key,T>. This iterator will be called I:

```
(*I).second
```

Dereferencing this iterator with operator*() yields a reference to a pair<Key,T>, of which the second (second) element of type T is now taken.

4.2 No. value_type is a pair, and the constructor for a pair is called.

Chapter 5

5.1
```
template <class InputIterator1, class InputIterator2>
inline bool equal(InputIterator1 first1,
                  InputIterator1 last1,
                  InputIterator2 first2)
{
    return mismatch(first1, last1, first2).first
           == last1;
}
```

5.2
```
template <class InputIterator1, class InputIterator2,
          class BinaryPredicate>
inline bool equal(InputIterator1 first1,
                  InputIterator1 last1,
                  InputIterator2 first2,
                  BinaryPredicate binary_pred)
{
    return mismatch(first1, last1, first2, binary_pred).first
           == last1;
}
```

5.3
```
#include<iostream>
#include<string>

template<class T>
class ostream_iterator
```

```
{
  public:
    ostream_iterator(ostream& o,
                const string& SepStr = string())
      : os(o), Separator(SepStr)
    {}

    ostream_iterator<T>& operator=(const T& x)
    {
        os << x << Separator;
        return *this;
    }

    ostream_iterator<T>& operator*() { return *this; }
    ostream_iterator<T>& operator++() { return *this; }
    ostream_iterator<T>& operator++(int) { return *this; }

  private:
    ostream& os;
    string Separator;
};
```

The interface of an ostream iterator requires the usual operators, although some of them, for example ++, do not have to do anything (see the end of Chapter 2, page 46). The ostream iterator provided by the STL in addition inherits from the superclass output_iterator in order to support the compiler during type checking.

5.4
```
template <class ForwardIterator, class Distance>
void rotate_steps(ForwardIterator first,
                  ForwardIterator last,
                  Distance steps)   // > 0 = right, < 0 = left
{
    steps %= (last - first);
    if(steps > 0)
        steps = last - first - steps;
    else
        steps = -steps;
    rotate(first, first + steps, last);
}
```

5.5
```
cout << "\n Stability (relative order) violated "
        "for the following value pairs:\n";
vector<double>::iterator stable_Iter1 = stable.begin();
while(stable_Iter1 != stable.end())
{
```

```
        //  search for counterpart in unstable[]
vector<double>::iterator unstable_Iter1 =
        find(unstable.begin(), unstable.end(),
            *stable_Iter1);

if(unstable_Iter1 != unstable.end())
{
    //  check all elements following after stable_Iter1
    //  whether they are also found in unstable[]
    //  after the position unstable_Iter1
    //  (if not: unstable sorting)
    vector<double>::iterator unstable_Iter2,
                            stable_Iter2 = stable_Iter1;

    stable_Iter2++;
    unstable_Iter1++;

    while(stable_Iter2 != stable.end())
    {
        unstable_Iter2 =
            find(unstable_Iter1, unstable.end(),
                *stable_Iter2);

        //  not found?
        if(unstable_Iter2 == unstable.end())
            cout << (*stable_Iter1) << ' '
                << (*stable_Iter2) << endl;
        stable_Iter2++;
    }
}
stable_Iter1++;
}
```

A.5 Overview of the sample files

`http://www.informatik.hs.bremen.de/~brey/stlbe.html` contains all the examples in this book.

The further directory structure is oriented by the book's chapters, with the names corresponding to the section numbers. Thus, the directory `k1/a3.4` belongs to Chapter 1, Section 3.4. Self-explanatory names, such as `k3/list`, are also often used. The include directory contains the template classes of this book together with auxiliary files for adaptation to the conditions of the compiler used.

On the following pages, the sample files are listed together with the page reference for this book.

File	Description	Page
include/checkvec	checked vector	203
include/dynpq	dynamic priority queue	255
include/graph	graphs	246
include/gra_algo	algorithms for graphs	264
include/gra_util	auxiliary functions for graphs	279
include/gr_input	reading of graph files	278
include/hashfun	hash address calculation	188
include/hmap	hash map	178
include/hset	hash set	189
include/place.h	class for places	263
include/setalgo	set algorithms	167
include/showseq	display of sequences	62
include/slist	singly linked list	9
include/sparmat	sparse matrix	223
include/myrandom	class for random numbers	120

Table A.1   Additions to the include directory.

A.5.1 Additions to the include directory

For simplicity, the files needed in many of the examples and therefore in many directories have been transferred into the include directory. This directory should be specified as a second standard include directory.

A.5.2 Files for the introductory examples

See Table A.2.

A.5.3 Files for the standard algorithms

The standard algorithms are described in Chapter 5, therefore no table is given. If needed, they can be found in the Contents. All files are located in the directory k5.

A.5.4 Files for applications and extensions

The files contained in Table A.3 refer to the examples of Chapters 6 to 11. They usually assume the files of Table A.1.

File	Description	Page
make.inc	include file for make	
readme	hints *read first!*	
alloc/myalloc.h	allocator class	285
alloc/main.cpp	example for the above	286
include/checkvec	checked vector	203
k1/a3.4/mainc.cpp	examples for interplay	6
k1/a3.4/mainstl.cpp	of STL elements	6
k1/a3.4/maint1.cpp		7
k1/a3.4/maint2.cpp		8
k1/a3.4/readme		
k1/a4/slist	singly-linked list	9
k1/a4/mainstl.cpp	example for slist	13
k1/a6/compare.cpp	example for comparison objects	23
k2/identify/identif.h	class for identifiers	42
k2/identify/identif.cpp	implementation of the above	43
k2/identify/main.cpp	application for the above	45
k2/identify/makefile	makefile for the above	
k2/istring.cpp	istream iterator application	39
k3/iterator/binsert.cpp	example for back inserter	72
k3/iterator/finsert.cpp	example for front inserter	73
k3/iterator/iappl.cpp	selection of implementation dependent on iterator type	65
k3/iterator/insert.cpp	example for insert iterator	74
k3/iterator/ityp.cpp	determination of iterator type	64
k3/iterator/valdist.cpp	determination of value and distance types	68
k3/list/identif.h	see above: k2/identify ...	42
k3/list/identif.cpp	see above: k2/identify ...	43
k3/list/id_main.cpp	list of identifiers	57
k3/list/makefile		
k3/list/merge.cpp	merging of lists	60
k3/list/readme		
k3/list/splice.cpp	splicing of lists	60
k3/vector/intvec.cpp	example with `int` vector	54
k3/vector/strvec.cpp	example with `string` vector	56
k4/div_adt.cpp	abstract data types stack, deque, priority queue	79
k4/map.cpp	example for a map	88
k4/setm.cpp	example for a set	85

Table A.2 Files for introductory examples.

File	Description	Page
k6/mainset.cpp	set algorithms	172
k7/mainseto.cpp	overloaded operators for sets	191
k7/maph.cpp	map with hash map	188
k8/crossref.cpp	cross-reference	194
k8/permidx.cpp	permuted index	196
k8/roget.dat	thesaurus file	199
k8/thesaur.cpp	program for the above	199
k9/a1/strcvec.cpp	string vector with index check	204
k9/a2/matmain.cpp	example with matrix	208
k9/a2/matrix	matrix class	206
k9/a2/matrix3d	three-dimensional matrix	210
k9/a3/divmat.cpp	various matrix models	218
k9/a3/fixmatr	fixed matrix for different memory models	213
k9/a4/sparse1.cpp	sparse matrix (variation 1)	219
k9/a4/main.cpp	example with sparse matrix	220
k9/a4/makefile		
k9/a4/mattest.cpp	run-time measurements	230
k9/a4/readme		
k9/a4/stowatch.h	stopwatch class	
k9/a4/stowatch.cpp	implementation of the above	
k10/extsort.cpp	external sorting	233
k10/extsort.t	templates for external sorting	234
k10/extsortq.cpp	external sorting with accelerator	239
k10/extsortq.t	templates for the above	240
k11/analyse/gra1.dat	graph data	254
k11/analyse/gra1u.dat	graph data	
k11/analyse/gra2.dat	graph data	255
k11/analyse/mainint.cpp	graph with integer edge weights	255
k11/analyse/empty.cpp	graph without edge weights	254
k11/dijkstra/gra2.dat	graph data	255
k11/dijkstra/mainplace.cpp	shortest paths (1) in a graph (Figure 11.8)	264
k11/dijkstra/mdi.cpp	shortest paths (2) in a graph	
k11/dynpq/maindpq.cpp	application of the dynamic priority queue	263
k11/toposort/main.cpp	topological sorting	271
k11/toposort/topo.dat	graph data	270

Table A.3   Files for applications and extensions.

References

Breymann, U. and Hughes, N. (1995). Composite Templates and Inheritance. *C++ Report*, No.7, September 1995, 32–40, 76

Cormen, T. H., Leiserson, C. E., and Rivest, R. L. (1994). *Introduction to Algorithms.* MIT Press

Hopcroft, J. E. and Ullman, J. D. (1979). *Introduction to automata theory, languages and computation.* Addison-Wesley

ISO/ANSI (1996). *Committee Draft.* ISO WG21/N0836, ANSI X3J16/96-0018 (January 1996)

ISO/IEC (1997). *Programming Language C++, Final Committee Draft.* ISO/IEC FCD 14882 (January 1997)

Josuttis, N. (1996). *Die C++-Standardbibliothek.* Addison-Wesley

Knuth, D. E. (1994). *The Stanford GraphBase.* ACM Press/Addison-Wesley

Kreft, K. and Langer, A. (1998). *The Standard C++ IOStreams.* Addison-Wesley

Lippman, S. B. (1995). *C++ Primer*, 2nd edition. Addison-Wesley

Maas, C. (1994). *Graphentheorie und Operations Research für Studierende der Informatik.* 2. Auflage, Wißner

Musser, D. R. and Saini, A (1996). *STL Tutorial and Reference Guide.* Addison-Wesley

Owsnicki-Klewe, B. (1995). *Algorithmen und Datenstrukturen.* 2. Auflage, Wißner

Sedgewick, R. (1992). *Algorithms in C++.* Addison-Wesley

Stepanov, A. and Lee, M. (1995). *The Standard Template Library.* Hewlett-Packard

Wirth, N. (1979). *Algorithmen und Datenstrukturen.* Teubner

Index